Knowledge-Based Systems

Rajendra Arvind Akerkar
Chairman, Technomathematics Research Foundation
and Senior Researcher, Western Norway Research Institute

Priti Srinivas Sajja
Sardar Patel University

JONES AND BARTLETT PUBLISHERS
Sudbury, Massachusetts
BOSTON   TORONTO   LONDON   SINGAPORE

World Headquarters

Jones and Bartlett Publishers
40 Tall Pine Drive
Sudbury, MA 01776
978-443-5000
info@jbpub.com
www.jbpub.com

Jones and Bartlett Publishers
Canada
6339 Ormindale Way
Mississauga, Ontario L5V 1J2
Canada

Jones and Bartlett Publishers
International
Barb House, Barb Mews
London W6 7PA
United Kingdom

Jones and Bartlett's books and products are available through most bookstores and online booksellers. To contact Jones and Bartlett Publishers directly, call 800-832-0034, fax 978-443-8000, or visit our website, www.jbpub.com.

Substantial discounts on bulk quantities of Jones and Bartlett's publications are available to corporations, professional associations, and other qualified organizations. For details and specific discount information, contact the special sales department at Jones and Bartlett via the above contact information or send an email to specialsales@jbpub.com.

Production Credits:
Publisher: David Pallai
Acquisitions Editor: Timothy Anderson
Editorial Assistant: Melissa Potter
Production Director: Amy Rose
Senior Marketing Manager: Andrea DeFronzo
V.P., Manufacturing and Inventory Control: Therese Connell
Composition: Northeast Compositors, Inc.
Cover and Title Page Design: Kristin E. Parker
Cover and Title Page Image: © Andrea Danti/Dreamstime.com
Printing and Binding: Malloy, Inc.
Cover Printing: Malloy, Inc.

Library of Congress Cataloging-in-Publication Data
Akerkar, Rajendra.
  Knowledge-based systems / Rajendra Akerkar, Priti Sajja.
    p. cm.
  Includes bibliographical references and index.
  ISBN-13: 978-0-7637-7647-3 (pbk.)
  ISBN-10: 0-7637-7647-5 (pbk.)
  1. Expert systems (Computer science) I. Sajja, Priti. II. Title.
  QA76.76.E95A443 2010
  006.3'3--dc22

                        2009019914

6048
Printed in the United States of America
13 12 11 10 09   10 9 8 7 6 5 4 3 2 1

To Rupali & Shreeram
—Rajendra Akerkar

To Srinivas & Abhignya
—Priti Srinivas Sajja

Contents

PREFACE

A *knowledge-based system* (KBS) is a system that uses artificial intelligence (AI) to solve problems. It incorporates a repository (database) of expert knowledge with utilities designed to facilitate the knowledge retrieval in response to specific queries, along with learning and justification, or to transfer expertise from one domain of knowledge to another. In particular, knowledge-based systems focus on using knowledge-based techniques to support human decision making, learning, and action. Such systems are capable of cooperating with human users and are being used for problem solving, training, and assisting users and experts of the domain for which the systems are developed. In some cases, KBSs are even better than humans are, as they are enriched with the virtues of efficiency and effectiveness. For instance, KBSs are able to diagnose diseases, repair electrical networks, control industrial workplaces, create geological maps, etc. Approaches have varied from simple rule-based systems (symbolic AI) to more complex models that use fuzzy logic and artificial neural networks (connectionist AI). Various hybridization of symbolic AI and connectionist AI are also explored in this book.

■ Reading Outcome

The basic purpose of this book is to:

- Develop an appreciation for knowledge-based systems and their architectures.
- Understand a broad variety of knowledge-based techniques for decision support and planning.

- Understand various methods for representing and reasoning under uncertainty.
- Understand and employ techniques to acquire knowledge from data.

■ Audience

The book is structured as a textbook, but it is accessible to a wide audience. It works as an introductory text on knowledge-based systems for advanced undergraduate or graduate students in computer science or related disciplines, such as computer engineering, philosophy, cognitive science, or psychology. It will be of more interest to the technically minded—the topics are technically challenging, focusing on learning by doing by designing, building, and implementing systems. This book is also suitable as a *self-study guide* for non–computer science professionals. For them, the book provides access to state-of-the-art knowledge-based systems and new concepts in artificial intelligence. Recent concepts, such as neural networks, fuzzy logic, generic algorithms, and hybrid/soft systems, are given proper attention with respect to knowledge-based systems. These concepts play a prominent role in the development of knowledge-based systems. However, due to time restrictions, it is difficult to cover all in one undergraduate or graduate curriculum. We feel that there is an urgent need for a single book covering these concepts at an advanced level. This text is a response to that need.

The book can be used in variety of ways. Industry or businesspeople can use this book not only to understand the fundamentals of knowledge-based systems, but also as a guide for building these systems in their own domain of expertise. On the other hand, those who do not wish to construct knowledge-based systems, but who wish to know the underlying details to be able to make intelligent decisions and deal with knowledge engineering efforts, will also find this book useful.

■ Prerequisites

The book assumes basic computer science skills that would be gained in the first year of a computer science or information technology degree program. Moreover, familiarity with mathematical concepts, such as set theory, relations, and elementary probability, as well as introductory concepts of artificial intelligence, such as predicate logic and searching will be an advantage.

■ How to Read This Book

The book is organized in twelve chapters. Each chapter is designed to be as independent as possible. The core of the book is Chapters 1 through 3. Thus, after reading these three chapters, the reader can start from any chapter among Chapters 4 through 9. Chapters 10 through 12 are brief case studies. Individual instructors may choose to omit or cover Chapters 4 through 9, depending on the specific course and its emphasis. Although instructors may wish to spend less or more time covering different topics in the book, we would nevertheless expect them to at least touch on the material in all of the chapters.

In Chapter 1, we briefly discuss the term artificial intelligence (AI) and various application areas. Also, the chapter provides a short overview of data pyramid and computer-based systems. The philosophy of knowledge-based systems (KBS) is introduced in this chapter, along with the different categories of KBS.

In Chapter 2, we present the structure of knowledge-based systems. We briefly discuss what knowledge is and its components. After presenting a brief introduction of every component of a typical knowledge-based system, we review inference techniques, such as forward and backward chaining, modes ponen, and modes tollens, and discuss conflict resolution strategies. Various application domains are also presented. Finally, we discuss advantages and limitations of knowledge-based systems.

In Chapter 3, we introduce a model specifically designed for KBS development, along with knowledge acquisition and existing techniques for it. We identify the main players in the knowledge-based system development team and further discuss the structure of a knowledge-based system. We elaborate on the main knowledge representation schemes for factual and procedural knowledge. We conclude our discussion by presenting various KBS tools.

In Chapter 4, we review the discipline of knowledge management. Knowledge management deals with knowledge as a main resource in modern organizations. This chapter covers perspectives on knowledge management, including technocentric, organizational, and ecological. We present the evolution and elements of knowledge management, along with the knowledge management process in depth. The organizational structure, roles, benefits, and challenges of knowledge management are also included in the discussion. The chapter concludes by categorizing knowledge management models into transaction models, cognitive models, network models, and community models. Existing models and knowledge modeling techniques are also discussed.

In Chapter 5, we deal with fuzzy logic and discuss the philosophical ideas behind it. We present the concept of fuzzy sets, consider how to represent a fuzzy set in a computer, and examine operations of fuzzy sets. Besides the different types of fuzzy membership functions, we also define linguistic variables and hedges. We then present fuzzy rules and explain the main differences between classical and fuzzy rules. We explore two fuzzy controllers and suggest appropriate areas for their application. The chapter concludes with brief introduction of Type 2 fuzzy logic and membership functions based on Type 2 fuzzy logic.

In Chapter 6, we explore agent-based systems, including topology of agents and advantages and characteristics of agents. A layered architecture of generic multiagent systems is proposed here. We also discuss knowledge-engineering-based methodologies. We conclude this chapter with two simple case studies.

In Chapter 7, we introduce artificial neural networks and discuss the basic ideas behind learning in a neural network. We present the concept of a perceptron as a simple computing element and discuss the perceptron learning rule. We explore the concept of the back-propagation learning algorithm. Finally, we briefly discuss self-organizing neural networks and probabilistic neural networks, as well as the relationship of neural nets with KBS.

In Chapter 8, we present an overview of genetic algorithms. We consider genetic algorithms, genetic cycles, and schemas. We demonstrate function optimization using genetic techniques. We also discuss ordering problems, schema, island genetic algorithms, and how to attempt problem solving using genetic algorithms. Finally, we consider the application of genetic algorithms to real-world problems and current research trends.

In Chapter 9, we consider soft intelligent systems as a combination of different intelligent technologies. First, we introduce soft computing and discuss its characteristics. Then we consider neuro-fuzzy systems, genetic-fuzzy systems, neuro-genetic systems, and neuro-fuzzy-genetic systems. We introduce a new soft computing constituent called chaos. Finally, we discuss applications of soft computing.

In Chapters 10 through 12, we present three distinct case studies, namely a multiagent e-learning solution, a diet planner, and a question-answering system.

Throughout the book, each chapter is enriched with applications and trends; warm-up questions for revision, exercises and projects to highlight certain aspects of covered material and to stimulate thought. Contents presented in the book and instructors manual enable students to develop a KBS project in parallel with studies.

■ Acknowledgments

We would like to thank a number of people who have helped us, both in general and in preparation of this text: Barry Levine, A. B. Cremers, M. R. Joshi, D. B. Choksi, Alla Khosrovyan, and Inessa Sahakyan. We have taught topics in this book in various appearances at different locations since 1996. The feedback from participants and colleagues at these venues has helped us to improve it significantly. We would also like to thank the students in courses we have taught with early notes of this draft at the Sardar Patel University, the Technomathematics Research Foundation, and the American University of Armenia, who provided precious support.

We would like to thank Jones and Bartlett Acquisitions Editor, Tim Anderson; Editorial Assistant, Melissa Potter; Production Director, Amy Rose and their staff for much appreciated help and support during this project.

Last, but not least, we are extremely grateful to our family members for their constant encouragement and support.

Rajendra Akerkar
Priti Srinivas Sajja

CHAPTER 1

Introduction to Knowledge-Based Systems

■ 1.1 NATURAL AND ARTIFICIAL INTELLIGENCE

The word "intelligence" comes from Latin "intelligo," which means "I understand." The basic meaning of intelligence is the ability to understand, or to "get it," so as to react. Intelligence is the computational part of the natural ability to achieve desired goals in the world. Living entities like people and animals have the ability to define their goals, plan accordingly, and react dynamically and quickly, according to the situation, using natural intelligence. The ability to respond quickly, to make sense out of ambiguous, contradictory, and incomplete information by recognizing the relative importance of the different elements of a situation, and to find similarities in dissimilar situations (and vice versa) comes from natural intelligence. Thus, intelligence involves learning, adopting, and applying problem-solving methods. Artificial intelligence (AI) is the development, to some extent, of similar kinds of abilities into a machine. AI is the science and engineering of making intelligent machines, especially by using computer programs. The term was coined by John McCarthy at the Massachusetts Institute of Technology in 1956. According to him, "AI is the branch of computer science concerned with making computers behave like humans." According to Rich and Knight (1991), "AI is the study of how to make computers do things, at which, at the moment, people are better."

Nevertheless, what seems intelligent to one person may not be so for another person, but the following characteristics are essential:

- Responds to situations flexibly
- Makes sense of ambiguous or erroneous messages

- Assigns relative importance to elements of a situation
- Finds similarities even though the situations might be different
- Draws distinctions between situations even though there may be many similarities between them

A machine is regarded as intelligent if it exhibits human characteristics generated through natural intelligence. In one way, Artificial Intelligence is the study of human thought processes and moving toward problem solving in a symbolic and nonalgorithmic way.

Artificial Intelligence is the branch of computer science that attempts to solve problems by mimicking human thought processes using heuristics and a symbolic and nonalgorithmic approach in areas where people are better. Here, "heuristic" means "rule of thumb," or a practical rule that does not give a guarantee of success. AI tries not only to provide solutions to problems for which there are no known efficient solutions, but also considers problems that can be solved, although the typical methods take an unrealistic (or infinite) amount of time. For example, optimization techniques and other problem-solving strategies may offer the best solution, but they can take a long time. Real-life decisions must be acceptable, should take a reasonable amount of time, and are not always the best. For example, deciding on a career and relevant courses of study must be made within a given time before admission to the courses closes.

Figure 1.1 shows the important constituents of an ideal AI definition, and Figure 1.2 shows the nature of an AI solution. Figure 1.3 shows four different areas of computing.

The goals of artificial intelligence systems can be divided into four categories (Russell & Norvig, 1995):

1. Systems that think like humans
2. Systems that think rationally

■ FIGURE 1.1
Constituents of
artificial intelligence

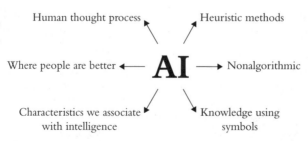

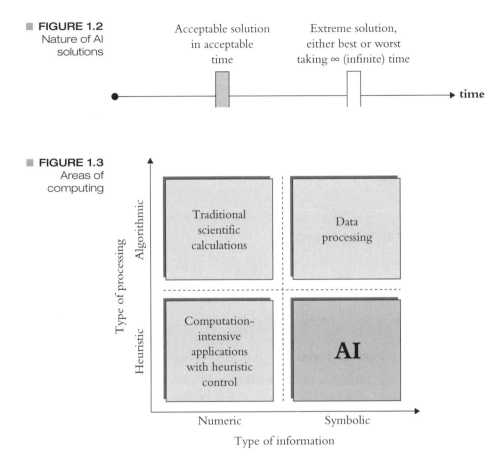

3. Systems that act like humans
4. Systems that act rationally

Just as the term "intelligence" has multiple interpretations, so does the field of artificial intelligence. Researchers are working toward various definitions of these goals, with a variety of approaches. After John McCarthy and other researchers' ambitious definition of AI, and after a few early failures, AI researchers started setting more realistic goals in the 1960s and 1970s, with a major focus on knowledge-based systems. During these years, expert systems technology was applied to many domains, ranging from medical diagnosis to inferring molecular structure to natural language understanding. The same period also witnessed early work on Artificial Neural Networks (ANNs) called perceptrons by Minsky and Papert (1969), which showed how the knowledge can be represented in a symbolic way, with the advantages of robustness, parallelism, and self-learning. After that, the late 1980s and 1990s saw a renewed interest in ANN research, when several different researchers invented the modified back-propagation learning algorithm. Continuing the excitement within the AI community, the field also witnessed the development of hybrid intelligent systems from 1990 onward. New paradigms, such as fuzzy logic, genetic algorithms, and agent technology, also have started to be applied to real-life problems.

■ 1. 2   TESTING THE INTELLIGENCE

To measure the degree of the intelligence and level of machine understanding achieved, various experiments have been introduced. The Turing test by Alan Turing (1950) and the Chinese Room experiment by John Searle (1980) are two important measures.

■ 1.2.1   Turing Test

Turing's 1950 article "Computing Machinery and Intelligence" discussed conditions under which a machine can be considered intelligent. He argued that if the machine could successfully pretend to be human to a knowledgeable observer, you certainly should consider it intelligent. However, a machine that passes the Turing test might be considered intelligent, but a machine could still be considered intelligent without knowing enough about humans to imitate one.

In this paper, Turing introduced the test as follows:

"A human judge engages in a natural-language conversation with one human and one machine, each of which try to appear human; if the judge cannot reliably tell which is which, the machine is said to pass the test. In order to test the machine's intelligence rather than its ability to render words into audio, the conversation is limited to a text-only channel, such as a computer keyboard and screen."

Turing originally suggested a test of a machine's ability to exhibit intelligence. Figure 1.4 illustrates the Turing test.

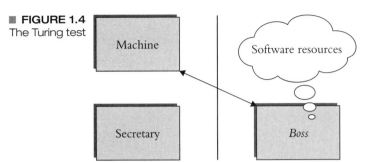

The Boss could not judge who was replying, thus the machine is as intelligent as the secretary.

■ 1.2.2 Weakness of the Turing Test

The Turing test will fail to test for intelligence in two circumstances. It tests for many behaviors that we may not consider intelligent, such as the susceptibility to insults or the temptation to lie. For example, a machine may well be intelligent without being able to chat *exactly* like a human. In addition, the test fails to capture the *general* properties of intelligence, such as the ability to solve difficult problems or come up with original insights. If a machine can solve a difficult problem that no person could solve, it would, in principle, fail the test.

■ 1.2.3 Chinese Room Experiment

In 1980, John Searle devised a thought experiment that he called the Chinese Room (Searle, 1980). The Chinese Room has shown that a symbol-processing machine like a computer can never be properly described as having a "mind" or "understanding," regardless of how intelligently it may behave. The experiment is as follows: A person who does not understand Chinese is able to communicate in Chinese solely by formal instructions. The person sits in a closed room—a *Chinese Room*—and is given questions from the outside written in Chinese characters. He transforms the Chinese characters into English characters solely through the completely formal, step-by-step guidance of an English rulebook. Thanks to the precise transformation rules, the results are flawless: Chinese replies to Chinese questions. Searle argues that the person, although people outside would think he spoke Chinese perfectly, would not understand the language at all. On the other

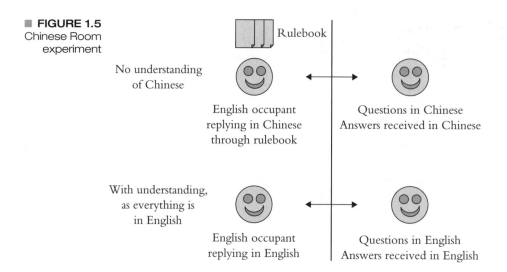

hand, in an *English Room* an English occupant outputs everything in English with a clear understanding of the communication process. This experiment is shown in Figure 1.5.

Searle repeated this experiment on himself and noted that he couldn't understand a single word of Chinese. He simply manipulated what, to him, were meaningless squiggles, using the book and whatever other equipment was provided in the room, such as paper, pencils, erasers, and filing cabinets. After manipulating the symbols, Searle produced the answer in Chinese. Since he could interact successfully, he supposedly passed the Turing test—however, without understanding a single Chinese word.

Searle argued that his lack of understanding showed that computers do not understand Chinese either, because they would be in the same situation as he was. They are mindless manipulators of symbols, just as he was. They don't understand what they're "saying," just as a person who does not understand Chinese does not know what he or she is saying. Since computers do not have a conscious mental state like "understanding," they cannot properly be said to have "minds."

■ 1.3 APPLICATION AREAS OF ARTIFICIAL INTELLIGENCE

Rich and Knight (1991) classified and described the different areas that artificial intelligence techniques have been applied to, as described in the following sections.

■ 1.3.1 Mundane Tasks

Plenty of real world tasks are so ordinary and seem unchallenging; they cannot attract much consideration by the way they are carried out. It is difficult to even notice small problems/actions and carve systematic solutions. Such so-called *simple* problems are actually very complex and require a high amount of knowledge. These tasks include balancing, planning, communication, etc. A list of such mundane tasks are given here:

- Perception (vision and speech)
- Natural language understanding, generation, and translation
- Commonsense reasoning
- Robot control

Attempts have been made for computers to see (by fitting them with television inputs) and hear (by fitting them with microphone inputs). These have achieved only limited success, since useful processing of complex input data requires understanding, and understanding, in turn, requires a large amount of knowledge about the things that are perceived. In AI, the process of perception is studied as a set of operations. A visual scene may be encoded by sensors and represented as a matrix of intensity values. These are processed by detectors that search for primitive picture components, like line segments, simple curves, corners, etc. These, in turn, are processed to infer information regarding the objects in the scene. The ultimate aim is to represent the scene by a suitable model. This model may be a high-level description of the scene—for example, *a hill with a tree on top*. The point of the whole perception problem is to provide a condensed version of the input from the unmanageably large amount of raw input data. The main difficulty, though, in perception problems is the enormous amount of candidate descriptions of a scene. One solution is to make a hypothesis of each description and then test it. When forming a hypothesis, a large amount of knowledge about the expected scenes is required.

It has been difficult to build computers that can generate and understand even fragments of a natural language like English. This is because language has developed as an effective communication medium between intelligent beings. It is seen as transmitting a bit of "mental structure" from one brain to another under circumstances in which each brain possesses large, highly similar mental structures that provide a common context. This similarity in context helps in generating and understanding highly condensed messages. Thus, natural-language understanding is a highly complex process of encoding and decoding. In order to build computer systems that can understand natural language, both the contextual knowledge and the process for making effective inferences are required. This is an important domain, which still fascinates a number of researchers.

Humans, even children, are able to successfully navigate their environment and manipulate things such as light switches and toy blocks. These tasks, although performed unconsciously by humans, involve a great deal of complexity. When we try to program machines to perform the same tasks, we see that this requires many of the capabilities used in solving more intellectually demanding problems. Research in robotics has helped to develop many AI techniques for modeling states of the world, and transformations from one state to another have been found.

■ 1.3.2 Formal Tasks

Formal tasks often deal with handling large and complex domain space for problem solving. Without AI intervention, it is difficult to solve such tasks. Finding a solution from a large search space and theorem proving are examples of such formal tasks. A few other tasks are:

- Games (chess, backgammon, checkers, etc.)
- Mathematics (geometry, logic, integral calculus, theorem proving, etc.)

Games can generate enormously sizeable search spaces. These are large and complex enough to require robust techniques for determining what alternatives to explore in the problem space. These techniques are called *heuristics* and comprise a key area of AI research. A heuristic is an effective but potentially imperfect problem-solving strategy. Much of what we commonly call intelligence seems to reside in the heuristics used by humans to solve problems. Contemporary successes in computer-based game playing include world championships in backgammon and chess.

Proving a mathematical theorem is an intensive intellectual task. It requires deductions from hypotheses and involves judgment. This judgment is based on a large amount of specialized knowledge and an accurate guess as to which previously proven theorem would help in the present proof. This helps to break the main problem into subproblems to be worked on independently. Several automatic theorem-proving programs have been developed that possess this ability to a limited extent. The formalization of deductive techniques using the language of predicate logic helps in understanding the components of reasoning more clearly. Many informal tasks, like making a fault diagnosis, can be formalized with theorem-proving problems. Hence, theorem proving is an important subfield of AI.

■ 1.3.3 Expert Tasks

Expert tasks are the tasks that require specialized knowledge to provide expert conclusions in the specific area. The following applications fall under this category.

- Engineering (design, fault finding, manufacturing, planning, etc.)
- Scientific analysis
- Medical diagnosis
- Financial analysis

One class of problems is concerned with specifying optimal schedules. A classic example is the *Traveling Salesperson Problem*, where the problem is to find a minimum distance tour, starting at one of several cities, visiting other cities only once, and then returning to the starting city. The problem becomes finding a minimum cost path over the edges of a graph containing n nodes such that each of the n nodes is visited only once. In such problems, the domain of possible combinations or sequences from which to choose an answer is large.

Brute-force attempts to generate a solution often lead to a *combinatorial explosion* of possibilities that exhaust the resources of even large computers. Such problems, called Nondeterministic Polynomial-complete problems by the computational AI researchers, have worked on methods for solving various types of combinatorial problems. The key to solving such problems is understanding the problem domain. Methods developed to solve combinatorial problems have proven to be helpful in solving other, less combinatorial, problems.

Expert systems are automatic consulting systems. They provide expert conclusions about specialized areas. Expert systems have been built in such a way that they can diagnose faults in military systems, such as aircrafts and radars; taxonomically classify members of a particular species; advise on possible chemical structures; evaluate potential ore deposits; diagnose diseases; and so on. There are two key components in the design of every expert system. One is the representation of knowledge, and the other is using this knowledge to draw conclusions. Representation of knowledge is difficult because expert knowledge can be imprecise and/or uncertain. In general, the knowledge is represented as a large set of simple rules. Knowledge is also represented in structures called *frames* and *scripts*. Conclusions are generally obtained through the technique of *rule-based deduction*. Other forms of deduction, such as probabilistic deduction, are also seriously being looked into.

To date, most of the successes of AI have been in the expert and formal task categories. It is ironic that the mundane tasks are thought to be so simple a child can do them at an early age. They have, however, proven to be difficult to formally describe. Research is continuing to push the edges of what we can do in these areas.

■ 1.4 DATA PYRAMID AND COMPUTER-BASED SYSTEMS

Artificial Intelligence systems use AI techniques, through which they achieve expert-level competence in solving problems in given areas. Such systems, which use one or more experts' knowledge to solve problems in a specific domain, are called *knowledge-based* or *expert systems*. Traditional information systems work on data and/or information. Figures 1.6 and 1.7 represent the data pyramid (modified–Eliot, 1934) showing relationships between data, information, knowledge, and intelligence. Figure 1.6 shows the convergence of data to knowledge by applying activities like researching, absorbing, acting, interacting, and reflecting. These activities are shown on the x-axis. While performing these activities, a human normally gains understanding

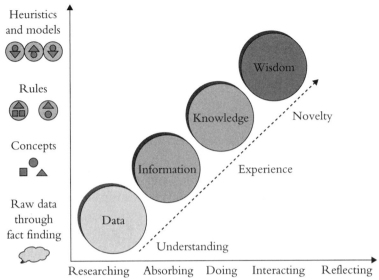

■ FIGURE 1.6
Convergence from
data to intelligence

Heuristics
and models

Rules

Concepts

Raw data
through
fact finding

Wisdom

Knowledge

Information

Data

Novelty

Experience

Understanding

Researching   Absorbing   Doing   Interacting   Reflecting

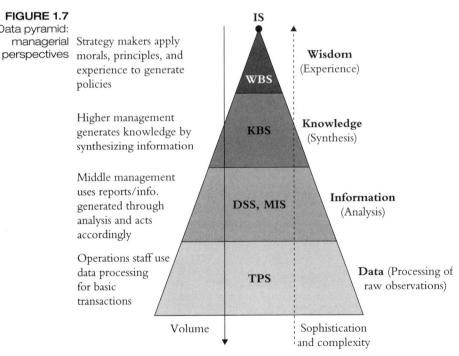

■ FIGURE 1.7
Data pyramid:
managerial
perspectives

Strategy makers apply
morals, principles, and
experience to generate
policies

Higher management
generates knowledge by
synthesizing information

Middle management
uses reports/info.
generated through
analysis and acts
accordingly

Operations staff use
data processing
for basic
transactions

IS

WBS

KBS

DSS, MIS

TPS

Wisdom
(Experience)

Knowledge
(Synthesis)

Information
(Analysis)

Data (Processing of
raw observations)

Volume

Sophistication
and complexity

and experience, and may come up with innovative ideas. The y-axis presents forms of convergence, which are namely raw observation, concepts, rules, and models and heuristics.

Figure 1.7 shows the data pyramid through management perspectives. The operational-level staff generally works with the structured environment and uses predefined procedures to carry out the routine transactions of the business, which are its base operations. To carry out these operations, the operational staff uses a system like a Transaction Processing System (TPS). With a structured environment and a set of predefined procedures, the development and automation of such TPS systems becomes easy. TPS considers raw observations of the field and processes them to generate meaningful information. This is the data level of the pyramid.

The information generated through these business transactions is analyzed to form routine and exceptional reports, which are helpful to the managers and executives when making decisions. The system that does this is called the Management Information System (MIS). TPS and MIS work on structured environments utilizing data and/or information.

Management also needs to make decisions considering the cost–benefit ratios of the different solutions available to effectively utilize scarce resources and environmental constraints. The system used for that is a Decision Support System (DSS). Unlike TPS, which uses databases only and works in structured environments, the DSS normally works on structured to semistructured environments and utilizes the model base and database for optimum utilization of resources.

Systems like TPS, MIS, and DSS carry out routine business transactions, provide detailed analysis of the information generated, and support the decision-making processes of the business. However, these systems neither make decisions themselves nor justify them with proper explanations and reasoning, as they do not possess the required knowledge. Higher-level management needs knowledge and wisdom for policy and strategy making; hence, there is a need for knowledge-based and wisdom-based systems (KBS and WBS, respectively). By applying morals, principles, and judgments to the decision taken, and after a level of maturity (experience) is gained, information can be generalized and converted into knowledge.

Many researchers are devoted to developing a truly intelligent system, and computer hardware and software innovations have started taking shape

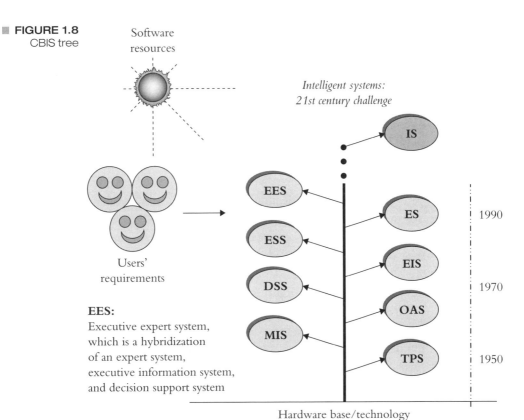

FIGURE 1.8
CBIS tree

in the last half-century. During this time, computer science has traversed the phases of "data," "information," and "knowledge." It is now the 21st century's challenge to develop a truly intelligent system. Figure 1.8 (Sajja & Patel, 1995) shows a typical information system in a tree form.

The following sections discuss the data, information, knowledge, and intelligence phases.

■ 1.4.1 Data

Factual, discrete and static things, and raw observations of the given area of interest are known as data. Information can be generated after systematic processing of such data. Data are often identified as numeric values within the environment. Data can also be observed as the transactional, physical records of an enterprise's activities, which are considered the basic building blocks of any information system. Unfortunately, we need to process the data before we can actually use it.

Ackoff (1989) writes, "Data are symbols that represent properties of objects, events, and their environments. They are products of observation. To observe is to sense. The technology of sensing instrumentation is, of course, to be highly developed."

According to Machlup (1983), "Data are the things given to the analyst, investigator, or problem-solver; they may be numbers, words, sentences, records, assumptions—just anything given, no matter what form and of what origin. This used to be well known to scholars in most fields: some wanted the word data to refer to facts, especially to instrument readings. [For those] who deal with hypotheses[e]s ... data are assumptions."

Though data are evidence of something, they need not be always true; however, there is a difficulty in "knowing" if data are true or not. This leads to further processing to generate information and knowledge from available data. For example, the temperature at a particular time on a given day is a singular item of data and is treated as a particular fact. There might be several such items, and these can be combined in various ways using the standard operations of logic. But according to Martin Frické (2007), there are also universal statements, such as, "Every day, the maximum temperature is above 50 degrees." However, from a logical point of view, such universal statements are stronger than items or compounds of items, and thus it is more difficult to be assured about their truth. Such data must be filtered further to generate necessary true information.

Above all, data might be empirical data, like daily temperatures, or nonempirical, like "Harry Potter studies at Hogwarts." It is hard to assign a truth value to fictitious nonempirical data.

■ 1.4.2 Information

All data are information. However, there is information that is not data. Such distinguished information can be considered processed data, which makes decision making easier. Processing involves an aggregation of data, calculations of data, corrections on data, etc., in such a way that it generates the flow of messages. Information usually has some meaning and purpose—that is, data within a context can be considered information.

In their book, *Working Knowledge*, Thomas Davenport and Laurence Prusak (1998) state that we add value to data in various ways:

- Contextualized: Tells us the purpose for which the data was gathered
- Categorized: Tells us the units of analysis or key components of the data
- Calculated: Tells us if the data was analyzed mathematically or statistically
- Corrected: Tells us if errors have been removed from the data
- Condensed: Tells us if the data was summarized in a more concise form

Further, information can be *processed, accessed, generated, transmitted, stored, sent, distributed, produced and consumed, searched for, used, compressed,* and *duplicated.* Information can also be of different types with different attributes. It can be *sensitive, qualitative,* or *quantitative.*

■ 1.4.3 Knowledge

Knowledge is considered a human understanding of a subject matter that has been acquired through proper study and experience. Information and data may be related to a group of humans and regarded as a collective mass, whereas knowledge is usually based on learning, thinking, and proper understanding of the problem area by an individual. Knowledge is derived from information in a similar way as information is derived from data. It can be considered the synthesis and integration of human perceptive processes that helps them to draw meaningful conclusions. According to Nonaka and Takeuchi (1995), knowledge is "justified true belief" related to human actions and is created from a flow of messages. Knowledge is generally personal, subjective, and inherently local—it is found "within the heads of employees" rather than existing objectively.

Wigg (1999) found that knowledge can be possessed outside of the human mind and suggested that executable programs (software agents) are capable of manipulating beliefs and judgments. He describes knowledge as "truths and beliefs, perspectives and concepts, judgments and expectations, methodologies and know-how, and is possessed by humans or other agents."

In the article "A Meta Data Repository is the Key to Knowledge Management," David Marco (2001) states that information is the data that tells about its business and how it functions. An extra step is applied to transform information into knowledge by identifying the three "Is" in the business, as follows:

- Impacts: Impact of the business on the target user group and market
- Interacts: How the business system interacts with users and other systems in the environment
- Influenced: How the business is influenced by competitors and market trends

In this case, knowledge is knowing how the system in a given domain works. It may be difficult to characterize knowledge; however, it can be represented as an intersection (multiplication) of information, ideas, and expertise, as denoted in Figure 1.9.

Within the field of knowledge management, two distinct and widely accepted types of knowledge exist: tacit and explicit. Tacit knowledge, as identified by Polanyi (1962), is knowledge that is hard to encode and communicate. It is ephemeral and transitory and "cannot be resolved into information or itemized in the manner characteristic of information." Further, according to Nonaka and Takeuchi (1995), tacit knowledge is personal, context-specific, and hard to formalize. On the other hand, explicit knowledge is exactly that kind of knowledge that can be encoded and is transmittable in language. It is explicit knowledge that most current knowledge management practices try to, and indeed are able to, capture, acquire, create, leverage, retain, codify, store, transfer, and share.

Knowledge is hidden in data and information like butter in milk. Data and information require suitable processing to generate structured meaningful information to aid decision making and gain expertise for problem solv-

■ **FIGURE 1.9**
Knowledge as a combination of information, expertise, and ideas

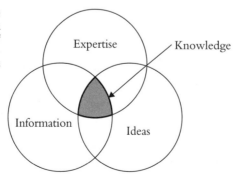

ing. That is, it is the level of processing that makes the content meaningful and applicable. Through proper processing, we can generate reports that aid decision making, concepts for learning, and models for problem solving.

■ 1.4.4 Wisdom and Intelligence

Knowledge of concepts and models leads to a higher level of knowledge called wisdom. One needs to apply morals, principles, and expertise to gain and utilize wisdom. This takes time and requires a kind of maturity that comes with age and experience.

The concept of wisdom has been explored by the ancient Greek philosophers, such as Plato and Aristotle, although it has not been a popular topic of discussion in recent times. There are several different strands of wisdom (Ryan, 2007). According to Martin Frické (2007), a person may have encyclopedic knowledge of facts and figures relating to the countries of the world, but that knowledge, by itself, will not make that person wise. Rather, a person becomes wise by applying knowledge to tricky problems of an ethical and practical nature and looking for possible solutions.

Wisdom is further enhanced by intelligence. Intelligence is the ultimate aim of an entity for better life.

■ 1.4.5 Skills Versus Knowledge

Skill in problem solving generally implies speed, efficiency, reduced errors, reduced cognitive load, robustness, etc. Knowledge, on other hand, allows humans to solve new problems through analogies, common sense, analysis, and so on. Most of the difficult and challenging problems, at least until now, do not have tractable algorithmic solutions. Many important tasks arise in complex sociophysical contexts that generally resist precise description and rigorous analysis—for example, planning legal reasoning, making a medical diagnosis, analyzing a military situation and machine diagnostics. Human experts achieve outstanding performance because they are knowledgeable and experienced. Another reason for focusing on knowledge lies in its intrinsic value. Knowledge is a scarce resource whose refinement and reproduction creates wealth.

Human knowledge is propagated through apprenticeship or training. With the use of knowledge, humans achieve outstanding success in solving difficult day-to-day problems. If the problem-solving knowledge from these human experts is extracted and put in a computer program, the program, too, should attain a high level of performance. Extracting knowledge from experts and putting it into computable forms will greatly reduce the cost of knowledge reproduction and exploitation. At the same time, refining knowledge can be speeded up by making private knowledge available for public test and evaluation.

■ 1.5   KNOWLEDGE-BASED SYSTEMS

A knowledge-based system (KBS) is one of the major family members of the AI group. With the availability of advanced computing facilities and other resources, attention is now turning to more demanding tasks that might require intelligence. Society and industry are becoming knowledge-oriented and relying on different experts' decision-making abilities to solve problems. A KBS can act as an expert on demand, anytime and anywhere. A KBS can save money by leveraging experts, allowing users to function at a higher level and promoting consistency. A KBS is a productive tool that offers collective knowledge of one or more experts.

Table 1.1 (Sajja, 2000) outlines the differences between traditional computer-based information systems (TPS, MIS, etc.) and knowledge-based systems.

The KBS started with expert systems, and many KBS solutions currently are in use. In fact, a KBS is a computer-based system that uses and generates knowledge from data, information, and knowledge. These systems are capable of understanding the information being processed and can make a decision based on it, whereas the traditional computer systems do not know or understand the data/information they process. Figure 1.8 represents the historical view of the computer-based information system in a tree form.

■ 1.6   OBJECTIVES OF KBS

KBS is an example of fifth-generation computer technology. Some of its objectives are as follows (Turban, 1990):

- Provides a high intelligence level
- Assists people in discovering and developing unknown fields
- Offers a vast amount of knowledge in different areas
- Aids in management of knowledge stored in the knowledge base

▥ **TABLE 1 Comparison of Knowledge-Based and Computer-Based Information Systems**

Traditional Computer-Based Information System (CBIS)	Knowledge-Based System (KBS)
Gives a guaranteed solution and concentrates on efficiency	Adds power to the solution and concentrates on effectiveness without any guarantee of solution
Data and/or information processing approach	Knowledge and/or decision processing approach
Assists in activities related to decision making and routine transactions; supports need for information	Transfer of expertise; takes a decision based on knowledge, explains it, and upgrades it, if required
Examples are TPS, MIS, DSS, etc.	Examples are expert systems, CASE-based systems, etc.
Manipulation method is numeric and algorithmic	Manipulation method is primarily symbolic/connectionist and nonalgorithmic
These systems do not make mistakes	These systems learn by mistakes
Need complete information and/or data	Partial and uncertain information, data, or knowledge will do
Works for complex, integrated, and wide areas in a reactive manner	Works for narrow domains in a reactive and proactive manner

- Solves social problems in a better way than the traditional computer-based information systems.
- Acquires new perceptions by simulating unknown situations
- Offers significant software productivity improvement
- Significantly reduces cost and time to develop computerized systems

Ultimately, the computer needs to have the capability to recognize continuous speech, process supervision, make intelligent decisions, perform self-repair, and augment the decision maker in general, through which productivity, efficiency, effectiveness, and quality of life can be improved.

▮ 1.7   COMPONENTS OF KBS

The KBS consists of a knowledge base and a search program called an inference engine (IE). The IE is a software program that infers the knowledge

■ **FIGURE 1.10**
General structure
of a KBS

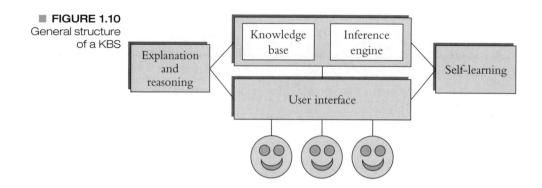

available in the knowledge base. The knowledge base can be used as a repository of knowledge in various forms. This may include an empty workspace to store temporary results and pieces of information or knowledge. Because an expert's power lies in his or her explanation and reasoning capabilities, the expert system's credibility also depends on the explanation and reasoning of the decision made or suggested by the system. Human beings can learn new things and sometimes forget knowledge that is not in regular use. Simulation of such learning is an essential component of a KBS. The life span of a KBS may vary according to the degree of such simulation. A KBS may be either manually updated (manual update) or automatically updated by a machine (machine learning). Ideally, the basic frame of a KBS rarely needs to be modified. In addition, there should be an appropriate user interface, which may have the natural-language processing facility. These components are shown in Figure 1.10.

■ 1.8 CATEGORIES OF KBS

According to the classifications by Tuthhill and Levy (1991), five main types of KBSs exist:

1. Expert systems
2. Linked systems
3. CASE-based systems
4. Database in conjunction with an intelligent user interface
5. Intelligent tutoring systems

■ 1.8.1   Expert Systems

The expert system (ES) is the pioneer of knowledge-based systems and the most popular. It replaces one or more experts for problem solving. They may be more useful in many situations than the traditional computer-based information system. Situations in which they are particularly useful include:

- When an expert is not available
- When expertise is to be stored for future use or when expertise is to be cloned or multiplied
- When intelligent assistance and/or training are required for decision making or problem solving
- When more than one expert's knowledge has to be grouped on one platform

Expert systems have the following benefits:

- Increased output and productivity
- Improved quality
- Reduced downtime
- Capturing scarce expertise
- Flexibility and reliability
- Integrated knowledge
- Educational benefits/ease of training
- Enhanced problem-solving capability
- Knowledge documentation and ease of knowledge transfer

■ 1.8.2   Database Management Systems in Conjunction with an Intelligent User Interface

Recent database management systems offer a user-friendly interface to the data being stored. With the help of a query language, information can be effectively extracted for users. However, such an interface is limited in that it cannot handle partial information in a natural language and cannot make or justify decisions for itself. An intelligent user interface can enhance the use of the content available in the traditional format. Interacting with users in their own language might increase the efficiency of decision making. An intelligent user interface also provides the facility of natural-language processing as an intelligent front end with a database. The knowledge-based systems generally do not permanently store the process history or intermediate knowledge, unless it is new inferred knowledge. At this time, the inferred knowledge and temporary results can be stored in the database. Such databases can be used in other application(s) in the same environment, if they contain useful and related information. Such an arrangement may be more useful when integrating intelligent systems with other existing systems.

■ 1.8.3 Linked Systems

Hypermedia systems, such as hypertext, hyperaudio, and hypervideo, are considered linked knowledge-based systems. Such linked systems contain nonsequentially linked text, audio, and video chunks generated during processing. These components are linked in such a way that they generate meaning and exhibit intelligence. In a network environment, like the Internet and intranets, these systems have their own importance. Multimedia-based linked systems are currently quite common.

■ 1.8.4 CASE-Based Systems

Intelligent systems for computer-aided software engineering (CASE) are another type of KBS. These systems guide the development of information/intelligent systems for better quality and effectiveness. Disciplines like systems analysis and design and software engineering can provide only guidelines to develop high-quality systems that meet user requirements in the most effective way. Here, the CASE-based system provides necessary guidelines to choose the model, acquire important requirements about the product being developed, design the framework of the systems accordingly, encode it, and test the information and/or knowledge-based system. These systems also help in risk management and support project management activities during development.

■ 1.8.5 Intelligent Tutoring Systems

Training, educating, and motivating users are important aspects of a tutoring system. Knowledge-based systems are used to train and guide students, trainers, and practitioners in specific areas and at different levels. Such systems are used to identify the users' level and other constraints to provide training in different technical and nontechnical areas. These systems are also useful in evaluating students' skills, preparing documentation of subject material, and managing the question bank for the subject.

One well-known branch of intelligent tutoring systems is dialog-based tutoring systems. The underlying metaphor of these systems is conversation, often in typed form to avoid the specialized algorithms needed for speech recognition, and often including nonverbal acts, such as pointing or graphics display, in addition to speech acts.

■ 1.9   DIFFICULTIES WITH THE KBS

■ 1.9.1   Completeness of Knowledge Base

Most of the systems have a great deal of limited knowledge about a focused subset of a problem and very little knowledge about anything else. Spring (2007) quotes an example as follows:

IF car will not start, THEN check battery.

The system has no information about the relationship between the battery and the car's ability to start—it only has the heuristic to check the battery in this instance.

■ 1.9.2   Characteristics of Knowledge

As knowledge plays a key role in problem solving and modeling natural intelligence, the knowledge base becomes a prime component of any knowledge-based system. To solve a simple real-life task, an extensive amount of knowledge is required. In addition, the knowledge is continuously changing. This makes the development of a knowledge-based system more difficult. (Akerkar, 2005)

■ 1.9.3   Large Size of Knowledge Base

As stated earlier, to solve even a simple problem, a large amount of knowledge is required. The voluminous knowledge base contains several "chunks" of knowledge in a variety of ontologies utilizing different representation techniques. Similar knowledge stored in different ontologies makes the knowledge base complex and unstructured. According to the nature and application of these knowledge components, they may be divided into different partitions or modules. An appropriate control strategy to maintain metaknowledge and to access the required knowledge from the proper partitions becomes trivial here. Without such control strategy, utilization of knowledge becomes difficult.

■ 1.9.4 Acquisition of Knowledge

Acquiring knowledge from one or more experts has always been a difficult, tedious, and costly process. The knowledge engineer, who is responsible for the acquisition process, should identify, "know," and represent the required knowledge, with the help of experts in forming and solving real-world problems, and representing it in the system. It is the knowledge engineer's knowledge that is reflected in the system, not the expert's knowledge. No predefined procedure is available to guarantee knowledge acquisition and representation. In addition, no lifecycle model is available specifically to develop knowledge-based systems. These systems are considered the same as other computer-based information systems for development purposes.

■ 1.9.5 Slow Learning and Execution

Once implemented, the KBS model is often slow and unable to access or manage large volumes of information; once implemented, it can be difficult to maintain. According to Spring (2007), solutions to these problems have been sought through better knowledge elicitation techniques and tools, better KBS shells and environments, improved development methodologies, knowledge-modeling languages, facilitating cooperation between KBSs and databases in expert and deductive databases, and techniques and tools for maintaining systems.

Above all, it is difficult for researchers to exactly mimic and generate humanlike reasoning and thought processes in a model of natural intelligence. A number of AI/KBS application areas also open up deep philosophical issues. This is a promising field of study whose primary concern is to discover more effective ways to understand and apply intelligent problem solving, planning, and communication skills to a wide range of practical problems.

■ 1.10 WARM-UP QUESTIONS, EXERCISES, AND PROJECTS

Warm-up Questions

1. What is the difference between data and information?

2. Why is the concept of knowledge different from the concepts of data and information?

3. What is the role of knowledge in decision making?

4. Visit http://www.thespoon.com/mimic/ to play with a system called Mimic. Mimic is learning how to talk without programmed responses. You can teach Mimic some lessons.

5. In artificial intelligence, any problem can be viewed as a system that we are attempting to analyze. What are the difficulties with this problem-solving strategy?

6. List four reasons for solving complex problems using artificial intelligence techniques.

7. Use your favorite search engine to discover whether the following tasks can already be solved by computers:

   a. Buying groceries on the Web

   b. Playing a game of chase at a competition level

   c. Writing a story

   d. Performing a complicated surgical treatment

   e. Proving new mathematical theorems

8. Consider the following topics and categorize them as either information or knowledge:

   a. The weather report of an unknown country

   b. An academic report from a university department

   c. The content of a reality show on TV

   d. A favorite author

9. Provide an example to explain how data can be transformed into knowledge.

10. List three fundamental questions that must be addressed while extracting knowledge from an expert.

11. What are the essential requirements for expert system development?

Exercises

1. Give your own definition of artificial intelligence and justify it with suitable examples.
2. What do you see as the future of AI? Justify your answer.
3. Comment on how reliable the Turing test is for testing artificial intelligence.
4. Define the terms knowledge and intelligence.
5. List two areas in the software development process in which an AI program might be useful.
6. What are the benefits of an intelligent tutoring system over a general e-learning tool?
7. List the main drawbacks of a knowledge-based system.
8. What are the basic characteristics of knowledge-based systems?
9. Given the differences between the architectures of stored-program computers and that of the human brain, what significance does studying the physiological structure and function of biological systems have for the engineering of knowledge-based programs? Justify your answer.
10. Discuss the possibility of a machine understanding a natural (human) language.

Projects

1. During your database systems course, you must have investigated how to design a software system for some of the following topics. If you incorporate intelligence into these systems, it can have many advantages. Suppose you are now assigned the task of adding intelligence to such a software system. Show how these systems can have built-in intelligence.

   a. Employer's payroll system
   b. Supermarket inventory management system
   c. Sales and marketing management system
   d. Hospital management system

2. The objective of this project is to give you a chance to research a topic from the following list. You must critically study the problem domain,

formulate interesting questions, and creatively analyze what you have studied during this research phase.

a. Cell phone selector system: This system helps users select the best possible cell phone to satisfy their needs.

b. Credit rater: This system helps evaluate a customer's credit.

c. Animal recognition system: This system assists in the recognition of an animal based on facts the user provides.

d. Market analysis system: This system helps in the analysis of the stock market.

e. Palm reading system: This system supports the analysis of a person's hand and making an inference based on such an analysis.

f. Online test system: This system aids in testing knowledge learned by a student in a specific course.

g. Farming system: This system helps in the management of diseases and pests on a farm. (You can select any type, e.g., vegetable farm, wheat farm, etc.)

h. Engineering system: You can select any specific engineering domain, such as designing an electric device, information security analysis, system monitoring control, designing topology networks in telecommunications, diagnostic system for real-time control, automation of a production process, redesigning engineering systems, and so on.

i. Customer personalization systems: This system assists a financial institution in personalizing their special gifts and promotional material for customers.

References

Ackoff, R.L. From data to wisdom, *Journal of Applied Systems Analysis,* vol.16, pp. 3–9, 1989.

Akerkar, R. *Introduction to Artificial Intelligence*, Prentice-Hall of India, 2005.

Buchanan, B.G. Four areas of computing, 2008. Retrieved from http://www.aaai. org/AITopics/assets/Page%20Art/aichart2.gif

Davenport, T. & Prusak, L. *Working Knowledge*, Boston: Harvard Business School Press, 1998.

Eliot, T.S. The Rock, London: Faber & Faber, 1934.

Frické, M. The knowledge pyramid: A critique of the DIKW hierarchy, *Journal of Information Science*, vol. 33(2), pp.163–180, 2007.

Machlup, F. Semantic quirks in studies of information. In: F. Machlup and U. Mansfield (ed.), *The Study of Information: Inter-disciplinary Message*, New York: Wiley, 1983.

Marco, D. A metadata repository is the key to knowledge management, *DM Review Magazine*, December 2001.

Minsky, M. L. & Papert, S. *Perceptrons: An Introduction to Computational Geometry*, Cambridge, Massachusetts: MIT Press, 1969.

Nonaka, I., & Takeuchi, H. *The Knowledge Creating Company*. New York: Oxford University Press, 1995.

Polanyi, M. *Personal knowledge: Towards a post critical philosophy*. London: Routledge and Kegan Paul, 1962.

Rich, E. & Knight, K. *Artificial Intelligence*, New York: McGraw-Hill Higher Education, 1991.

Russell, S. & Norvig, P. *Artificial intelligence: A modern approach*, Prentice Hall Series, 1995.

Ryan, S. *Wisdom (Stanford Encyclopedia of Philosophy)*, 2007. Retrieved from http://plato.stanford.edu/entries/wisdom/

Sajja, P. S. & Patel, S. M. A multi-layer knowledge-based system adviser for small-scale and cottage industries, *Proceedings of 1st International Conference on Cognitive Systems*, pp.311–320, New Delhi, 1995.

Sajja, P. S. *Knowledge-based systems for socio-economic rural development*, PhD Thesis, Sardar Patel University, India, 2000.

Searle, J. R. Minds, brains and programs. *Behavioural and Brain Sciences*, vol.3, pp. 417–457, 1980.

Spring, G. Artificial intelligence in transportation, 2007. Retrieved from http://onlinepubs.trb.org/onlinepubs/circulars/ec113.pdf

Turban, E. Decision support and expert systems, Macmillan Publication, 1990.

Turing, A. M. Computing machinery and intelligence. *Mind*, vol.59, pp. 433–460, 1950.

Tuthhill, S. & Levy, S. Knowledge-Based Systems: A Manager's Perspective, TAB Professional Reference Books, 1991.

Wigg, K.M. Successful knowledge management is an integrated whole—Not an assembly of individual pieces. In the proceedings of *Knowledge*, London, vol.1, pp. 179–202, 1999.

CHAPTER 2

Knowledge-Based Systems Architecture

■ 2.1 SOURCE OF THE KNOWLEDGE

The data pyramid discussed in Chapter 1 shows that knowledge is difficult to acquire directly—it needs to be processed from the raw observations and information from the domain. The basic source of the knowledge is the human mind. Another often-accessed resource for knowledge is data and information from the environment. Experience of working in a given domain, survey results, media reports, case studies, and experts are the means through which knowledge can be acquired. However, no formal method exists for knowledge acquisition, such as the fact-finding methods suggested in the disciplines software engineering or systems analysis and design disciplines (see Figure 2.1).

■ **FIGURE 2.1**
Sources of
knowledge

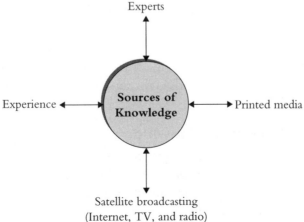

Knowledge in any field is usually of two types:

- Public knowledge—Public knowledge includes the published definitions, facts, and theories, available in textbooks, journals, research papers, and so on. But public knowledge is not the only source of human expertise.
- Private knowledge—Human experts generally possess private knowledge. Private knowledge consists largely of rules of thumb, also called heuristics. Heuristics enable human experts to make educated guesses when necessary, recognize promising approaches to problem solving, and deal effectively with faulty or incomplete data.

■ 2.2 TYPES OF KNOWLEDGE

■ 2.2.1 Commonsense and Informed Commonsense Knowledge

Commonsense knowledge and informed commonsense knowledge possess general principles and concepts of the domain. Commonsense knowledge is general knowledge about a domain that an average person is expected to know—this person need not be an expert. An example of commonsense knowledge is "All people who do not exercise gain weight." Informed commonsense knowledge is knowledge of a given domain that is common for all experts within the domain. An example is "Because of hormonal imbalances, a person also may become overweight."

■ 2.2.2 Heuristic Knowledge

Heuristic knowledge is a practical rule of thumb applied to problem solving that does not give a guarantee of success. Heuristic comes from the Greek *heuriskein*, which means "to find." It pertains to the process of gaining knowledge or some desired result by intelligent guesswork rather than by following some pre-established formula. It is a rule of thumb or an argument derived from experience.

■ 2.2.3 Domain Knowledge

This type of knowledge refers to a specific area of application, such as chemical analysis or drug designing in bioinformatics. Domain knowledge is knowledge that is specific to the domain, rather than general knowledge or commonsense knowledge.

■ 2.2.4 Metaknowledge

Knowledge about knowledge is known as metaknowledge. Metaknowledge is helpful when searching required knowledge and applying it to problem solving. It gives an idea about the ontology (the scheme in which the domain knowledge is represented) and its usefulness for problem solving, matching characteristics of problems and situations where metaknowledge can be applied and hence, increasing the ease of operation.

■ 2.2.5 Classifying Knowledge According to Its Use

Knowledge can also be divided according to its use as conditional knowledge, utility knowledge, action knowledge, and goal knowledge, as described in the following sections.

2.2.5.1 Conditional Knowledge

This is knowledge that provides information about certain constraints and prerequisites. For example, a car must have fuel to run and a driver needs to have a key to start the car.

2.2.5.2 Utility Knowledge

This is knowledge or information that provides utility functions on future states. For example, knowledge of an alarm available in an elevator is an example of utility knowledge.

2.2.5.3 Action Knowledge

The knowledge that leads to the best course of action, given the current information, is called action knowledge. This knowledge specifies the next action to be performed.

2.2.5.4 Goal Knowledge

Knowledge that represents goals by specifying a high utility on a desired future state is known as goal knowledge.

■ 2.2.6 Classifying Knowledge According to Its Nature

Another way of classifying knowledge is to determine whether it is tacit or explicit. Tacit knowledge is usually embedded in the human mind through experience. Explicit knowledge is that which is comparatively easy to extract and codify into various sources, such as books, media, reports, and so on.

■ **FIGURE 2.2**
Explicit and tacit
knowledge

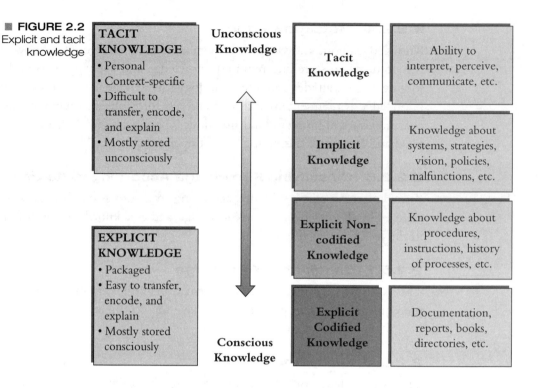

Figure 2.2 shows the different types of knowledge, along with their characteristics.

Knowledge can be permanent, static, or dynamic as shown in Table 2.1.

■ **TABLE 2.1 Types of Knowledge**

Knowledge Type	Meaning	Example
Permanent	Knowledge that never changes, like physical laws	The earth moves around the Sun
Static	Knowledge that is constant over a given period	Policies and procedures
Dynamic	Knowledge that is continuously changing	Prices of shares and gold

■ 2.3   DESIRABLE CHARACTERISTICS OF KNOWLEDGE

Desirable characteristics of knowledge are discussed in Table 2.2.

■ TABLE 2.2 Characteristics of Knowledge

Naturalness	Ease of representing knowledge in its native form
Transparency	Ease of identifying stored knowledge
Adequacy and completeness	Ability of knowledge to contain all components required to solve the problem
Modularity	Ease of storing knowledge components in parts to form a lower-level reusable component library, which leads to increased cost-effectiveness and structuredness by providing high reusability
Usefulness	Extent to which the knowledge is useful to solve a problem in the domain
Explicitness	Ease of representing the knowledge directly
Ease of operation, easy to access, and efficient	Ease of obtaining, applying the knowledge to problem solving, and analyzing the results

■ 2.4   COMPONENTS OF KNOWLEDGE

Knowledge consists of procedural and declarative components. Declarative knowledge is a descriptive representation of knowledge consisting of factual statements and information. These are rules and facts. Declarative knowledge is easy to acquire and document in the knowledge base.

Procedural knowledge results from the intellectual skills to do something. These skills used to make decisions are difficult to explain for most situations. That is why it is comparatively difficult to work with such knowledge. Procedural knowledge generally encompasses a sequence of actions, along with the expected results. Commonsense knowledge and heuristic knowledge are examples of procedural knowledge. The following section describes in detail the various components of knowledge.

■ 2.4.1   Facts

Facts represent sets of raw observation, alphabets, symbols, or statements. Examples of facts are as follows:

- The Earth moves around the Sun.
- Every car has a battery.

■ 2.4.2 Rules

Rules encompass conditions and actions, which are also known as antecedents and consequences. Examples of rules are:

- If there is daylight, then the Sun is in the sky.
- If the car does not start, then check the battery and fuel.

A knowledge-based system that consists only of rules is called a rule-based system. To deal with uncertainty, the rules incorporate uncertainty factors.

■ 2.4.3 Heuristics

Besides rules and facts, the knowledge base is enriched with heuristics. Heuristics are the way to represent problem-solving experiences within the knowledge base. They are solutions that an expert employed in a similar situation. Since heuristics are not developed from a standard formula or process, they do not give a guarantee of success. Rules and facts are easy to acquire and document. On other hand, heuristics are generally stored in the minds of experts (albeit subconsciously) in the form of tacit knowledge; hence, heuristics are difficult to characterize, formulate, and document. Examples of heuristics are as follows:

- If there is total eclipse of the Sun, there is no daylight, even though the Sun is in the sky.
- If it is a rainy season and a car was driven through water, your silencer would have water in it, so it may not start.

■ 2.5 BASIC STRUCTURE OF KNOWLEDGE-BASED SYSTEMS

A knowledge-based system is the software containing a source of knowledge called a knowledge base. It is a mechanism for referring to existing knowledge and generating new knowledge—that is, inference, reasoning, and explanation. Figure 2.3 illustrates the basic components of a typical knowledge-based system.

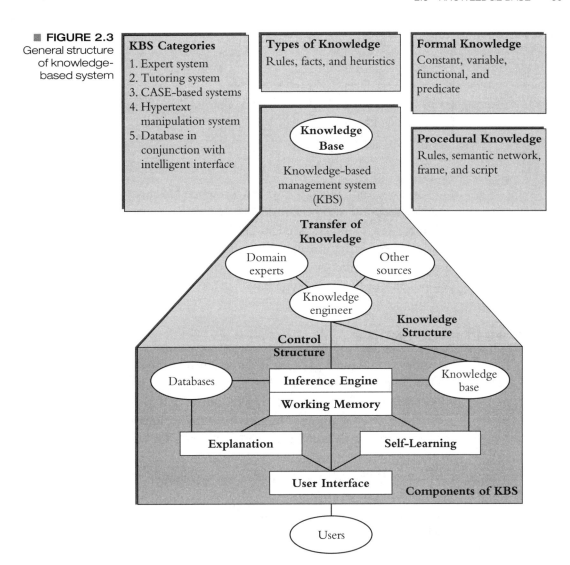

■ FIGURE 2.3
General structure of knowledge-based system

KBS Categories
1. Expert system
2. Tutoring system
3. CASE-based systems
4. Hypertext manipulation system
5. Database in conjunction with intelligent interface

Types of Knowledge
Rules, facts, and heuristics

Formal Knowledge
Constant, variable, functional, and predicate

Knowledge Base
Knowledge-based management system (KBS)

Procedural Knowledge
Rules, semantic network, frame, and script

Transfer of Knowledge

Domain experts

Other sources

Knowledge engineer

Knowledge Structure

Control Structure

Databases

Inference Engine

Working Memory

Knowledge base

Explanation

Self-Learning

User Interface

Components of KBS

Users

■ 2.6 KNOWLEDGE BASE

The knowledge base is the key component of a knowledge-based system. The quality and usefulness of the system is directly related to the knowledge represented in it. The knowledge base contains all types of knowledge in a given form. It is obvious that the knowledge base must contain the domain

FIGURE 2.4
Components of
knowledge base

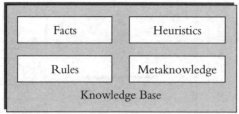

knowledge within which the system is intended to solve the problem. Meta-knowledge should also be stored. As stated earlier, metaknowledge is defined as knowledge about knowledge. This generally includes knowledge about ontology—the structure in which the domain knowledge is represented, along with the target application and methods of use. Figure 2.4 shows the components of the knowledge base.

■ 2.7   INFERENCE ENGINE

An inference engine is a software program that refers the existing knowledge, manipulates the knowledge according to need, and makes decisions about actions to be taken. It generally utilizes pattern matching and search techniques for conclusions. Through these procedures, the inference engine examines existing facts and rules and adds new facts when possible. In other words, an inference engine not only refers the knowledge available within the knowledge base, but also infers new knowledge as needed. It also decides the order in which inferences are made. There are two common rules for deriving new facts from rules and known facts. These are modus ponens and modus tollens.

■ 2.7.1   Modus Ponens

Modus ponens is a common inference strategy. It is simple and easy to understand. The framework can be given as follows:

The rule states that when A is known to be true and a rule states "If A, then B," it is valid to conclude that B is true.

An example can be given as follows:

Rule: IF the teacher is present in the class

THEN students must be present in the class

Given fact: The teacher is present and teaching in the class on the given day

Conclusion: Students must be present in the class

■ 2.7.2 Modus Tollens

Modus tollens is given as:

When B is known to be false and a rule states "If A, then B," then A is false.

An example can be given as follows:

Rule: IF the teacher is present in the class

THEN students must be present in the class

Given fact: Students were absent on the given day

Conclusion: The teacher must be absent, which is a new fact

In simple rule-based systems, there are two kinds of inferences: *forward chaining* and *backward chaining*. Figure 2.5 shows the typical inference cycle.

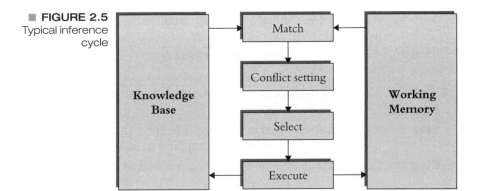

■ **FIGURE 2.5**
Typical inference cycle

■ 2.7.3 Forward Chaining

Environmental inputs and data are stored in working memory. The input of the working memory triggers rules for which conditions match the new data and constraints. These rules then perform their actions. The actions may add new data to memory, thus triggering more rules, and so on. This is also called *data-directed* inference, because an inference is triggered by the arrival of new data in working memory.

An inference engine using forward chaining searches the inference rules until it finds one where an 'IF' clause is known to be true. When found, it can conclude, or infer, the 'THEN' clause, which results in the addition of new information to its dataset.

Figure 2.6 represents the algorithm for forward chaining.

■ 2.7.4 Backward Chaining

The system needs to know the value of a piece of data or a hypothesis. It searches for rules whose conclusions mention this data. Before it can use the rules, the system must test their conditions. This may entail discovering the value of more pieces of data and so on. This is also called *goal-directed* inference, or *hypothesis-driven*, because inferences are not performed until the system is made to prove a particular goal or question.

■ **FIGURE 2.6**
Forward chaining

Step 1: Consider the initial facts and store them in working memory of the knowledge base.
Step 2: Check the antecedent part (left side) of the production rules.
Step 3: If all the conditions are matched, fire the rule (execute the right side).
Step 4: If there is only one rule, do the following:
Step 4.1: Perform necessary actions.
Step 4.2: Modify working memory and update facts.
Step 4.3: Check for new conditions.
Step 5: If more than one rule is selected, use the conflict resolution strategy to select the most appropriate rules and go to Step 4.
Step 6: Continue until an appropriate rule is found and executed.

■ **FIGURE 2.7**
Backward chaining

Step 1: Start with a possible hypothesis, say H.

Step 2: Store the hypothesis H in working memory, along with the available facts. Also consider a rule indicator, R, and set it to Null.

Step 3: If H is in the initial facts, the hypothesis is proven. Go to Step 7.

Step 4: If H is not in the initial facts, find a rule, say, R, that has a descendent (action) part mentioning the hypothesis.

Step 5: Store R in working memory.

Step 6: Check conditions of R and match with the existing facts.

Step 7: If matched, then fire the rule R and stop. Otherwise, continue to Step 4.

Figure 2.7 represents the algorithm for backward chaining.

■ 2.7.5 Forward Versus Backward Chaining

Data-driven reasoning, or forward chaining, is appropriate when:

- There exists sufficient information about an environment to conclude a final decision
- There is a single initial state
- It is difficult to form a goal to verify

Forward chaining starts with some facts and applies rules to find all possible conclusions. Forward chaining is applicable when a goal state is unpredictable or unimportant. In the situation where the goal state is not important but the continuous improvement in the development process must be given more emphasis, forward chaining is to be utilized—for example, the quality improvement phase in the software development process, or improving a business process through which a high-level goal can be achieved. In these situations, goals are either very high or too idealistic to achieve, or can be achieved only through improved procedures.

Goal-directed inference, or backward chaining, is appropriate when:

- The goal is given or obvious
- Environmental constraints or data are not clear
- Relevant data must be acquired during the inference process
- A large number of applicable rules exist

Backward chaining starts with the desired conclusion(s) and works backward to find supporting facts. However, any backward-chaining rule system can be rewritten as an equivalent forward-chaining system. If you already know what you are looking for, backward chaining may be a good solution.

This method often provides better justification or explanation for how you arrived at a particular goal. If explanation and reasoning are important to the users according to the nature of the application, backward chaining is appropriate. Examples of such applications are systems used in learning and training and making medical diagnoses.

If there are few goals and a small number of rules dealing with a large number of facts, again backward chaining is more suitable because it avoids unnecessary efforts to input large amounts of data. However, the backward-chaining methods are not good for the application that needs cross-referencing or data mining to match multiple documents with each other.

Backward-chaining systems manage their subgoals automatically, which is the major attraction of this strategy. However, backward chaining is more limited than forward chaining. Many tasks are difficult or impossible with the backward-chaining method. Backward-chaining systems are good for diagnostic and classification tasks, but they may yield poor results for tasks like planning, design, process monitoring, and so on.

Example: This example illustrates the forward-chaining technique in a medical diagnosis domain. Suppose we have a working memory consisting of the following assertions:

1: runny nose

2: temperature = 104°F

3: headache

4: cough

The rules in our rule base are:

R1: if (nasal congestion and virosis), then diagnose (influenza) exit

R2: if (runny nose), then assert (nasal congestion)

R3: if (body aches), then assert (itchiness)

R4: if (temp > 100), then assert (fever)

R5: if (headache), then assert (itchiness)

R6: if (fever and itchiness and cough), then assert (virosis)

Then the execution is as follows:

First R2 fires, so (nasal congestion) is added to working memory.

R4 fires, so (fever) is added to working memory.

R5 fires, so (itchiness) is added to working memory.

R6 fires, so (virosis) is added to working memory.

R1 fires, diagnosing the ailment as (influenza) and exits.

Example: This example illustrates the backward-chaining technique in the same medical diagnosis domain. We have rules 1 through 6, as with the previous example, and four assertions. The goal is diagnosis (influenza).

Initially, R1 fires: Since the goal, diagnosis (influenza), goes with the conclusion of the rule R1, new goals are created: (nasal congestion) and (virosis), and back chaining is recursively used with these recent goals.

R2 fires, matching the goal nasal congestion. A new goal is created: (runny nose). Back chaining is recursively used. Since (runny nose) is in working memory, it returns true.

R6 fires, matching the goal virosis. Back-chaining recursion takes place with new goals: (fever), (itchiness), and (cough)

R4 fires, adding the goal (temperature > 100). Since (temperature = 104) is in working memory, it returns true.

R3 fires, adding the goal (body aches).

On recursion, there is no information in working memory or rules that match this goal. Therefore, it returns false and the next matching rule is chosen.

Here, the rule is R5, which fires, so the goal (headache) is added. Since (headache) is in working memory, it returns true.

The goal (cough) is in working memory, so that returns true.

Finally, the entire recursive procedures have returned true. This proves the result.

■ 2.7.6 Conflict Resolution Strategies for Rule-Based Systems

For rule-based systems, forward and backward chaining work in cycles by managing and updating the concerned facts and hypotheses of goals in working memory. Based on the content of working memory, appropriate rules from the rule base are selected and triggered. The collection of triggered rules is known as a conflict set. Out of the rules in the conflict set, the inference engine selects one rule based on some predefined criteria. This process is called conflict resolution. Opaque relationships between rules, an ineffective search strategy within the knowledge base, and an inability to learn are the major hurdles of the conflict resolution strategy.

The most common and simple strategy to resolve the conflict is to select the first rule from the conflict set. Here, the order in which rules are stored in the conflict set is very important. Sometimes, the priorities can be set to the rules and the rule with the highest priorities can be selected. One may consider a heuristic approach by managing a simple pointer referencing how frequently the rule is fired to set the priority. Another approach is to select the rule with more details or constraints, or that was recently updated.

Selecting rules randomly is also another possible alternative to resolving the conflict. The function that generates the random rule identifiers may be based on a formula learned through references. Also, it is possible to construct multiple versions of the knowledge base and/or conflict set and use many rules in parallel. Another alternative is to define a search space and apply special-purpose search algorithms, like a heuristic search or hill-climbing search, on it.

■ 2.8 SELF-LEARNING

Self-learning is a scientific task that enables the knowledge-based system to learn automatically from the inference process, cases executed, and environment. To carry out such tasks, one needs to have a control mechanism that discovers general conjectures and knowledge from specific data and experience, based on sound statistical and computational principles.

■ 2.9 REASONING

The capability and quality of a knowledge-based system or human expert depend upon the ability to reason and explanations provided by experts.

When the knowledge-based system makes a decision, it needs to justify it—especially when the system is not being told explicitly how to perform the given task. For instance, suppose an information retrieval program "knows" only that "animals breathe oxygen" and that "all dogs are animals"; then the system may answer perfectly questions like:

Do animals breathe oxygen? Yes.
Are all dogs animals? Yes.

If we ask, "Do dogs breathe oxygen?" then the program must use reason to answer the query. In problems of any complexity, the ability to do this becomes increasingly important. The system must be able to deduce and verify a multitude of new facts beyond those it has been told explicitly.

■ 2.10 EXPLANATION

Presenting the chain of reasoning from the strategic knowledge available in the knowledge base does not let a human user easily understand that reasoning. From such knowledge, the rules used by the knowledge-based system are compiled, and this knowledge is used to provide more abstract explanations of the system's reasoning. This is also known as the explainable expert system approach. Another alternative approach is the reconstructive explainer approach. This approach deals with the development of specific dedicated procedures for explanation and reasoning to justify decisions made by the knowledge-based system.

■ 2.11 APPLICATIONS

The knowledge-based systems can be used in a wide range of applications. A few areas are discussed in the following sections.

■ 2.11.1 Advisory Systems

Knowledge-based systems are comparatively more effective than other computer-based advising methods because they are goal-oriented, deal with uncertainty, are adaptive, and are able to explain their actions. A small-scale business advisory system and a course selection system for students are the examples of this category.

■ 2.11.2 Health Care and Medical Diagnosis Systems

Diagnosing is the process of finding fault in a system or determining an ill state in a living system, based on interpretation of potentially noisy or incomplete data. With the help of knowledge-based systems, dermatology reports, sonography reports, computerized axial tomography (CAT) scan reports, and so on, can be easily analyzed and doctors' decisions can be cross-referenced. For diet, weight loss, and child health purposes, knowledge-based systems can be developed and made available anytime, anywhere, through the platform, much like the Internet.

■ 2.11.3 Tutoring Systems

The tutoring system needs to interact with users in a friendly, customized way by identifying their level and providing methods to access the learning material in a cost-effective way. Users may talk with the system in their "natural" language, receive material according to their style and need, and demand for explanation and reasoning.

Intelligent tutoring systems may appear to be monolithic systems, but for the purposes of conceptualization and design, it is often better to think of them as consisting of interdependent components. There are five major components of such systems, namely, the student module, the pedagogical module, the domain knowledge module, the communication module, and the expert module.

■ 2.11.4 Control and Monitoring

Monitoring means to continuously interpret signals and take necessary actions accordingly when intervention is required. Such monitoring can be applied to an artificial life support system attached to a patient after surgery, for example.

■ 2.11.5 Prediction

Prediction means to forecast the course of the future from a model of the past and present. This process is dynamic, time-consuming, and deals with diverse areas giving hints about the future. A knowledge-based system predicting market trends for the purposes of better portfolio management and fruitful investments is an example of this category.

■ 2.11.6 Planning

A plan is a program of actions that can be carried out to achieve goals by satisfying certain environmental constraints. Such a plan helps in using scarce resources in an effective way by presenting a sequence of actions to be performed. For example, the manufacturing and service division requires good designs and planning solutions to guarantee success. Activities related to software development also require creating plan and monitoring phases. The knowledge-based system also allows little deviation from the plan. The degree of such deviation without disturbing the overall objective is determined by the knowledge-based system. The same is also applicable to design.

■ 2.11.7 Searching Larger Databases and Data Warehouses

Searching and retrieving information from one or more large databases is not an easy job. Especially when the source databases are spread over a distributed platform like the Internet, the knowledge-based methods of searching are helpful to efficiently retrieve information. With the help of a knowledge-based system, the information can be extracted from one or more search engines, ranked according to a user profile, and filtered according to the user's cutoff point.

■ 2.11.8 Knowledge-Based Grid and Semantic Web

A knowledge-based system can be used to map the different ontologies on the semantic web to avoid redundant information and manage web resources in a meaningful way. The knowledge-based system automates the process the management of resources on a grid; through which it facilitates storage, retrieval, and utilization of the resources on demand.

■ 2.12 KNOWLEDGE-BASED SHELL

A knowledge-based shell is a suite of software that allows construction of a knowledge base and interaction with it using an inference engine. A knowledge-based shell provides a fully developed knowledge-based system with an empty knowledge base. Utilities like inference, explanation, reasoning, and learning are available in ready-made fashion. That is why such a shell is the most suitable tool for the experts who cannot develop a knowledge-based system themselves. If necessary, a sensory interface and knowledge update facility is provided; it can serve as a general-purpose framework for the knowledge-based system.

Various knowledge-based system development tools are available. They differ in the level of flexibility they provide in the system and in the range of knowledge representation, reasoning, and other intelligent techniques they support. They also differ in the interoperability level and systems users can develop using those tools. The shell comprises the inference and explanation facilities of a knowledge-based system, without the domain-specific knowledge. This is beneficial to nonprogrammers, who can include their own knowledge on a problem of similar structure but reuse the reasoning mechanisms. A different shell is required for each type of problem, but one shell can be used for many different domains. Thus, selecting a shell with the wrong reasoning strategy for the problem will create more difficulties than it solves.

■ 2.13   ADVANTAGES OF KNOWLEDGE-BASED SYSTEMS

The following sections describe the major advantages of using knowledge-based systems.

■ 2.13.1   Permanent Documentation of Knowledge

A knowledge engineer acquires knowledge from multiple experts and other resources, such as media and the Internet. He represents it in a well-designed knowledge base. The knowledge would be permanently documented for future use.

■ 2.13.2   Cheaper Solution and Easy Availability of Knowledge

Knowledge-based system development is often considered large, complex, and costly. However, creating the knowledge base is one-time cost. After cloning it into multiple copies, it is easy to utilize the knowledge among multiple sites. This breaks monopolies of experts and makes knowledge acquisition and utilization easier. Such cloning also increases the degree of reproducibility and distribution of expertise, as many copies of the knowledge-based system can be made. On other hand, training new human experts is time-consuming and expensive. Knowledge-based systems save cost, time, and effort.

■ 2.13.3 Dual Advantages of Effectiveness and Efficiency

The knowledge-based system, being a computer-based system, already has efficiency-oriented parameters like speed, accuracy, control, and long-term storage of content. By adding the knowledge component, it also becomes effective. It is more efficient than human experts are and, at the same time, tries to become as effective as human experts. This gives the dual advantages of efficiency and effectiveness.

■ 2.13.4 Consistency and Reliability

With the knowledge component added in the system and the ability to act effectively, reliability increases. In addition, fraud and errors can be prevented. Information is available quickly for decision making with proper justification. When the amount and level of knowledge increases, that will result in more reliable decision making and decrease the risk of false decision making, which is an added advantage for a knowledge-based system.

■ 2.13.5 Justification for Better Understanding

The credability and quality of experts depend on the ability to justify their decisions. Knowledge-based systems provide this through brief reasoning and detailed explanations in users' native (natural) language. Better understanding of the decisions concluded by the system leads to the greater reliability and increased scope. This results in improved quality of the system.

■ 2.13.6 Self-Learning and Ease of Updates

With the help of the inference engine, the knowledge base undergoes continuous updating. A knowledge-based system provides updates through automatic machine learning, or the expert or knowledge engineer can manually update it. The domain knowledge of such a system must be tested and undergo updates from time to time; however, the inference framework and control logic may not need frequent revision. Ideally, the inference engine, which provides control knowledge, should not be changed unless there is a drastic constitutional change in the structure of the system. Such self-learning increases the adoptability and flexibility of the system.

■ 2.14   LIMITATIONS OF KNOWLEDGE-BASED SYSTEMS

■ 2.14.1   Partial Self-Learning

As stated earlier, the knowledge-based system can justify its decision making and is able to learn. Since the source that is being mimicked—the human brain—is not fully known, the knowledge-based system can achieve human-like learning in a limited manner. In addition to a great deal of technical knowledge, human experts have common sense. It is not yet completely known how to provide knowledge-based systems with common sense. Case-based reasoning and neural networks incorporate learning in a limited fashion. However, human experts automatically adapt to changing environments, whereas knowledge-based systems must be explicitly updated.

■ 2.14.2   Creativity and Innovation

One cannot expect machines to behave with humanlike creativity. Human experts can respond creatively to unusual situations and apply intuition, whereas knowledge-based systems can, at most, deal with the five basic senses. Knowledge-based systems do not posses any methodology, or even a conceptual framework, to deal with creativity, innovation, and common sense.

Humanlike five senses are partially implemented using artificial (AI) techniques within the knowledge-based system. The vision, listening, smell, taste, and touch functions are developed in such a way that they cannot fully support activities related to perception, emotion, and enjoyment. The main reason for this is that the knowledge-based systems are currently dependent on symbolic input, whereas humans have a wide range of sensory experience.

■ 2.14.3   Weak Support of Methods and Heuristics

Knowledge-based systems cannot function at their full potential when no answer exists or when the problem is outside their area of expertise. If heuristics have been used to search for a suitable model from the model base or a solution from the search space, the success of such systems depends on the quality of the heuristics. The knowledge engineer is responsible for the heuristic development; thus, the knowledge-based systems are dependent on the knowledge engineer for representative domain and control knowledge.

■ 2.14.4 Development Methodology

Developing a system is an art as well as a science. Even for the typical information system, there is no set formula for the development. Disciplines like systems analysis and design and software engineering provide only guidelines and lifecycle models for the development, which are common for all information systems. No development model exists for the knowledge-based system. The information and knowledge possess different characteristics and hence, the typical information system development model may not be suitable for the knowledge-based system. Moreover, knowledge-based computer-aided software engineering (CASE) tools support the information system development, as well as KBS development.

■ 2.14.5 Knowledge Acquisition

Knowledge acquisition is the transformation of knowledge from the forms in which it is available in the world into forms that can be used by a knowledge-based system. Besides development of the suitable models for knowledge-based systems, one may think about the knowledge-finding methods, which are special-purpose fact-finding methods for the knowledge acquisition. The knowledge that is stored in an expert's mind is implicit and tacit in nature; hence, it is difficult to extract with typical fact-finding techniques.

In terms of knowledge management, an organization's value depends on intangible assets, which exist in the minds of employees, in databases, and in myriad documents. Knowledge management technologies capture such intangible elements in an organization and make it globally available. The most popular method of mapping the knowledge of a domain is to use an ontology describing such a domain.

■ 2.14.6 Structured Knowledge Representation and Ontology Mapping

Chunks of knowledge within the knowledge base are available at times in a redundant fashion. When the same knowledge is presented through different ontologies, it may be treated as different each time. The mapping functions of the ontology, or knowledge structure on which knowledge chunks are represented, can be considered. Such mapping effectively reduces the size and complexity of the knowledge base.

One may manage the large size of a knowledge base by dividing the knowledge into multiple reusable partitions according to their representation strategies (ontologies), nature, and application. Such a multilayer knowledge-based system has the advantages of a structured approach and reusability.

■ 2.14.7 Development of Testing and Certifying Strategies and Standards for Knowledge-Based Systems

Knowledge-based systems are meant to work in a narrow domain. Hence, such systems have limited scope and are often developed in an ad hoc manner, which leads to comparatively difficult-to-maintain, nonreliable, and nonrigorous systems. A major drawback of the current state of acceptance of knowledge-based software is the lack of standardization. To test intelligence, the Turing test and Chinese Room methodologies are available. However, these methods have their own limitations and focus either only on the content of the knowledge base or on how they interact with users. Other important procedures such as representation, development of facilities such as inference, self-learning, and explanation require dedicated techniques for verification and validation. That is, verification and validation methods are required not only for the full-fledged knowledge-based system, but also at every stage of the development process. Acquired knowledge must be tested before representing it in the knowledge base. Similarly after acquisition, representation, and self learning, the knowledge base content must be tested for newly contributed knowledge. Standards offered by disciplines such as software engineering are meant for general information systems. For the knowledge-based system, verification and validation techniques and quality metrics are still needed. Such standards will ensure the quality of the system and serve as the basis of certification.

■ 2.15 WARM-UP QUESTIONS, EXERCISES, AND PROJECTS

Warm-up Questions

1. Which inference rule is suitable for proving that the statement "All humans have two legs. Sam is a human. Thus, Sam has two legs." is true? Justify your answer.

2. Can you identify the components of knowledge that are present within knowledge representation systems?

3. Such components of knowledge have intuitive analogies in the parts of natural language speech. Can you think of these analogies?

4. When can we say that a rule is proved?

5. Illustrate how the process of deduction works using facts and rules.

6. What is metaknowledge? Why is it essential in a knowledge-based system?

7. Why do you feel knowledge-based systems are better than human capabilities?

8. Explore a fascinating system developed by Computer Associates, Aion BRE, to identify the characteristics of the knowledge-based system. You can find material on the World Wide Web.

9. Propose any two potential benefits of using a knowledge-based system shell. What are the weaknesses?

10. Download a personal edition of Visual Prolog at http://www.visual-prolog.com/vip6/Download/default.htm. Explore how to use it by creating your own projects, based on examples provided at http://www.visual-prolog.com/vip/example/

11. List advantages and disadvantages of rule-based systems.

12. What type of knowledge is each of the following statements an example of?

    a. Find the cost of an apartment. If the cost is more than $150,000, do not go for it; otherwise, purchase the apartment.

    b. An alcoholic person often suffers from liver problems.

Exercises

1. What is the value of having the knowledge of a knowledge-based system separate from its control?

2. List and define the major components of an expert system.

3. Suppose you wish to use a knowledge-based system to provide a medical diagnosis. Illustrate the essential reasoning methods and the main knowledge-based system features needed for this.

4. Consider a knowledge-based system that has the following three propositions in its current knowledge base:

   a. $\neg Bird(x) \vee Flies(x)$

   b. $\neg Bird(y) \neg \vee Swims(y)$

   c. $Bird(Kuku)$

   Show formally the circumstances under which the system can logically conclude the proposition:

   d. $\neg Flies\ (kuku)$.

5. Translate the following knowledge base into the predicate logic:

   a. Jack and Jill are children.

   b. Everyone loves either a Jack or a Jill.

   c. Anyone who likes children has a friend.

   d. Everyone has a friend.

   Prove that everyone has a friend (sentence d) follows from sentences a, b, and c.

   a. $\forall x(J(x) \rightarrow C(x)) \wedge (K(x) \rightarrow C(x))$

   b. $\forall y \exists z(J(x) \vee K(x)) \wedge L(y,z)$

   c. $\forall r(\exists s L(r,s) \wedge C(s)) \rightarrow \exists q F(r,q)$

   d. $\forall x \exists y F(x,y)$

6. Consider the following set of facts:

   - All people that are not sick and are smart are happy.
   - People that read are smart. Happy people have exciting lives.
   - Healthy people are not sick.

Illustrate how your set of rules could be used in a backward-chaining manner to find out if some particular person has an exciting life.

7. Let us consider the following animal identification problem. The knowledge needed for the problem consists of the following set of rules:

   a. If the animal has hair, then it is a mammal.
   b. If the animal gives milk, then it is a mammal.
   c. If the animal has feathers, then it is a bird.
   d. If the animal flies and it lays eggs, then it is a bird.
   e. If the animal is a mammal and it eats meat, then it is a carnivore.
   f. If the animal is a mammal and it has pointed teeth and it has claws and its eyes point forward, then it is a carnivore.
   g. If the animal is a mammal and it has hoofs, then it is an ungulate.
   h. If the animal is a mammal and it chews cud then it is an ungulate.
   i. If the animal is a mammal and it chews cud, then it is even-toed.
   j. If the animal is a carnivore and it has a tawny color and it has dark spots, then it is a cheetah.
   k. If the animal is a carnivore and it has a tawny color and it has black stripes, then it is a tiger.
   l. If the animal is an ungulate and it has long legs and it has a long neck and it has a tawny color and it has dark spots, then it is a giraffe.
   m. If the animal is an ungulate and it has a white color and it has black stripes, then it is a zebra.
   n. If the animal is a bird and it does not fly and it has long legs and it has a long neck and it is black and white, then it is an ostrich.
   o. If the animal is a bird and it does not fly and it swims and it is black and white, then it is a penguin.
   p. If the animal is a bird and it is a good flyer, then it is an albatross.

   Assume a set of initial facts: the animal gives milk; it chews cud; it has long legs, long neck, tawny color, and dark spots are all TRUE for the animal we want to identify. Assume the following set of premises:

   1. The animal is a giraffe.
   2. The animal is a penguin.
   3. The animal is a mammal.

Using the repeated application of the modus ponens inference rule, determine whether premises 1–3 hold.

Projects

1. Design a framework for a knowledge-based online help desk to assist call center executives to help customers solve their problems. You may select any domain of your choice—for example, camera manufacturer or home appliance retailer. Keep in mind that you are going to apply concepts learned in this chapter (especially Sections 2.2 to 2.9).

2. This project is a continuation of Project 2 in Chapter 1. Based on a preliminary study of the selected topic, prepare a project description, including a literature survey of existing similar systems and specifications of user requirements.

References

Brachman R., Levesque H., eds. *Readings in Knowledge Representation*, Los Altos: Morgan Kaufman. 1985.

Nilsson N. Logic and artificial intelligence, *AI*, 47:31–56, January 1991.

Rich E. and Knight K. *Artificial Intelligence*, second edition, New York: McGraw Hill, 1998.

Winston, P. *Artificial Intelligence*, third edition, Boston: Addison Wesley, 2001.

CHAPTER 3

Developing Knowledge-Based Systems

■ 3.1 NATURE OF KNOWLEDGE-BASED SYSTEMS

Knowledge-based systems (KBS) are quite different from other computer-based information systems, such as Transaction Processing Systems (TPS), Management Information Systems (MIS), and Decision Support Systems (DSS). Knowledge-based systems deal with knowledge and work at an unstructured level. They can justify their decisions and have the ability to learn. This is the main reason why a knowledge-based system must be conceived and developed in a different way. Many knowledge-based systems possess excellent knowledge of the domain in depth; however, they may not satisfy users' needs or may not be operationally feasible. A large amount of domain knowledge and control logic does not guarantee users' acceptance. A knowledge-based system must be user-friendly, too. Other reasons knowledge-based system development fails are cost, level of risk, and level of effort required. Especially when readymade solutions are available, the development results in a waste of labor, time, and money. This chapter discusses the difficulties in knowledge-based system development and the different development phases.

■ 3.2 DIFFICULTIES IN KBS DEVELOPMENT

There are many possible approaches to developing a knowledge-based system: the software can be purchased readymade, the required system can be built in-house, or the development can be outsourced. Many people go for purchasing or outsourcing the development task instead of developing the system in–house because of the aforementioned reasons, which are discussed further in the following sections.

■ 3.2.1 High Cost and Effort

Developing a KBS is costly and tedious. Though it offers a high level of customization in a specific domain and solves problems in a more humanlike fashion, people may not prefer to develop the system. The readymade solutions do not offer a high level of customization, but they do provide quick, comparatively error-free, cheaper, and ready-to-use solutions. Some companies prefer to outsource the development task in order to take advantage of quick, cheap customization, provided such a resource is available.

■ 3.2.2 Dealing with Experts

Developing a KBS may require highly knowledgeable experts, including a knowledge engineer and field experts. Since experts often are rare commodities in their given fields, acquiring knowledge for the system can become a difficult task.

■ 3.2.3 The Nature of the Knowledge

If an expert is not available, his or her knowledge cannot be shared with the knowledge engineer. Even if the knowledge is available, it can be difficult to interpret and transfer it into a knowledge base using a suitable knowledge representation scheme. Moreover, this knowledge needs to be continuously updated.

■ 3.2.4 The High Level of Risk

Developing a knowledge-based system is somewhat risky because the development cost is high. First, as mentioned, it is difficult to acquire knowledge from experts; second, once such a system is developed, it always needs to be updated, which increases the cost of the system. Another factor that increases the cost and risk associated with the system is the amount of heuristics stored in the knowledge base. Expert knowledge is more valuable than facts. Yet, it is the heuristic type of knowledge that gives real power to the knowledge-based system. Heuristics are nothing but practical rules; hence, there is no guarantee of a solution. This is another reason why a KBS carries a certain level of risk.

According to Elias and Hassan (2004), the present trend exists towards ready-to-use, generalized software packages. Such an approach saves time, because many facilities, such as searching, inference, reasoning (control knowledge), and so on, are available readymade—one only has to acquire and store domain knowledge through a user-friendly editor. This leads to comparatively low development cost as time, resources, and errors can be reduced and better flexibility can be achieved. However, specific requirements cannot be accommodated with such generalized software and such a system cannot be merged into an existing system/environment. Attributes like reliability, market trend, usefulness, performance, and so on must be taken into consideration when deciding which development route to take.

Many software engineering models are available when developing the typical information system, as mentioned. Some examples of the development methodology, to name a few, are prototype, structured approach, and the classical model. The classical model freezes the requirements early in the process, forming a Software Requirements Specification (SRS) document, which cannot be further modified. In many cases, the SRS is considered an agreement between the developer and the users. Moreover, such a model does not involve the users much, except when considering their requirements. The prototype, iterative development, and rapid business application development models involve users more, but do not provide methods to collect, encode, and verify expert knowledge. It must be noted that disciplines like systems analysis and design and software engineering only provide guidelines for the information system development, as systems development is an art and a science.

With knowledge-based systems, the resource persons are generally experts. However, it is difficult to extract this knowledge through current fact-finding methods, such as interviews, questionnaires, reviewing records, and observation. (Facts can be extracted using these techniques.) Problem-solving scenarios and proper simulation of the environment lead to easy extraction of knowledge. Above all, the knowledge is voluminous and continuously changing, so the typical data structure will not be able to completely possess the knowledge.

■ 3.3 KNOWLEDGE-BASED SYSTEMS DEVELOPMENT MODEL

There is a need for a methodological approach that considers the characteristics of the knowledge-based system and presents a corresponding development lifecycle model. Figure 3.1 describes this method.

Figure 3.1 shows the basic activities of knowledge-based systems development, namely (i) knowledge acquisition; (ii) feasible requirement elicitation; (iii) strategy selection and overall design of KBS; (iv) ontology selection and knowledge representation; (v) system development and implementation; and (vi) testing, implementation, and training. These six activities are broadly divided into four main phases: analysis, design, detailed design, and implementation. The knowledge engineer and his or her team play a key role in knowledge elicitation, designing systems, developing, testing, and

■ **FIGURE 3.1**
Development methodology for a knowledge-based system

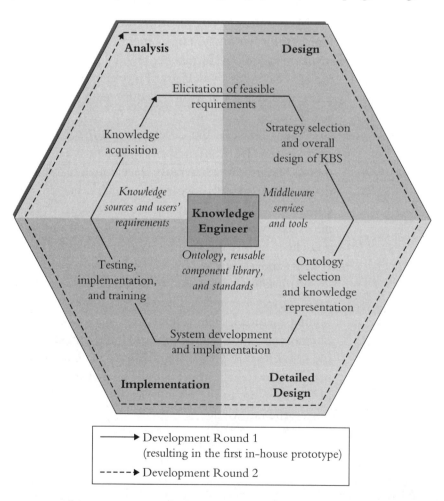

implementing the KBS system. Tools, services, and standards help with these tasks to some extent. The requirements can be extracted from the knowledge sources and users (see Chapter 2).

During the first development round, the knowledge engineer begins to understand the environment and the problems, and prepares the list of requirements by frequently visiting experts and users. After identifying the feasible requirements in technical, economical, and operational terms, the broad design of the system is prepared and distributed among the team members for detailed development. Once the modules are ready, a prototype is prepared. The first prototype is implemented and tested against the standards and list of requirements. Such testing generally leads to the identification of hidden requirements. With these additional requirements and the problems raised by the users and experts, another round starts, involving additional requirements collection, design, and development. There may be multiple such rounds until the desired level of quality or of users' satisfaction is achieved. The following section discusses two major activities in depth: knowledge acquisition and knowledge representation of the proposed model. The typical knowledge acquisition activities are shown in Figure 3.2.

■ **FIGURE 3.2**
Activities in the knowledge acquisition process

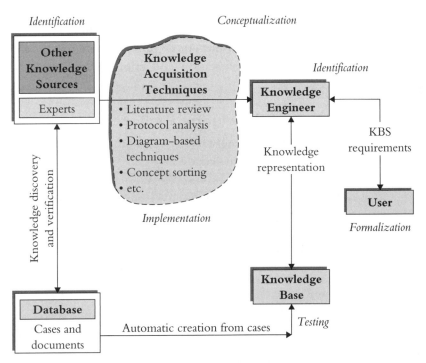

■ 3.4 KNOWLEDGE ACQUISITION

Knowledge is acquired from various sources, such as media, the Internet, printed material and documents, reports, and experts. The process of knowledge acquisition also involves a variety of personnel, such as the knowledge engineer, domain expert users, and programmers. See Chapter 2 for more information on these sources.

■ 3.4.1 Knowledge Engineer

This is the individual who is responsible for the analysis, design, and development of the knowledge-based system.

■ 3.4.2 Domain Experts

Experts are those people in the field who are consulted when a problem arises. They use their knowledge to reliably make decisions, know when exceptions are to be made, and explain their decisions. Experts play a key role in making decisions; the abilities to communicate and explain are valuable when it comes to developing a knowledge-based system as the quality depends upon the successful and proper documentation provided by the experts in the knowledge base of the system.

The knowledge acquisition process emphasizes capturing experts' thoughts and experiences. Typical fact-finding methods may be helpful here to some extent; however, more important are specific knowledge acquisition methods such as elicitation, collection, analysis, modeling, and validation of knowledge.

■ 3.4.3 Knowledge Elicitation

This is a type of knowledge acquisition in which the domain expert is the only source of knowledge.

■ 3.4.4 Steps of Knowledge Acquisition

Generally, the following steps are carried out for knowledge acquisition.

Step 1: Find suitable experts and a knowledge engineer. The creditability of a knowledge-based system is directly related to the amount of expertise/knowledge it possesses. Experts are the main sources of the domain knowledge. The knowledge representation scheme and inference mechanism, etc., can be designed and implemented by the knowledge engineer (who is an expert in KBS development). However, for the domain specific knowledge, one is dependent on the experts of the given field. Finding experts is not difficult, but convincing them to share their knowledge may be. Ideally, knowledge engineers work with one expert at a time; however, many experts' knowledge must be combined and presented in the knowledge base.

Step 2: Proper homework and planning. The knowledge engineer, who is responsible for acquiring knowledge from various sources, must first understand the background information, any available knowledge, and problems of the domain to prepare himself or herself for the acquisition process. The knowledge engineer presents problems to the expert to extract the sufficient amount of knowledge. He or she may utilize appropriate tools, if any, to support the acquisition process. In addition, when and where meetings with experts will take place in order to acquire their knowledge must be planned.

Step 3: Interpreting and understanding the knowledge provided by the experts. The knowledge-based system represents the knowledge of the knowledge engineer, not the experts. Hence, it becomes necessary for the knowledge engineer to get a complete understanding of the experts' knowledge before representing it in the knowledge base. Interpreting the knowledge correctly is also helpful in providing insight into the underlying reasoning model.

Step 4: Representing the knowledge provided by the experts. Once the knowledge acquisition process is started, the knowledge engineer needs to record it immediately in a temporary knowledge-representation scheme. If the representation scheme is suitable, it can be used as the permanent version. This is important, as the knowledge acquired may be interpreted in many different ways.

■ 3.5 EXISTING TECHNIQUES FOR KNOWLEDGE ACQUISITION

Depending on the type and nature of the knowledge, different techniques for acquisition are used. Figure 3.3 summarizes the knowledge acquisition techniques described in the following sections.

■ 3.5.1 Reviewing the Literature

The preliminary knowledge that is readily available from media, the Internet, and other sources can be reviewed without burdening the experts for this knowledge, given that their time is valuable.

■ 3.5.2 Interview and Protocol Analysis

This technique includes structured (e.g., a planned interview with trained personnel) and unstructured interviews with challenging problem scenarios. For the unstructured interview, the knowledge engineer must remain abreast of new trends and problems in the environment. The knowledge engineer asks spontaneous questions based on the response of the experts. This saves time and opens new dimensions and aspects of the knowledge acquisition process. On the other hand, the knowledge engineer prepares himself or herself for the structured interview. In this case, spontaneous problems should be considered in a limited way as the interviewer might not be sufficiently trained. This increases the amount of time required for preparation and the cost for training, but offers good control in managing the acquisition process if more than one engineer or expert is working in a field for the project.

Protocol analysis is a kind of interview in which the domain expert is asked not only to solve a problem, but also to think aloud while doing so

■ FIGURE 3.3
Knowledge acqui-
sition techniques
for different
types
of knowledge

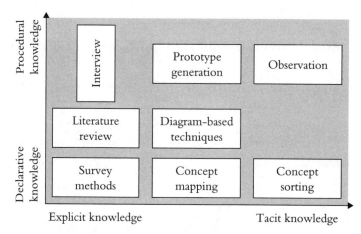

(an online protocol analysis). With an offline protocol analysis, the verbal protocol will be gathered after the expert solves the problem. Qualitative expert knowledge—also called tacit knowledge—is typically acquired with this technique. It helps identify various types of knowledge, such as goals, decisions, relationships, and attributes.

■ 3.5.3 Surveys and Questionnaires

When gathering quantitative factual knowledge—also called explicit knowledge—surveys and questionnaires are useful. The processes are comparatively easy and recommended to automate the efficient processing of the collected knowledge and analyzing the results.

■ 3.5.4 Observation

Observing experts in a live environment sometimes gives a better picture of the solution strategy and may help clear up any confusion.

■ 3.5.5 Diagram-Based Techniques

These techniques include the use of process-flow diagrams, conceptual maps, and event and state charts to clarify the conceptual and logical frameworks of the system.

■ 3.5.6 Generating Prototypes

Experts have acquired a high amount of tacit knowledge, which is difficult to extract without using scenarios or problems. Domain experts often share their knowledge through the use of anecdotes and examples, but for a knowledge-based system, more general principles are required. For the domain experts, a working prototype can be developed to collect necessary knowledge.

■ 3.5.7 Concept Sorting

Concept sorting is a psychological technique that is useful in tapping an organization's knowledge. The knowledge engineer performs the following steps during the process:

Step 1: Consider a textbook or ask a domain expert for the basic concepts and standards of the domain. Then codify each major concept on separate cards.

Step 2: With the help of a textbook or experts, arrange these cards into various groups according to their use.

Step 3: The knowledge engineer asks the expert questions regarding the order and placement of the concept cards in order to arrive at conceptual knowledge.

Step 4: Steps 2 and 3 are repeated until the expert is finished answering questions asked by the knowledge engineer and/or a sufficient amount of knowledge is acquired.

Step 5: If the expert runs out of knowledge, the knowledge engineer takes any three cards and asks for the relationship between the cards.

■ 3.6 DEVELOPING RELATIONSHIPS WITH EXPERTS

Before meeting the experts, the knowledge engineer is supposed to acquire explicit knowledge from the available sources so as to utilize the expert's valuable time most effectively. Making a good impression on the expert positively affects the knowledge extraction process. The knowledge engineer may use psychology, informed common sense, and domain knowledge to attract the expert's respect and attention. The knowledge engineer should use domain language jargon and show glimpses of informed common sense about the domain to create a sense of trust and reliability. If the project is going to take a long time, the knowledge engineer may develop personal working relationships with experts.

The location for the knowledge acquisition session must provide the basic facilities and necessary tools. The style of expert and type and nature of knowledge are the main factors in determining the location and required facilities. For example, if the concept-sorting technique is going to be used, the concept cards and comfortable seating arrangements must be available. The location should be quiet and free from interruption—for this reason, the expert's office is not an ideal location.

■ 3.7 SHARING KNOWLEDGE

Experts have gained their knowledge by learning and practicing in different situations and different places. One expert, having the same qualifications and background as another, will have a different knowledge base if learned and practiced in a different setting. They may share the meaningful outcomes of their learning process to enrich and generalize their knowledge. Conferences, symposiums, seminars, books, magazines, and journals are just some of the ways they can share their knowledge; others are described in the following sections.

■ 3.7.1 Problem Solving

In this style, the expert solves a real-life problem and the knowledge engineer observes him or her doing so. This is very similar to the fact-finding method, observation, discussed in Section 3.5.4.

■ 3.7.2 Talking and Storytelling

In this style, the expert shares his or her knowledge by explaining logical, procedural, and conceptual fundamentals of the domain. However, the practical training may be overlooked, as the storytelling may not incorporate observations of real problem-solving scenarios.

■ 3.7.3 Supervisory Style

In this style, the expert supervises the process of problem solving, and if there is some confusion or difficulties, may take over the process. In fact, the expert may be hard-pressed to not take over the process, in order for the knowledge engineer (or others who are learning) to solve the problem for him- or herself. Figure 3.4 illustrates three different types of knowledge sharing.

■ 3.8 DEALING WITH MULTIPLE EXPERTS

While an expert is a reliable knowledge source, he or she may make mistakes. It is always desirable to collect the views and knowledge from multiple

■ **FIGURE 3.4**
Knowledge sharing
techniques

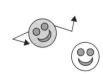

Problem-solving
type

Talking and story-
telling type

Supervisor
type

experts, cross–verify them, and represent the views and knowledge in the system. This increases the system's reliability and depth.

■ 3.8.1   Handling Individual Experts

With this process, the expert's knowledge is acquired on an individual bases. Such an individual assessment gives full freedom and opportunity to both the knowledge engineer and the expert to elaborate on this knowledge without many restrictions.

■ 3.8.2   Handling Experts in Hierarchical Fashion

Here, the knowledge developer meets the expert, who is most important in the organization hierarchy, early in the knowledge-capture process to clarify the objectives, key functions, and plan. The knowledge engineer may seek necessary permission to access resources and get information about personnel or specialists in the domain. The knowledge engineer may then meet the other experts individually or in a group according to requirements.

■ 3.8.3   Small-Group Approach

Experts are classified into various small groups according to the type of knowledge required and their expertise. Different knowledge acquisition techniques are applied in each group, which also helps clarify the suitability of certain techniques. The experts' responses are monitored, and the functionality of each expert is tested against the expertise of the others. There may be conflict when experts' opinions differ. Figure 3.5 shows three strategies for dealing with multiple experts.

■ **FIGURE 3.5**
Dealing with
multiple experts

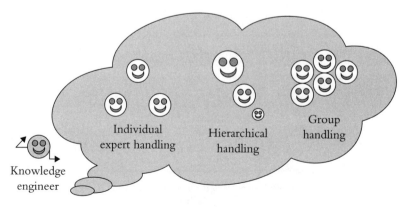

■ 3.9   ISSUES WITH KNOWLEDGE ACQUISITION

Some of the most important issues in knowledge acquisition are as follows:

- Most knowledge rests with experts, so it cannot be extracted directly.
- Experts have vast amounts of knowledge, but it is continuously changing. Thus, this knowledge can be said to have a "shelf life."
- Experts are rare, and it is difficult to prepare them for the knowledge acquisition process. Experts may not have the required attitude to communicate their knowledge, or may have insufficient time or resources to do so properly. Some do not want to share their knowledge.
- Sometimes knowledge is subconscious; in such cases it is difficult for the expert to interpret or explain that kind of innate knowledge.
- An expert is not always correct. Experts frequently provide incomplete and even incorrect knowledge, or may not be able to articulate their knowledge at all.
- No single expert knows everything; one has to contact multiple experts.
- The knowledge engineer is supposed to acquire knowledge from multiple experts. However, opinions among multiple experts may differ significantly.

■ 3.10   UPDATING KNOWLEDGE

The development of knowledge-based systems is not a one-time job. What ensures the quality of the system is the domain knowledge incorporated within it. The control logic, such as the inference engine and searching mechanism framework, may not be changed, yet the knowledge base undergoes continuous updating. There are three means by which updates can be made, which are discussed in the following sections.

■ 3.10.1   Self-Updates

The system may learn from the cases it handles and update itself accordingly. Such self-learning is known as automatic learning or machine learning.

■ 3.10.2   Manual Updates by Knowledge Engineer

The knowledge engineer keeps a constant eye on the trends and advancements of the domain and updates the knowledge base as needed.

■ 3.10.3   Manual Updates by Experts

The knowledge-based system is developed in conjunction with a general editor or knowledge acquisition tool. The editor facilitates gathering the expert's knowledge by asking interactive questions, considering the answers given, and storing the appropriate content in the knowledge base. The editor may achieve this using the standard knowledge acquisition techniques.

Figure 3.6 presents the different approaches to updating the knowledge.

■ 3.11   KNOWLEDGE REPRESENTATION

Knowledge representation is a methodology by which a suitable ontology (structure) is selected to represent a given knowledge component in such a way that operations like storage, retrieval, inference, and reasoning are facilitated without disturbing the required characteristics of the knowledge components. With knowledge representation, real-world knowledge is used for problem solving and reasoning.

A good knowledge representation strategy acts as a medium to achieve computation efficiency, human expression, and basis for reasoning. It is a kind of knowledge structure (more than a data structure) that enables easy operations on the knowledge it possesses. The basic difference between a data structure and a knowledge structure is that data structures contain data and provide an access mechanism (for reference only) for the stored data, whereas the knowledge structures contain knowledge to provide reasoning and inference to achieve intelligent problem solving. That is, the knowledge structure incorporates a special representation scheme and offers methodology to access knowledge. A knowledge structure can hold data and information, but a data structure does not contain knowledge or a support mechanism to access it. The process of inference is an example of such an advanced knowledge accessing technique, which is not needed when a data

■ **FIGURE 3.6**
Knowledge
updates

Self-update by
system

Update by knowledge
engineer

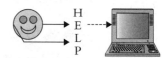

Update by expert
through interface

FIGURE 3.7
Data structures
and knowledge
structures

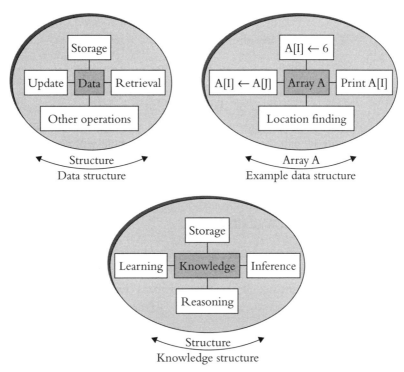

structure is used. Figure 3.7 represents the basic difference between data structures and knowledge structures.

It is said that knowledge is power. However, the power of the knowledge lies in the way it is expressed and used for problem solving. For any human being, or artificially intelligent machine for that matter, there is a need for an efficient knowledge representation facility that does the following:

1. It should be able to represent (hold) the given knowledge to a sufficient depth.
2. It should preserve the fundamental characteristics of knowledge, such as completeness, accessibility, transparency, naturalness, and so on (see Chapter 2 for more knowledge characteristics).
3. It should be able to infer new knowledge.
4. It should be able to provide reasoning and explanation.
5. It should be adaptive enough to store updates and support incremental development.

6. It should be an independent lower-level component so that it can be reused in other places.

Also, it should be noted that no more than required knowledge is available in a knowledge representation strategy.

Depending on the type of knowledge, the representation scheme can be finalized. The knowledge representation scheme can be classified into two broad categories: (i) factual knowledge representation and (ii) procedural knowledge representation. The following sections describe factual knowledge and procedural knowledge in detail.

■ 3.12 FACTUAL KNOWLEDGE

Factual knowledge is also known as formal knowledge and can be represented using first-order logic supporting constants, variables, functions, and predicates. It also uses symbols such as And ($\land$), Or ($\lor$), Not ($\sim$), Implies ($\Rightarrow$), There exists ($\exists$), For all ($\forall$), and so on to make meaningful compound statements.

■ 3.12.1 Constants

Constants are those symbols that do not change—they represent a specific type of fixed knowledge. For example, the Earth moves around the Sun. This can be considered as a universal truth, which cannot be changed during execution of the knowledge-based system.

■ 3.12.2 Variables

Variables take different values within a fixed domain. All humans, all cars, all dogs, and all computer e-mail addresses are variables. The value of such variables may change during the execution of the system from time to time. For example, the knowledge that "all humans breathe oxygen" is applicable to every element that is "human."

■ 3.12.3 Functions

Functions are the sets of instructions that carry out processes and return a predefined value. The example of such a function is Father ('Harry') returns 'James.' It is a function that outputs a string (here 'James' by considering the parameters used along with the function 'Father' (here 'Harry').

■ 3.12.4 Predicates

Predicates are special functions that return only Boolean values, either "True" or "False." The predicates are special types of functions that return only Boolean (true/false) values. The function Father ('Harry') discussed in the previous subsection is a string type and returns 'James.' The function Father ('Harry,' 'James')returns true if 'James' is the father of 'Harry.' Note that Father ('James,' 'Harry') returns false.

■ 3.12.5 Well-Formed Formulas

A well-formed formula (WFF) is a string of symbols that is generated by a formal language. That is, a string is a member of the language generated by the grammar of the language. A formal language can be identified with the set of its WFFs. Figure 3.8 provides examples of constants, variables, functions, and predicates, along with a WFF.

The organization system of a library, a taxonomy of web pages, and bibliographic knowledge can be efficiently stored using factual knowledge.

■ 3.12.6 First-Order Logic

First-order logic is generated by combining predicate logic (language-like representation of knowledge that facilitates inference using predicate calculus) and propositional logic (logic based on propositions, which are statements that are either true or false).

Propositional logic is useful, but it has a major shortcoming: We cannot generalize sentences. Predicate logic overcomes this by allowing us to *quantify* variables. To do this, predicate logic introduces two quantification symbols:

- *Universal quantification*: $\forall x$.
- *Existential quantification*: $\exists x$.

■ FIGURE 3.8
Examples of
factual knowledge
representation

Constant:	RAM, LAXMAN
Variable:	Man
Function:	Elder (RAM, LAXMAN) returns any value, here, RAM
Predicate:	Mortal (RAM) returns a Boolean value, here, True
WFF:	'If you do not exercise, you will gain weight' is represented as: $\forall x[\{Human(x) \wedge {\sim}Exercise\ (x)\} \Rightarrow Gain\_weight(x)\ ]$

This enables us to give some general sentences over those possible in propositional logic:

$\forall x.\text{Man}(x) \Rightarrow \text{Mortal}(x)$. All men are mortal.

$\forall x \exists y.\text{Father}(x,y)$. Every man has a father.

First-order logic is powerful and expressive. However, such a high degree of expression sometimes complicates the process of inference. Also, it is not possible to represent generalized knowledge, such as "Sweety eats everything that she likes." It is difficult to mention each thing that Sweety likes in a few rules. First-order logic may not be helpful in creating references to other sentences; hence, high-order logic is required.

■ 3.13 REPRESENTING PROCEDURAL KNOWLEDGE

Procedural knowledge represents how to reach a solution in a given situation. It can be thought of as "know-how." For example, to find whether "RAM" is older than "LAXMAN," we first have to find their ages and then compare them. In any situation, procedural knowledge is after-the-fact reflection, as the procedures cannot be exactly molded into words. Many decision-making situations use tacit knowledge, which is difficult to express in words. Such knowledge is nothing but the steps in a procedure; hence, it is known as procedural knowledge. This is similar to declarative knowledge, except that tasks or methods are being described instead of facts or things. Examples of procedural knowledge are rules, strategies, procedures, and models.

■ 3.13.1 Production Rules

With production rules, knowledge is represented as a sequence of conditions and the appropriate actions. The general format of the rule is as follows:

If <conditions>, then <actions>

Rules are simple and easy to understand, implement, and modify. Also, with rules, it is easy to incorporate uncertainty. However, the problems with this knowledge structure are the increased size of the knowledge base and there is no efficient way to specify relationships between rules. Because the rules are simple, to solve a real-life application in knowledge-based fashion, a large number of rules are needed. Such a high volume increases the difficulties in acquiring, documenting, and encoding the rules into the knowledge base.

Rules permit the generation of new knowledge in the form of facts that are not initially available but that can be deduced from other knowledge parts. These facts are generated as the conclusions of rules are applied. The deduction procedure using facts and rules works as follows:

1. Knowledge exists in the form of facts and rules.
2. New facts are added.
3. Combining the new facts with the existing facts and rules leads to the deduction of further facts.

This kind of deduction forms the source of a symbolic reasoning that uses knowledge structures. However, with symbolic reasoning, a knowledge-based system does not assure that the system will produce accurate results. Inaccurate knowledge will lead to imperfect conclusions. Therefore, the quality of the knowledge that a rule-based system employs is a critical determinant of how well the system performs.

Rules are generally not suitable for modeling complex real-world relationships and creating real-world models, but instead can be used to represent procedural or shallow knowledge.

■ 3.13.2 Semantic Networks

Semantic networks are graphical descriptions of knowledge composed of nodes (objects or concepts) and links (arcs) that show hierarchical relationships. The link carries semantic information, such as the *is_a*, *type_of*, and *part_of* links. Because of their hierarchical nature and their ability to represent class relationships through links, semantic networks can show inheritance. A semantic network stores the relationships efficiently, provided they are generic and standard. Figure 3.9 shows a small example of a semantic network.

Semantic networks contain various links and follow a specialized hierarchy. All of the relationships shown in the network do not have to

■ **FIGURE 3.9**
An example of a
semantic network

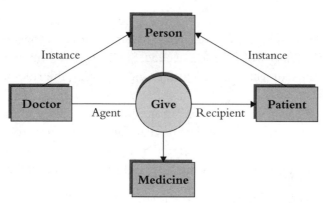

be inherited. Generally, the inherited relationships are further constrained to narrow the domain. An example of such a constrained extension follows:

All patients have complaints (symptoms). A heart patient has chest pain and high blood pressure. That is, high blood pressure and chest pain are specific symbols short-listed from the set of possible symptoms, with constraints that can narrow the search space to diagnose the correct disease.

A semantic network is easy to create and maintain, and provides efficient storage. However, it is comparatively inefficient at reasoning. Semantic networks are normally considered specifications, and do not allow exceptions or default knowledge.

The main inference mechanism used here is to follow links between nodes. This can be achieved by two approaches:

- Intersection search: Begin the search out of two nodes and find the intersection that gives the relationship among the objects. With this process, one can assign a special tag to each visited node.
- Inheritance: The *is_a* and *instance* representation provides a mechanism for implementation.

The intersection search has merit because it provides fast parallel implementation, whereas inheritance provides a means of dealing with default reasoning.

Even if the usual features of semantic networks are employed in several large knowledge-based systems, this is a hierarchical classification of knowledge. For us, such classification is a natural reasoning process, but not so much for machines. Hierarchical classification leads to enhanced generalization, information reduction, and significantly increased performance.

■ 3.13.3 Frames

Frames—first proposed by Marvin Minsky, who has made important contributions to AI, cognitive psychology, computational linguistics, and robotics—have been the primary attempt to mimic human reasoning and knowledge in a hierarchical representation. They are descriptions of conceptual and default knowledge about a given entity. Frames can be logical or physical. Examples include a bike, a teacher, and a course. A frame contains different elements known as slots. Slots are the building blocks defined by the knowledge engineer. The example shown in Figure 3.10 shows a frame for a bike.

A frame organizes knowledge—typically according to cause-and-effect relationships. The slots of a frame contain items like rules, facts, videos, references, and so on. Besides the typical components like the frame name and other slots, it may contain pointers to other frames or procedures. These procedures include default inference, consistency, and checking procedures. However, frames are static and contain only default knowledge. Hence, they are useful for storing routine events.

The slot of a frame is further divided into one or more facets. A facet may be any of the following:

• Explicit or default values
• A range of values
• An if-added type of procedural attachment, which is an attachment that specifies an action to be taken when a value in the slot is added or modified

■ **FIGURE 3.10**
An example of a
frame

Name:	Power bike
Broad Category:	Land vehicle
Subcategory:	Gearless
Fuel Type:	Gas
Cost:	$350
Capacity:	Two persons
Speed:	160 km /hour

- An if-needed type of procedural attachment, which triggers a procedure to handle an exception or to get values that the slot does not have
- Other components, which may be references to other frame or other knowledge

A frame-based system interpreter must be capable of the following in order to exploit the frame slot representation:

- Check for a slot value that is correct and within specified range, which is then added to the frame, depending on the domain attribute
- Dissemination of *definition* values
- Inheritance of default values
- Computation of the value of a slot as required
- Checking whether the correct number of values has been computed

The principle of frames has been further enhanced and refined in the object-oriented programming paradigm and the multiagent system.

■ 3.13.4 Scripts

A script is a knowledge representation structure for a specific situation. With a frame, one can incorporate only default knowledge about an entity. The script contains slots, such as objects, their roles, entry and exit conditions, and different scenes describing a process in detail. Scripts provide the framework for the actions to be carried out. Based on the sequence of scenes within the frame, it can predict events and answer questions. The unusual events are easily identified because they are not included as default knowledge. Figure 3.11 represents a script for driving to the hospital.

Scripts are beneficial because they demonstrate causal relationships between events.

■ 3.13.5 Hybrid Structures

The knowledge structures discussed in the earlier sections have their own advantages and limitations. The knowledge base generally consists of more than one knowledge structure, depending on the requirements. Some applications may require a hybrid knowledge structure that incorporates more than one representation scheme. Procedural rules already have been included in frames. Similarly, a semantic network presents inherited relationships in

■ **FIGURE 3.11**
An example of a
script

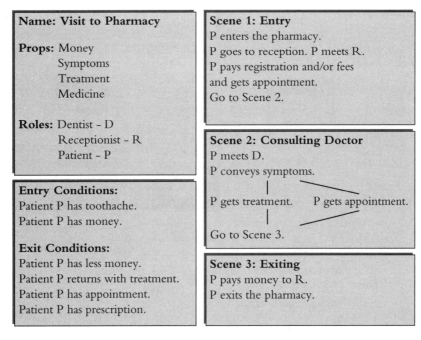

Name: Visit to Pharmacy

Props: Money
      Symptoms
      Treatment
      Medicine

Roles: Dentist - D
      Receptionist - R
      Patient - P

Entry Conditions:
Patient P has toothache.
Patient P has money.

Exit Conditions:
Patient P has less money.
Patient P returns with treatment.
Patient P has appointment.
Patient P has prescription.

Scene 1: Entry
P enters the pharmacy.
P goes to reception. P meets R.
P pays registration and/or fees
and gets appointment.
Go to Scene 2.

Scene 2: Consulting Doctor
P meets D.
P conveys symptoms.

P gets treatment.   P gets appointment.

Go to Scene 3.

Scene 3: Exiting
P pays money to R.
P exits the pharmacy.

graphical format but not the default static knowledge. If the node representing an object within the given semantic network is enriched with the default knowledge (or a reference to it) and with if-needed/if-added procedural attachments within the node, the advantages of frames and semantic networks can be achieved simultaneously. One may develop the necessary inference and reasoning procedure for the hybrid infrastructure proposed. This situation is demonstrated in Figure 3.12.

In the same fashion, scenes of scripts may incorporate default knowledge and rules to create a hybrid script. Such a hybrid structure minimizes the requirements of defining and linking the default knowledge separately. When it is needed (in between the procedures), the default knowledge is readily available. However, before combining the knowledge structure like this, one must ensure the level of modularity needed and that there is no need for the default knowledge to remain independent to solve other problems within the domain. A knowledge structure, like a script or a frame, should not be invoked frequently to get the default knowledge. Instead, one may put a slot containing references (paths) to the frames within the script.

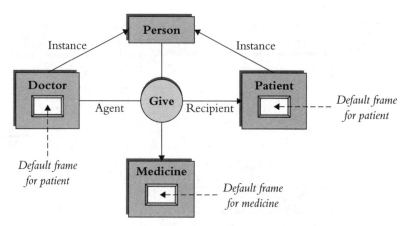

Ronald Brachman (Brachman, 1985) designed a network notation for his Knowledge Language One (KL-ONE), which is the ancestor of existing hybrid systems. Almost 20 popular knowledge representation and reasoning systems have been implemented in the KL-ONE tradition (Akerkar, 2001). Brachman drew a clear distinction between the different kinds of links in a semantic network.

The basic unit of information (i.e., frames) in KL-ONE is called a Concept, which denotes a set of objects. A Concept has a set of components, each denoting a property that must be true of each member of the set. Specifically, one type of component is a *Roleset* that is analogous to a "slot" in a "frame-like" language. For instance, we can construct a Concept denoting the set of all people where each person has a mother tongue:

PERSON is a Concept and has a Roleset mother tongue.

Unlike semantic networks, domain-dependent relationships are not represented as links, but as Concepts and Rolesets. Descriptions are separated into two basic classes of Concepts: primitive and defined. Primitives are domain Concepts that are not fully defined and thus all Concepts denoting "natural kinds" (e.g., person, trees, birds) are primitive. For example:

PERSON is a primitive Concept subsumed by MAMMAL and has a Roleset mother tongue with a number restriction of exactly one with a value description of LANGUAGE.

That means, each person is a mammal and has exactly one mother tongue that must be a language.

Defined Concepts are complete definitions. For example, PARENT:

```
PARENT is a nonprimitive Concept is subsumed by PERSON and has a
Roleset Child with a number restriction of one or more and a value
description of PERSON.
```

It means a parent is a person who has at least one child who is also a person.

■ 3.13.6 Semantic Web Structures

The Semantic Web was thought up by Tim Berners-Lee, inventor of the World Wide Web (WWW), Uniform Resource Identifier (URI), Hypertext Transfer Protocol (HTTP), and Hypertext Markup Language (HTML). The Semantic Web is an evolving extension of the WWW in which the semantics of information and services on the Web is defined, making it possible for the Web to "understand" and satisfy the requests of people and machines to use its content (Berners-Lee et al., 2001).

In general, the Semantic Web deals with the syntaxes that use URIs. Examples of such syntaxes are Resource Description Framework (RDF) and eXtensible Markup Language (XML). Special languages have been created for ontology mapping and inference. An example of such language is DARPA Agent Markup Language (DAML) [http://www.daml.org/], which was created by the Defense Advanced Research Projects Agency (DARPA) [http://www.darpa.mil/].

The simplest way to deal with knowledge representation on the Internet is to embed the reference path (URL) of a knowledge structure, as defined in RDF or an equivalent tool, into the application. One may create tags to incorporate fuzziness and uncertainty with rules using XML. Sajja (2007) in her paper has described a fuzzy XML model to access distributed databases. Ranking (by importance and usage) the associations instead of the content/ node is another alternative to represent knowledge on the Web.

Recently, knowledge-based systems began dealing with information described in Semantic Web languages like Web Ontology Language (OWL) and RDF, and providing services such as storing, reasoning, querying, and debugging. There are two basic requirements for these systems. First, they have to satisfy the application's semantic requirements by providing sufficient reasoning support. Second, they must scale well in order to be of practical use. Given the sheer size and distributed nature of the Semantic Web, these requirements impose additional challenges beyond those addressed by earlier knowledge-based systems.

Wider recognition of World Wide Web Consortium (W3C) recommendations, such as RDF and OWL, has led to modern tools and products from both emerging and mainstream industries (Akerkar, 2009). As semantic technologies prove their value with targeted applications, opportunities to consider applying them as business enablers increase. Knowledge management is a key enabler for improving organizational performance through the better use of intellectual assets; in addition, many businesses must deal with knowledge services that form larger parts of the global economy. Consequently, recent examples exist in which organizations have applied semantics to improve on traditional knowledge-management approaches or to realize emerging knowledge-services requirements.

■ 3.14   USERS OF KNOWLEDGE-BASED SYSTEMS

The first user of the knowledge-based system is the knowledge engineer, who acts as a tester. The expert also tests the system and gives valuable suggestions. When it is commercially available for use, the KBS can be used as an "assistant" to carry out intended tasks and as a "colleague" to cross-reference decisions made by other experts in the field. For novice learners, the knowledge-based system can be used as "trainer" and as a "tutor."

■ 3.15   KNOWLEDGE-BASED SYSTEM TOOLS

Certain key consequences of research into knowledge-based systems have been progresses in programming languages and software development environments. Due to idiosyncratic artificial intelligence techniques, KBS programmers have been forced to develop an intense collection of programming methodologies.

Often, programmers prefer an artificial-intelligence programming language designed for large, complex real-life knowledge-based systems. The two main AI languages are Program Logic (PROLOG) and List Processing (LISP). PROLOG is a logic-based language with a set of facts, rules, and goals. It attempts to prove assumed goals by applying rules to known facts. PROLOG uses backward chaining. That is, it starts with the goal and works backward toward the known facts. The goal is eventually reduced to simple facts. In LISP, facts and procedures are developed and presented in the form of a list.

Both PROLOG and LISP are old special-purpose programming languages, and provide a good understanding of the basics of AI programming. However, these languages are not widely used to develop commercial applications.

Many languages have been developed based on PROLOG and LISP. An example of such a language is C Language Integrated Production System (CLIPS). Another example is Java Expert System Shell (JESS), which is available for free on the Internet [http://herzberg.ca.sandia.gov/jess/], although a license is needed for commercial applications. JESS is directly integrated into the Java Virtual Machine (JVM) and hence, it offers the added advantages of platform independence and object orientation. CLIPS and JESS are discussed further in the following sections.

Other programming environments include knowledge-structuring techniques, for instance, object-oriented programming. Trace packages allow a programmer to rebuild the execution of a complex algorithm and make it possible to resolve the complexities of heuristic search. Many important knowledge-based systems could have been built without such tools and techniques, and many of these techniques have become standard tools for software engineering. Several knowledge-based systems are also produced in conventional programming languages—namely, C++ and Java.

With regard to Web-based environments, Artificial Intelligence Markup Language (AIML) is also available, which is a derivative of XML [http://docs.aitools.org/aiml/spec/]. Its goal is to enable pattern-based, stimulus-response knowledge to be served, received, and processed—both on the Web and offline—in the manner that is presently possible with HTML and XML. Languages like AIML allow knowledge-based applications and general-purpose shells to be developed. Consider, for example, Program D, which is the most widely used free ("open source") AIML bot platform in the world [http://aitools.org/Program_D]. Program D contains features that support knowledge base creation, utilization, and testing. Program D is packaged with an AIML Test Suite that verifies that the program itself complies to

AIML specifications. The program code can also be downloaded from the given site and modified to develop various knowledge-based applications. It is the most feature-complete, best-tested implementation of the current AIML specifications.

For knowledge acquisition in particular, tools like Protégé [http://protege.stanford.edu] help in the development of knowledge-based systems.

One interesting product, developed by an Indian company called iKen Studio [http://www.ikenstudio.com], is a complete online Web-based development framework to construct and deploy knowledge-based systems. It is available as a Software as a Service (SaaS) model only. The company can give free access to those who are interested in using it online for personal or prototype purposes.

Many other visual tools are available for developing knowledge-based systems: such as MATLAB [http://www.mathworks.com], Java Neural Network Simulator (Java NNS) [http://www.ra.cs.uni-tuebingen.de/software/JavaNNS/welcome_e.html], and Predict [http://www.neuralware.com/]. Expert system shells are also available, such as eg2Lite [http://www.expertise2go.com/webesie/e2gdoc/], TMYCIN [http://www.cs.utexas.edu/~novak/tmycinb.html], and Vidwan [http://www.cdacmumbai.in/index.php/cdacmumbai/research_and_publications/research_groups/kbcs_artificial_intelligence/products/vidwan], to develop customized knowledge-based systems.

■ 3.15.1   C Language Integrated Production System (CLIPS)

3.15.1.1   The Basics

There are several general-production system languages; however, CLIPS and JESS are the two most popular. JESS is written in Sun's Java language. It extends features of CLIPS by providing the ability to use scripting applets and interface with the Web.

CLIPS can be downloaded for free from http://www.ghg.net/clips for noncommercial use. The package is downloadable as a collection of source files or as an executable. To start CLIPS from the shell in Unix, type `clips`. If you are using a Windows or Mac operating system, double-click the

CLIPS icon. You will get a window with nothing in it but the command prompt CLIPS>. For the time being, this is where you type your commands and programs. To exit CLIPS, type (exit) or shut down the program. Note that CLIPS commands are always encased in parentheses, as in (assert (foo)). Here is a list of some important ones:

(exit)   Shuts down CLIPS

(clear)   Removes all program and data from memory

(reset)   Removes dynamic information from memory and resets the agenda

(run)   Executes a CLIPS program

The CLIPS shell provides the crucial elements of an expert system, that is:

- A global memory for data, called a fact-list or instance-list
- A knowledge base
- An inference engine to control the execution of rules

Moreover, CLIPS has pattern-matching abilities, extended math functions, conditional tests, and object-oriented programming (COOL: Clips Object-Oriented Language), with abstraction, inheritance, encapsulation, polymorphism, and dynamic binding.

There are eight primitive data types in CLIPS: float, integer, symbol, string, and four address types. Numbers (floats and integers) are represented using the usual syntax, with e for exponentiation. Strings are defined using double quotes, for example: "Ram". All other sequences of characters that do not contain delimiters (<new line>, <tab>, <,>, <">, <(>, <)>, <□>, <|>, <<>, and <~>), and that do not start with ? or $? are symbols. Numbers, strings, and symbols entered in CLIPS are treated as constants and always evaluate to themselves.

Relationships and functions can have any number of arguments, and are written with the following syntax:

```
(<function name> <arg1> <arg2>...)
```

3.15.1.2 The Rete Algorithm

The Rete algorithm was proposed to improve the speed of forward–chaining rule systems by limiting the effort required to recompute the conflict set after a rule is fired. It takes advantage of two empirical observations:

- *Temporal redundancy*: The firing of a rule usually changes only a few facts, and only a few rules are affected by each of those changes.
- *Structural similarity*: The same pattern often appears on the left side of more than one rule.

The Rete algorithm employs a rooted acyclic directed graph, the Rete, where the nodes represent patterns, and paths from the root to the leaves represent left sides of rules. The Rete consists of the *root node*, one-input *pattern nodes*, and two-input *join nodes*. The algorithm keeps information associated with the nodes in the graph up-to-date. When a fact is added or removed from working memory, a token representing that fact and operation is entered at the root of the graph. Then it is broadcast to its leaves, amending as appropriate the information associated with the nodes. When a fact is modified, the old fact is deleted and the new one is added.

The disadvantage of the algorithm is that it requires a great deal of memory.

3.15.1.3 Facts

A fact is a piece of information and is created by *being asserted* onto the fact database using the assert command.

We will give an illustration of it:

```
CLIPS>(assert (color red))
<Fact-0>
```

The <Fact-0> part is the response from CLIPS. It indicates that a new fact (fact number 0) has been cited on the fact database.

The deffacts statement allows the user to define a group of facts:

```
CLIPS> (deffactsrabbits
(rabbit spot)
(rabbitrintintin)
(rabbitfido))
```

The undeffacts statement can be used to eliminate a (deffact) from memory. Facts may be pulled back in rule actions, but you should attach the fact address to a variable on the left side of the rule. It is also possible to list the fact set using (list-deffacts) or to delete a fact set using (undeffacts <deffacts-name>).

3.15.1.4 Rules

In order to define a rule, you should use defrule:

```
CLIPS> (defrulesibling-1 ; rule name
(brother-of ?b1 ?b2) ; condition
=> ; then arrow
(assert (brother-of ?b1 ?b2))) ; action
```

Here, the expressions ?b1 and ?b2 are variables. You can use the (run) command to execute rules. Likewise, rules can have multiple conditions and actions and an optional comment:

```
(defrule rule-name "optional comment"
(condition-1)
...
(condition-n)
=>
(action-1)
...
(action-m))
```

If all of the patterns of a rule's condition match the facts, the rule is activated and put on the plan or agenda. A plan is a collection of activations, which are those rules that match pattern entities. Any number of activations may be on the plan. CLIPS decides which one to fire and then executes its actions. You can check what is on the plan at any time by executing the (agenda) command.

■ 3.15.2 Java Expert System Shell (JESS)

3.15.2.1 The Basics

JESS stands for Java Expert System Shell. It was developed by Ernest Friedman-Hill at Sandia National Laboratories. It is a rule engine and scripting environment similar to CLIPS that was developed by the National Aeronautic and Space Administration (NASA). JESS is a forward-chaining production system that uses the Rete algorithm. It was written using the Java platform of Sun Microsystems. JESS is free for academic purposes and can be downloaded from http://herzberg.ca.sandia.gov/jess/

The JESS general architecture is shown in Figure 3.13.

JESS has the same basic properties CLIPS has, but its language lacks a few advanced features. For instance, the CLIPS user has a choice of seven conflict resolution strategies in rule firing, while JESS only has the two most important ones, namely *depth (LIFO)* and *breadth (FIFO)*. In JESS, when the depth strategy is in effect, more recently activated rules are fired before less recently activated rules of the same salience. When the breadth strategy is active, rules of the same salience fire in the order in which they are activated. However, in either case, if several rules are activated simultaneously the order in which these several rules fire is unspecified, implementation-dependent, and subject to change. Additionally, it is possible to implement your own strategies in Java by creating a class that implements the `jess.Strategy` interface and then specifying its class name as the argument to `set-strategy`.

The conditional tests (`and` and `or`) are not available in JESS in the left side of rules. Moreover, JESS does not implement modules.

However, JESS has some advantages over CLIPS. The Java language implementation makes JESS the choice for developing Web-based expert systems, even if it is also possible to use CLIPS with C++ in a Common Gateway Interface (CGI) script. JESS enables the user to put multiple expert systems in one process. Java threads can be used to run these systems in parallel.

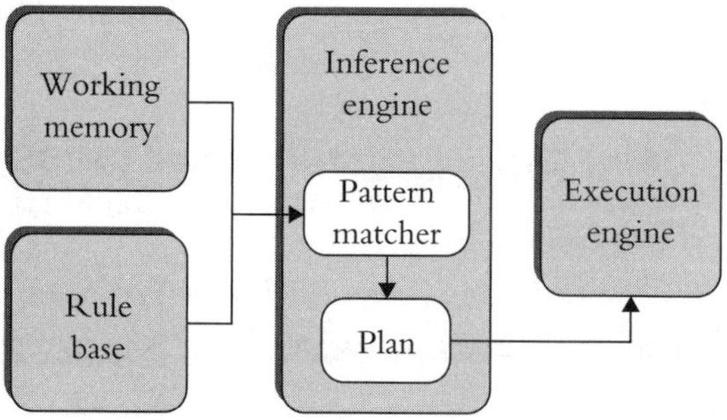

■ FIGURE 3.13
JESS architecture

To run JESS, just type

```
> jess
```

Typing this command, will put display the "Jess>" prompt. You will interact with this shell. To exit from this shell, type

```
Jess> (exit)
```

It is possible to use Unix system commands from the "Jess>" prompt, as follows:

```
Jess>(system pwd)
/users/rakerkar/jess
Jess>
```

Despite the fact that you can write Java programs and use the Rete engine, it is possible to interact just with the JESS shell. You can define facts and rules from the command prompt. JESS stores them in its internal knowledge base, but never gives you access after you clear the memory. Thus, it is better to enter your script in a separate file and call that file from the JESS prompt. You are free to use any editor to edit your file. For example, if the file name is math.clp, you can load it by typing

```
Jess> (batch math.clp)
Jess>
```

You can write comments by preceding them with a ";" character.

All of the facts that you provide obtain an ID and are entered into the knowledge base. The rules are entered into the rule base. When you execute a JESS program, it runs as long as it doesn't find any rule to fire or gets a termination signal, which is (halt), equivalent to exit()/System.exit() in other languages.

In essence, when a JESS program is executed, rules are fired that modify the knowledge base until the goal is reached. After you load your program using the batch function, you should use the reset command to clear the working memory and load the facts into it. To run your program, use the run command. For example:

Jess> (batch math.clp) loads the facts and rules into the knowledge base.

Jess> (reset) clears the working memory and loads the facts and rules into working memory.

Jess> (run) runs the script. Jess> (clear) clears JESS.

After using the clear command, the reset or run commands will not work. You will have to reload the facts and rules into the knowledge base using the (batch) function after using the clear command.

JESS allows floating point and integer numbers, which behave just as they do with any other language.

The Boolean values in JESS are TRUE and FALSE (they are case-sensitive). The JESS equivalent of C's NULL or Java's null is nil.

Strings should be enclosed between double quotes. You can use the escape (esc) character on the keyboard if you want JESS to ignore double quotes. str-length can be used to find the length of a string. str-cmp will let you compare two strings. It returns 0 if the two strings are identical; otherwise, it returns a negative or positive value.

```
Jess> (str-length "where")
5
```

A list consists of an enclosing set of parentheses and zero or more symbols, numbers, strings, or other lists:

```
Jess> (+ 5 3)
8
```

Three logical operators are available in JESS: and, or, and not.

As with any other programming language, JESS allows the use of if-then-else statements and while loops.

```
(if <expression> then <action>+ else <action>+)
(while <expression> do <action>+)
```

Common functions in JESS are:

(reset): Resets the working memory

(clear): Clears JESS

(`facts`): Shows facts currently in working memory

(`rules`): Shows rules currently in working memory

(`batch <filename>`): Sends the shell the file content

(`run`): Starts the engine

(`apply`): Calls a function on a given set of arguments

(`build`): Parses and executes a function from a string

(`open <filename> id w`): Opens a file in write mode

(`read t`): Reads from standard input

(`read id`): Reads the file content

(`printout t "…" crlf`): Prints to standard output

(`printout id "…" crlf`): Prints to a file

(`exit`): Exits the shell

3.15.2.2 Facts

The facts are stored in the knowledge base. You can use `assert` to add a fact to the knowledge base. `assert` is especially helpful when you want to add a fact to a knowledge base when a rule is fired or during the execution of the program. You can remove facts using `retract`.

3.15.2.3 Rules

Rules are responsible for taking actions based on the facts in the knowledge base. The rules have a left side and a right part, with the `implies` operator in between. JESS fires all the rules continuously as long as the conditions on the left are satisfied.

The JESS rule syntax is as follows:

```
(defrule <rule-name> {;optional comment}
<condition-element-1>
<condition-element-2>
...
<condition-element-k>
=>
<action-1>
...
<action-m>
)
```

JESS can be used in two overlapping ways. First, it can be a rule engine—that is, a special kind of program that efficiently applies rules to data. A rule-based program can have thousands of *rules*, and JESS will continually apply them to data in the form of a *knowledge base*. In general, the rules represent the heuristic knowledge of a human expert in a domain, and the knowledge base represents the state of an evolving situation.

JESS is also a general-purpose programming language; thus, it can directly access all Java classes and libraries. For this reason, JESS is frequently used as a dynamic scripting or rapid application development environment. While Java code generally must be compiled before it can be run, a line of JESS code is executed immediately upon being typed. This allows you to experiment with Java application programming interfaces (APIs) interactively and build up large programs incrementally. It is easy to extend the JESS language with new commands written in Java or in JESS itself, and so the JESS language can be customized for specific applications.

JESS is, therefore, useful in a wide range of situations. However, one application for which JESS is not so well suited is as an applet intended for Internet use. JESS's size (a few hundred kilobytes of compiled code) makes it too large for applet use, except on high-speed local area networks (LANs). Furthermore, some of JESS's capabilities are lost when it is used in a browser. For example, access to Java APIs from the JESS language may not work due to security restrictions in some browsers. When building Web-based applications using JESS, you should strongly consider using it on the server side.

■ 3.16   WARM-UP QUESTIONS, EXERCISES, AND PROJECTS

Warm-up Questions

1. List the activities of a knowledge engineer during KBS development.
2. Describe the tools and techniques available to assist the knowledge engineer in carrying out these activities.
3. There are five distinct phases when transforming human knowledge into some form of KBS. The knowledge engineer plays a prominent role in these phases. What are these five phases and what duties do they contain?

4. List the words you might want to use to describe the characteristics of a software professional.

5. If you are a knowledge engineer, what particular knowledge would you expect to find in the following domains:

   a. A university

   b. A wild animal

   c. A cactus

6. Explain the purpose of the following elements of a knowledge-based system:

   a. Expert

   b. Repository

   c. Acquisition module

   d. Knowledge base

   e. Inference engine

   f. User

   g. Interface

7. List the shortcomings of a typical knowledge-based system.

8. Evaluate the basic advantages and disadvantages of interviews as a method of knowledge acquisition.

9. Clarify how the distortion between the knowledge engineer and the knowledge base can be purged.

10. Consider the limitations of basic software engineering lifecycle models in terms of KBS development, and justify the necessity for a methodology when developing a KBS.

11. Compare and contrast frames and object-oriented programming.

12. Describe the concept of inheritance in the context of frames.

Exercises

1. Define a production system. How can such a system be used for either data- or goal-driven problem solving?

2. List three reasons why the production system offers an important "architecture" for computer-based problem solving.

3. Compare and contrast the knowledge-based system development model with the general software product development model.

4. A temperature regulator device can be considered to have some intelligence. It makes decisions to turn the furnace or air conditioner on or off. Using *if-then* rules, describe a definition of the device's function. One of the rules might be the following:

   if room_temperature > setting + 3°, *then* put_on_air

   You may design rules in such a way that only one rule is valid at any given temperature.

5. Describe the role of the knowledge engineer and his/her relationship with other key members in the knowledge acquisition process.

6. What is semantic knowledge representation?

7. Shades of meaning are always difficult to represent with a knowledge representation language. For example:

   a. Gopal nibbled at the pizza.

   b. Gopal ate the pizza.

   c. Gopal devoured the pizza.

   d. Gopal inhaled the pizza.

   e. Gopal dined on the pizza.

   Distinguish the use of semantic networks and logic for their efficacy at representing minor variations of meaning. List the problems and advantages of each. Which is suitable for this particular problem?

8. Suppose your software firm allocates you the task of building a brand new knowledge-based system to observe the blood flow rate of patents in a hospital. Your firm says you must use PROLOG, LISP, or Java for this system, and it must have the structure of a typical knowledge-based system, such as separate rules, inference engine, and conflict resolution. Moreover, you are not supposed to use an expert system shell. Which language would you choose to write your system? Why?

9. Explain the differences in meaning of the following predicate logic statements. Note any that are equivalent.

$$\forall X.(elephant(X) \rightarrow sees\_proboscis(X)).$$
$$\forall X.(elephant(X) \land sees\_proboscis(X)).$$
$$\exists X.(elephant(X) \rightarrow sees\_proboscis(X)).$$
$$\exists X.(elephant(X) \land sees\_proboscis(X)).$$

10. Consider any problem domain and represent the knowledge in the frame-based system.
11. What are the disadvantages of frame-based knowledge representation?
12. Give your opinion, with a brief justification, about suitable programming languages to implement a semantic network and frames.
13. Give an example of a problem that you think would be a suitable candidate for knowledge-based programming. Justify your answer.

Projects

1. This is an extension of Project 2 in Chapter 2. Based on your detailed project description, work out the system design. Then brainstorm on development tools, implementation strategies, and a prototype. During the current project phase, you will have to practice concepts learned in this chapter. You will learn various techniques in subsequent chapters in this book, which will help you understand and incorporate changes in the original design. At that point, you will concentrate on system design changes, user interface, and new features to be implemented in the project. You should follow a knowledge engineering approach while preparing a complete project report, evaluation plan, and working prototype.
2. Search the World Wide Web for information about JESS. Prepare your term paper on this rule engine. List the advantages of using *deftemplate* facts rather than ordered facts in the JESS program.

References

Akerkar, R. *Foundations of the Semantic Web*, Daryaganj, New Delhi: Narosa Publishing House, 2009.

Akerkar, R., & Duthie, R. KRIS: Knowledge Representation Formalism, *Proceedings of International Symposium on Artificial Intelligence (ISAI'2001),* 2001.

Berners-Lee, T., Hendler, J., & Lassila. O. The Semantic Web, *Scientific American, 284*(5), 35–43, 2001.

Brachman R. & Schmolze J. An Overview of the KL-ONE Knowledge Representation System, *Cognitive Science, 9*(2), 1985.

Elias, M. A. & Hassan, M. G. *Knowledge Management*, Prentice Hall, NJ: Pearson Education, Inc., 2004.

Forgy, C. L. Rete: A Fast Algorithm for the Many Pattern/Many Object Pattern Match Problem, *Artificial Intelligence, 19*, 17–37, 1982.

Friedman-Hill, E. J., *JESS in Action*, Greenwich, CT: Manning Publications, 2003.

Giarratano, J., *Expert Systems: Principals and Programming*, Boston: PSW-Kent, 1989.

Sajja, P.S. Knowledge representation using fuzzy XML rules for knowledge-based adviser, *International Journal of Computer, Mathematical Sciences, and Applications, 1*(2–4), 323–330, 2007.

CHAPTER 4

Knowledge Management

■ 4.1 INTRODUCTION TO KNOWLEDGE MANAGEMENT

Knowledge has an effect on real-life business problems. However, it is nothing but the understanding that people have developed while solving problems using information and data. Knowledge is a kind of intellectual capital whereby a business achieves strategic and competitive advantages, and an organization achieves success if it can meet users' continuously changing needs in a value-added way through its products, processes, and people. The people within the organization are the main resources for capturing, using, and sharing knowledge.

Knowledge management (KM) is a discipline that deals with an integrated approach to identifying, managing, and sharing different types of knowledge assets within various components of the business.

According to Skyrme (2002), knowledge management can be defined as "the explicit and systematic management of vital knowledge and its associated processes of creating, gathering, organizing, diffusion, use and exploitation, in pursuit of organizational objectives."

Assets managed by a knowledge management system may be either explicit or tacit. Explicit knowledge assets are generally documents, reports, policies, files, and databases. Explicit knowledge is easy to represent and communicate through words and symbols. Tacit knowledge is generally embedded in procedures and people. The vital knowledge of a business is embedded primarily in organizational practices, insights, norms, and key people who are responsible for the practices. During the knowledge management process, tacit knowledge must be explicitly represented in a system-readable form to support further operations on it. During management activities, processes such as identification, acquisition, organization, representation, use, sharing, and conversion (innovation) are incorporated to get optimum usage of this vital knowledge for the organization.

With the help of such knowledge management, the organization gains better understanding, sharing, and utilization of existing knowledge. All of the knowledge management activities result in documentation of this knowledge in the form of a centrally available repository. This repository contains knowledge assets such as business processes, customers, key people of the business, organizational memory, and relationships. For example, in a typical manufacturing factory, information held by key people who are responsible for carrying out transactions such as new product design, inventory control, contract renewals, and other related information is stored in a centralized repository. The remedies and solution strategies are also stored there. This will be helpful to the organization when training personnel and making decisions in the absence of key people. Such repositories can be used to obtain competitive advantages and offers a new platform and an opportunity to create innovative knowledge to satisfy customers' needs.

Organizations that have been thwarted by usual KM practices are paying more attention to how knowledge flows through their business. *Social network analysis* plays an important role in this respect. It is a process of mapping a group's contacts (whether personal or professional) to pinpoint who knows whom and who works with whom. A social network analysis is not a substitute for conventional KM tools such as knowledge databases or portals, but it can offer organizations a basis for how best to progress with KM initiatives. As part of a larger KM strategy, social network analysis can help organizations identify key leaders and then set up mechanisms so that those leaders can pass on their knowledge to the group.

■ 4.2 PERSPECTIVES OF KNOWLEDGE MANAGEMENT

Knowledge management is an interdisciplinary area requiring technical, organizational, and interpersonal skills. The following sections describe the broad perspectives of knowledge management.

■ 4.2.1 Technocentric

According to the technocentric perspective, as the name denotes, the main emphasis is on the technological aspects of knowledge management. The technological aspects include storage mechanism, representation schemes, and dissemination software to make the knowledge available to a large audience in a secured way.

■ 4.2.2 Organizational

The main procedures and business routines of an organization are the focus of this perspective. This aspect of knowledge management focuses on the ways an organization's operations are carried out, the key persons involved in these operations, and the organization's best practices.

■ 4.2.3 Ecological

Here, the emphasis is on the relationships between the knowledge, people, and environmental factors. According to the ecological perspective, the components of the knowledge management system must not have an adverse effect on the organization's environment, relationships with outside entities, or other ecological factors like government policies, the vision and the ethical values of the organization, and interpersonal relationships within the organization. The resulting knowledge management system is flexible enough to accommodate environmental changes.

■ 4.3 WHAT DRIVES KNOWLEDGE MANAGEMENT?

The need for competitive advantages and to manage the organization's intellectual assets leads the knowledge management practice. Systematic knowledge management often leads to high-level innovation, better customer service, and consistency, along with other organizational benefits. This inspires more organizations to opt for the systematic, organization-wide knowledge management.

Things that drive the knowledge management processes are discussed in the following sections.

■ 4.3.1 Size and Dispersion of an Organization

It is difficult for large organization with multiple employees and complex procedures to manage its intellectual assets. Moreover, the knowledge is dispersed across multiple geographic locations in a distributed fashion. In this situation, a virtual repository of organizational knowledge is quite valuable. For example, knowledge of who knows what can be helpful when making critical business decisions. This also helps in the globalization of the business.

■ 4.3.2 Reducing Risk and Uncertainty

Dependency on the people who have critical knowledge is risky, but this risk can be reduced by collecting and managing this knowledge. Knowledge should be always available on demand and in a timely fashion. That way, risks and uncertainty involved with the business are minimized.

■ 4.3.3 Improving the Quality of Decisions

Ready access to knowledge helps management make better decisions. It opens up new opportunities and even creates new knowledge to support innovative decisions. This directly improves the business's performance.

■ 4.3.4 Improving Customer Relationships

Predicting and satisfying customers' needs in a value-added way is one of the key components to achieving success in a business. By storing the related knowledge, customer services can be improved—customers do not have to depend on a single person, whose absence or lack of knowledge can cause customer relations to suffer. Rather new alternatives can be invented to carry out these tasks in a cheaper, simpler, and quicker fashion.

■ 4.3.5 Technocentric Support

As discussed earlier, knowledge management is a multidisciplinary field, and one of the related perspectives has to do with technology. As technology advances, it becomes easier to serve both customers and employees through better services and high-quality, timely decisions. Advancements like the Internet enable multiple users to simultaneously access business knowledge and provide advantages like high accessibility and availability of information and knowledge (anywhere, anytime). The knowledge management system makes the organization less dependent on people and even creates new knowledge. The systems and/or tools used to manage the knowledge can be created in a tailormade fashion or customized from readymade generalized packages. Such a knowledge management system also helps in generating routine documentation and making common business decisions. That is, the advantages of automation and technology are better achieved in a knowledge-oriented fashion.

■ 4.3.6 Intellectual Asset Management and Prevention of Knowledge Loss

The knowledge of an organization is available without barriers of geographic location, time, and availability of experts. Once the necessary knowledge is documented, a backup is always kept in a safe location as an extra precaution. This makes it easy to manage the resources and perform cloning, sharing, testing, and so on.

■ 4.3.7 Future Use of Knowledge

In addition to the routine procedures of discovery, use, sharing, and so on, the stored knowledge can be used for training the experts. Such material can be used along with a particular case during a brainstorming analysis to track mistakes and learn from them when handling similar cases.

■ 4.3.8 Increase Market Value and Enhance an Organization's Brand Image

The cheaper, better, and quicker solutions a knowledge management system can provide make all beneficiaries of the system happy. The customers feel they can rely on the organization, which improves the company's brand image. The knowledge gained from customer feedback and expert opinion improves the quality of the product and services of the company, resulting in increased market value of the product.

■ 4.3.9 Shorter Product Cycles

Because the organization is not dependent on a particular expert and business decisions are made in a knowledge-oriented way from any location, the business transaction cycle is shorter. Hence, the organization satisfies customers' and employees' needs in a better, quicker fashion.

■ 4.3.10 Restricted Access and Added Security

With the technocentric approach to knowledge management, the knowledge is made available to select people. This can be done through passwords, access rights, or other utilities. Such restricted access makes the information more secure and offers a clear view of the picture by hiding unnecessary details. For example, final decisions and product design specifications can be viewed by a select group of employees. Instead of elaborating the complete procedure entailed to reach the specifications, this approach provides a clear picture of the work to do and hides unnecessary details. Details about the product specification can be made available but access is restricted.

■ 4.4   TYPICAL EVOLUTION OF KNOWLEDGE MANAGEMENT WITHIN AN ORGANIZATION

■ 4.4.1   Ad-hoc Knowledge

In this scenario, there is no formal procedure for knowledge management in the organization. However, the organization may use an informal system. Sometimes, knowledge management is in practice only while dealing with interdepartmental issues.

■ 4.4.2   Sophisticated Knowledge Management

In this case, an organization might have adopted a formal knowledge management process, but only practices certain phases of it.

■ 4.4.3   Embedded Knowledge Management

In this scenario, an organization may have critical processes and a knowledgeable expert who has a high degree of knowledge regarding the organization's business and its knowledge assets.

■ 4.4.4   Integrated Knowledge Management

All of the tasks, major operations, and subsystems of an organization are contained in a knowledge management system, and knowledge is shared through a common integrated environment, like an intranet in a local area network (LAN) or a portal on the Internet.

■ 4.5   ELEMENTS OF KNOWLEDGE MANAGEMENT

There are a few core elements of a knowledge management process—namely, skilled people, processes, strategy, and technology—which serve as the basis of the knowledge management system. Organizational factors, such as

■ **FIGURE 4.1**
Elements of knowl-
edge management

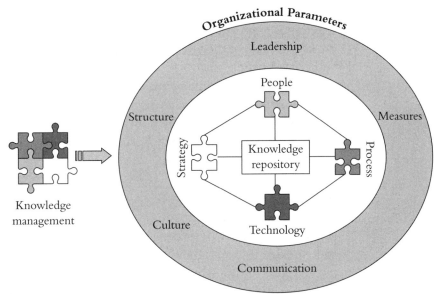

■ **FIGURE 4.1** Elements of knowledge management

leadership, structure, culture, and communication methodologies, have an effect on these core elements. Figure 4.1 describes the knowledge management elements and how they relate to the organizational factors.

■ 4.5.1 People and Skills

It is now clear that the highly skilled work force, with its expertise in a given domain, is one of the critical factors of success in any business. From performing routine procedures and basic transactions of the business to the strategic policy determination, organizations are dependent on their human resources. In other words, the organization's brand image and success directly depend on the highly skilled people working at different levels of the organization. On one hand, this trained and skillful work force helps an organization achieve desired milestones through their skills, knowledge, and experience. However, the organization is dependent on these people. There is a risk that such people may leave to pursue other opportunities and the knowledge they have earned will be lost. Since experts are rare commodities in their field, they are highly mobile.

Because of this high mobility, the expert's valuable knowledge should be transferred into the knowledge repository, where it can be permanently preserved and used. Experts themselves may be utilized to contribute to the development process of this knowledge repository, which is why they are the basic source of the tacit knowledge at the discovery phase of the system. Concerned people may play different roles, not only in providing knowledge, but also in conceiving, planning, developing, and maintaining the organizationwide knowledge management system. The KM team (which is a group of experts responsible for developing the knowledge management system in an organization), management, personnel, and users are the main people involved in the process.

■ 4.5.2 Procedures

Standard procedures and basic operations within an organization normally generate the explicit knowledge, which can be easily collected, organized, and encoded into the knowledge repository. Besides these routine transactions, reports regarding project monitoring, learning plans, meeting agendas, outcomes, and so on can be captured systematically for future use.

■ 4.5.3 Strategy and Policy

The long-term vision and promises made by the organization to its customers regarding product quality and services must be kept in the mind before capturing, storing, and using the knowledge for the organization.

■ 4.5.4 Technology

The appropriate tools and methodologies are essential factors when developing a knowledge management system. Knowledge acquisition techniques, knowledge representation structures, knowledge sharing tools, and communication tools, such as a website, a newsletter, mailings, etc., can be made available through such technology.

■ 4.6 THE KNOWLEDGE MANAGEMENT PROCESS

As mentioned, people, procedures, strategy, and technology play a variety of roles in providing, sharing, and documenting knowledge for future use. The knowledge management process encompasses the phases of knowledge discovery, knowledge documentation, knowledge sharing, and knowledge use. Figure 4.2 shows the conceptual process of knowledge management.

■ **FIGURE 4.2**
Conceptual
process of
knowledge
management

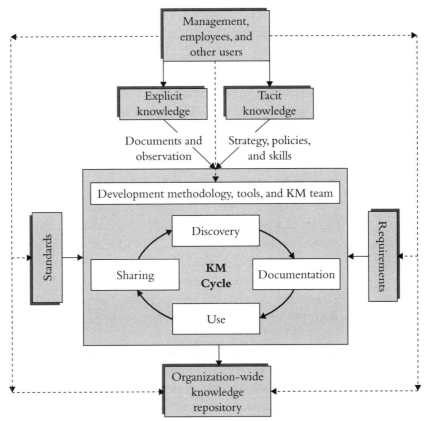

■ **FIGURE 4.2** Conceptual process of knowledge management

■ 4.6.1 Knowledge Discovery and Innovation

The knowledge discovery phase encompasses activities regarding the identification and acquisition of knowledge. Basic sources of knowledge are people, policies, and procedures. Generally, tacit knowledge is extracted from people and policies, and explicit knowledge is obtained from processes, documentation, and reports. Besides discovering the "known" entities for further representation into the repository for future use, one may have to think about creating new knowledge. Such creation of knowledge may be considered "knowledge innovation." The embedded knowledge within the organization's strategy, ideas, and vision can be identified, structured (embedded knowledge is highly unstructured), and codified into the repository.

■ 4.6.2 Knowledge Documentation

The discovered knowledge is sorted according to its application and nature. This generates a new category of knowledge, called metaknowledge, which is necessary to understand how the knowledge is stored and documented. For such sorting and classification, industry-specific structures or classification strategies are used. The power and usefulness of the stored knowledge often depends on the representation schemes utilized. This process usually involves information professionals like knowledge engineers.

■ 4.6.3 Knowledge Use

Once the knowledge is documented in the repository, it is used and reused as part of a work process. It may be used to solve problems, support business-related decisions, and train the work force within an organization. With every cycle, there is a possibility of generating new useful knowledge, which must be incorporated into the repository. The repository needs to be updated regularly so that new lessons learned and innovative knowledge generated from the knowledge management cycle can be incorporated into it.

■ 4.6.4 Knowledge Sharing Through Pull and Push Technologies

When the content of the repository is sent to the necessary people in a routine, well-defined fashion, it is called "information push." When the repository is utilized as needed, and content is fetched to solve a specific problem, it is called "information pull." The repository must be available centrally so that all necessary users can handle it, contribute to it, and use it as and when required.

Figure 4.3 presents a detailed development process for a knowledge management system.

■ 4.7 KNOWLEDGE MANAGEMENT TOOLS AND TECHNOLOGIES

■ 4.7.1 Tools for Discovering Knowledge

Techniques like creative abstraction, simulation, interactive sessions, meetings, and morphological analysis can be used for knowledge identification and innovation. These techniques provide a platform to discuss knowledge relating to a product and/or processes. Such a discussion may lead not only

■ FIGURE 4.3
Detailed
knowledge
management
development
process

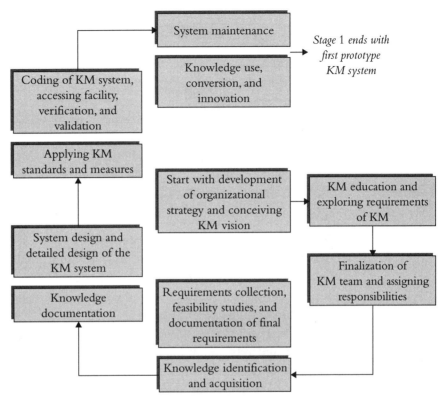

to extraction of the existing knowledge, but also to the creation of innovations, because it provides an opportunity to explore various alternatives to complete a given task. Some organizations employ an information audit to identify the knowledge needs and limitations of the existing methods of doing business. In addition to meetings and discussions, formal presentations and conceptual mapping of employees' knowledge can be used to extract knowledge. Also, with the help of intelligent agents, such as semantic search and information retrieval agents, such tasks can be carried out. Figure 4.4 summarizes these knowledge discovery tools.

■ 4.7.2 Tools for Documenting Knowledge

In the absence of high quality documentation, an organization may face difficulties in launching new knowledge management applications and modifying existing ones. Moreover, it becomes difficult and/or costly to introduce

FIGURE 4.4
Knowledge
discovery tools

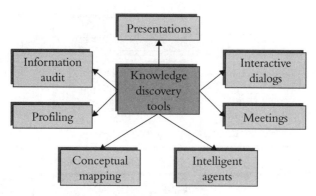

new policies for the organization. Proper documentation preserves an organization's valuable knowledge and prevents loss of knowledge if an employee leaves the company, as well as increasing decision-making productivity. The typical process of documentation incorporates authoring, testing, editing, and correcting errors according to the comments made by the documents' authors or committees.

As stated earlier, knowledge documentation encompasses the organizing, encoding, and representation techniques. Design methods like algorithms, product data management, a thesaurus (to find similar entities represented by different names for proper indexing), knowledge trees, and metadata tools (keywords, index, etc.) are helpful in organizing and representing the collected knowledge. Tools like SNOWBALL (Ford & Wood, 1991) can also be utilized. Such tools support the flexible use of both computer- and paper-based representations. Some authority tools like TT Author (http://www.tt-s.com/en/software/tt-knowledge-force/tt-author.html) help to create documentation and learning programs (Web-based training) in a single operation. Figure 4.5 illustrates some knowledge documentation tools.

■ 4.7.3 Tools for Sharing and Using Knowledge

Typical document management systems and a centralized knowledge repository facilitate using and sharing the collected knowledge. If the organization covers a large geographic area, a website or portal can be used. Users may form groups according to their needs and requirements. Cross-functional teams, which are comprised of people with different disciplines and from different organizational units, are formed to share informal knowledge.

FIGURE 4.5
Knowledge
documentation
tools

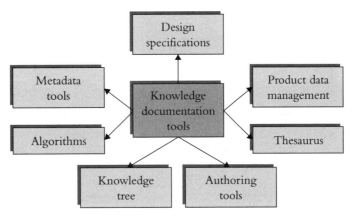

Sometimes, human-oriented factors, such as office design (which takes care of people flow, special conference rooms, etc.), are considered to provide a better working environment. Management may introduce a set of best practices, like small gradual improvements through Total Quality Management (TQM) at various levels of the organization, share fairs, business meetings, and so on.

To use the collected knowledge effectively, there must be a high degree of accessibility. However, from the knowledge base directly such high-level knowledge cannot be retrieved without a proper procedure. Here, an object-oriented paradigm helps. A bundle of knowledge and utilities that provide access are packed in a user-friendly way, which makes the embedded knowledge widely available. Such multiple-access mechanisms provided in machine-readable form serve as an intelligent agent to support business decisions. Because this knowledge is readily available, further explanation and reasoning can be provided on request, which increases the system's ease of use. Similarly, networking, Web-enabling, or proper marketing enhance the use of the documented knowledge. Figure 4.6 shows the tools for using and sharing knowledge.

Some general collaborative technologies, such as e-mail, document management, and an intranet, can be used in one or more ways for knowledge management. Examples include Enterprise Information Portals (EIP), Content Management Systems (CMS), categorization and visualization software (to suggest keywords or visualize the core concept in a given document), and profiling experts for their knowledge, when required.

■ **FIGURE 4.6**
Tools for shar-
ing and using
knowledge

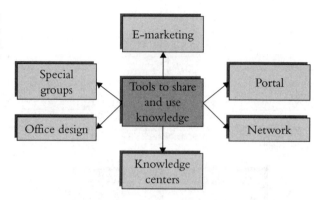

■ 4.7.4 Technologies for Knowledge Management

There are four prominent technologies for knowledge management:

1. **Managing knowledge:**

   In general, artificial intelligence, and, in particular, knowledge-based systems, are an excellent platform for capturing, sharing, and applying certain types of knowledge. Knowledge-based systems were designed primarily to apply knowledge automatically. In many KM contexts, we just want a tool to support knowledge capture, discovery, and sharing—we may not need automatic application. However, the ability of knowledge-based systems to apply knowledge can be useful for knowledge sharing: There are knowledgeable individuals who are not considered experts. Knowledge can be specific without being at an expert level, and having knowledge is not the same thing as being able to apply it effectively. Thus, knowledge-based systems are excellent at representing many forms of additional expertise.

2. **Preserving and applying human expertise:**

   Knowledge-based systems can be viewed as technologies for knowledge management. They offer potential solutions to problems that are detected, analyzed, and prioritized through knowledge management.

3. **Using history explicitly as knowledge:**

   Case-based reasoning (CBR) is an exceptional technology for making use of historical knowledge. The CBR paradigm covers a range of different methods for organizing, indexing, retrieving, and utilizing the knowledge retained in past cases. Cases may be kept as concrete experiences, or a set of similar cases may form a generalized case. Cases may be stored as separate knowledge units or split up into subunits and distributed within the knowledge structure. Cases may be indexed by a prefixed or open vocabulary and within a flat or hierarchical index structure. The solution from a past case may be directly applied to a present problem, or modified according to differences between the two cases.

In CBR, the initial description of a problem defines a new case. This new case is used to retrieve a case from the collection of previous cases. The retrieved case is combined with the new case and revised into a solved case—that is, the proposed solution. Through the revision process, this solution is tested for success and repaired if it fails. During the retain process, useful experience is retained for future use, and the case base is updated by a new learned case or by modification of some existing cases. General knowledge (i.e., main dependent knowledge) supports the CBR process. The CBR cycle is shown in Figure 4.7.

The CBR provides quick answers to new problems, even in complex domains and when there is a lack of complete information, provided many previously solved cases are available. Case-based reasoning is applicable to a wide range of real-world situations, ranging from knowledge-rich situations, in which the construction of solutions is

■ **FIGURE 4.7**
Case-based
reasoning cycle

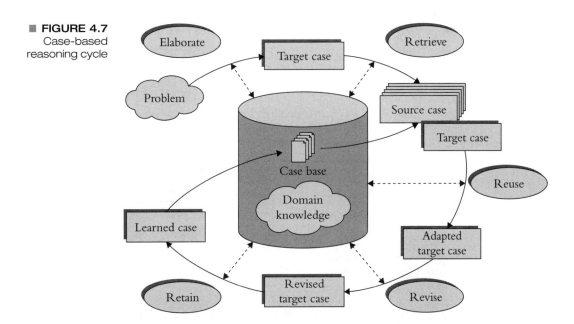

complex, to knowledge-poor situations, in which cases provide the only available knowledge. Researchers have shown that CBR has the capability for developing knowledge-based systems more efficiently than with rule- or model-based approaches. The CBR approach combines the efficiency of data management and retrieval of database systems with the intelligence and power of the KBS inference engine.

4. Discovering new knowledge:

Data mining (DM) techniques can be used for building and discovering new organizational knowledge, which could lead to a better performance. Data mining is intended to provide support in the complex data-rich but information-poor situations.

The process of knowledge discovery is shown in Figure 4.8. It usually involves an interactive sequence of the following steps: data cleaning, data integration, data selection, data transformation, modeling, pattern evaluation, and knowledge representation. During the preprocessing steps—that is, data cleaning and integration—data are analyzed in order to remove noise and inconsistencies. The resulting preprocessed data are stored in a data warehouse. During the modeling step, intelligent techniques are used to extract and evaluate data patterns. The relevant patterns can be presented to users using visualization and representation techniques.

Data mining is mostly used by organizations with a rigorous consumer focus (Akerkar, 2008). These organizations are typically focused

■ **FIGURE 4.8**
Knowledge
discovery process

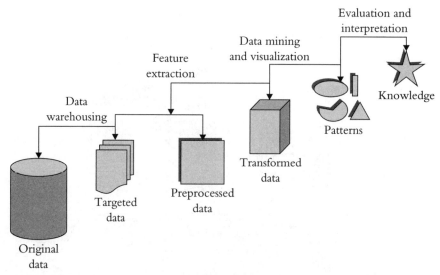

on trade, finance, communication, and marketing. Data mining enables these companies to determine relationships among *internal* factors, such as price, product positioning, or staff skills, and "external" factors, such as economic indicators, competition, and customer demographics. It enables them to determine the impact on sales, customer satisfaction, and corporate profits. The goal of KM in this context is to make more effective and efficient use of available DM techniques.

■ 4.8   KNOWLEDGE MANAGEMENT MEASURES

It is obvious that the qualitative and intangible things, like knowledge, are difficult to measure. Patents, copyrights, goodwill, research and development outputs, and so on cannot be valued by the standard measures or metrics. For verification, validation, and certification of the knowledge management system, there is a need for standards and measures. Measures like *Tobin's q,* which is a comparison of market value of an organization against the total assets value, is an attempt at identifying an organization's intellectual strength; however, it does not provide a direction for KM system development.

Considering the KM development procedure and its applications in typical organizations, factors like cost, benefits, market value increase through knowledge management, total amount of knowledge invented, customer satisfaction, performance of the work group, improved relationships, and so on are considered parameters whereby the success and suitability of a knowledge management system can be measured.

There are many KM measures, both established and emerging. According to Knowledge Management Online [http://www.knowledge-management-online.com/KM-Measures.html], three good sources of further measures are as follows:

- **APQC:** The American Productivity and Quality Centre published works on KM measures
- **BSI:** The British Standards Institute, KMS/1 Knowledge Management published KM measures
- **Sveiby:** Karl Eric Sveiby published KM measures

Besides these, House of Quality, Benchmarking, KM Balanced Score Cards, Knowledge Orientation Matrix, and The KM Maturity Model are popular techniques for understanding KM metrics.

■ 4.9 KNOWLEDGE MANAGEMENT ORGANIZATION

A knowledge management system presents the organization's intellectual as-sets in a systematic way to better utilize and implement the knowledge and experience of the organization's members. To achieve such documentation and safekeeping of the knowledge for better utilization, the organization often needs to be restructured. Figure 4.9 presents the general structure of a KM organization.

In general, three groups of experts who need to work together as teams of knowledge partners are users, knowledge professionals (including librar-

■ **FIGURE 4.9**
Organizational
structure of
a knowledge
management
system

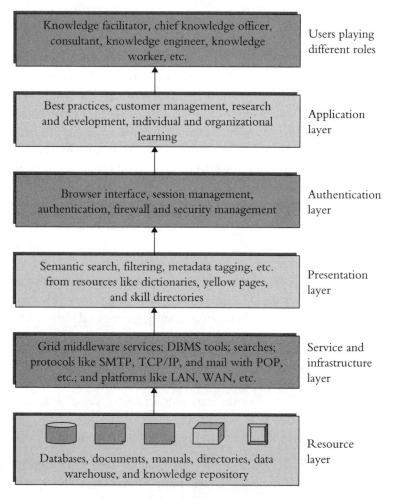

Knowledge facilitator, chief knowledge officer, consultant, knowledge engineer, knowledge worker, etc.

Users playing different roles

Best practices, customer management, research and development, individual and organizational learning

Application layer

Browser interface, session management, authentication, firewall and security management

Authentication layer

Semantic search, filtering, metadata tagging, etc. from resources like dictionaries, yellow pages, and skill directories

Presentation layer

Grid middleware services; DBMS tools; searches; protocols like SMTP, TCP/IP, and mail with POP, etc.; and platforms like LAN, WAN, etc.

Service and infrastructure layer

Databases, documents, manuals, directories, data warehouse, and knowledge repository

Resource layer

ians), and technology experts. Users are the individuals in the organization who are personally involved in the act of creating and using knowledge. This group includes professionals, technologists, managers, and others who possess and apply both tacit knowledge and explicit knowledge. The knowledge and expertise they have is specialized and focused on the organization's domain of activity.

Knowledge professionals are the individuals in the organization who have the skills, training, and know-how to organize knowledge into systems and structures that facilitate the productive use of knowledge resources. They include librarians, records managers, archivists, and other information specialists.

Knowledge technology experts are the individuals in the organization who have the specialized expertise to fashion the knowledge infrastructure of the organization. This group includes system analysts, system designers, software engineers, programmers, data administrators, network managers, and other specialists who develop knowledge-based systems and networks. There are specific roles and responsibilities for these knowledge management workers, such as knowledge facilitator, chief knowledge officer, knowledge engineer, and knowledge worker. These roles and responsibilities are discussed in the next section.

■ 4.10 KNOWLEDGE MANAGEMENT ROLES AND RESPONSIBILITIES

For better knowledge management system development and effective use of the knowledge repository generated through the system, new roles and responsibilities are identified. These roles and responsibilities are dispersed both within the organization and outside it. These roles generally are filled by the existing employees of the organization rather than employees hired specifically for this purpose. However, regular employees may not have expertise in specific tasks, such as knowledge acquisition, conversion, and representation. For this reason, some dedicated roles needs to be created and assigned to outside experts.

As mentioned in the previous section, examples of the knowledge management roles include chief knowledge officer, knowledge facilitator or administrator, knowledge manager, knowledge worker, and knowledge consultant. However, these roles may vary for different organizations based on the nature of the business.

■ 4.10.1 Chief Knowledge Officer (CKO)

The CKO is the leader of the knowledge management team and is responsible for the development and usage of the knowledge management system. The CKO may conceive the special role to identify tasks to be carried out, and to disseminate the tasks within the team. Besides strategic leadership, the CKO is responsible for critically examining how this knowledge is managed and used, and making sure the process is efficient. This person may review new knowledge and mark it for inclusion in the knowledge repository, depending on its usefulness and suitability. As a leader, the CKO is responsible for communicating to higher management and convincing them to promote knowledge management activities within the organization.

■ 4.10.2 Knowledge Engineer (KE)

The KE is the developer and administrator of the organizational knowledge repository. This person leads the processes of analysis and design. The KE also solves problems that arise in development and usage and performs other troubleshooting tasks as needed. This person is the key to ensuring that the complete business knowledge is represented in the system.

■ 4.10.3 Knowledge Facilitator (KF)

Facilitating knowledge usage at multiple sites simultaneously requires one or more KFs, depending on the organization's size and span. The KF understands the detailed logic of the organization's business cycle and underlying principles, processes, tools, and technologies for the knowledge management system in use. This person inspires others to use the knowledge management system to get maximum organizational and individual benefits from it. Sometimes, the KE is responsible for marketing the knowledge management system, both within and outside the organization, based on this person's awareness of the communication and collaboration required to fully explore the benefits of the knowledge management system.

■ 4.10.4 Knowledge Worker (KW)

If the roles in knowledge management are thought of as a tree, the KW is at the leaf level. The basic responsibilities of the KW are to use, reuse, and apply the documented knowledge effectively and carry out the business procedures in such a way that the minimum amount of resources, information, time, and efforts are used to meet the required goal.

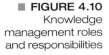

FIGURE 4.10
Knowledge
management roles
and responsibilities

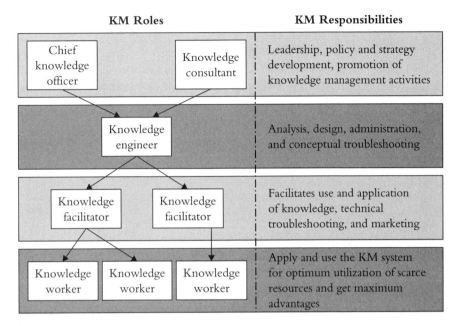

■ 4.10.5 Knowledge Consultant (KC)

The KC's work parallels that of the CKO by contributing to the development of strategy, vision, and risk analysis. The KC generally audits the plan for the knowledge management activities and supports development of knowledge management objectives and policies. This person's responsibilities may include identifying and suggesting a strategy to support organizational knowledge management activities.

Figure 4.10 shows a tree diagramming the roles and responsibilities for knowledge management activities.

Besides these roles, knowledge catalogers, media specialists, and researchers in the field of competitive intelligence are required to create an organizational network and related links.

■ 4.11 KNOWLEDGE MANAGEMENT MODELS

Knowledge management is a complex, dynamic procedure because this system mainly deals with intangible knowledge, people, and strategies. The development of the knowledge management system requires a holistic and comprehensive approach. Just defining knowledge management cycles, the organizational structure, and knowledge categories may not offer the holistic

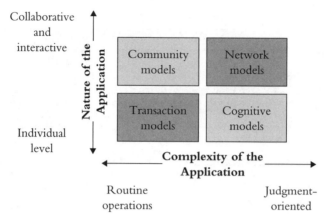

view and sound conceptual background of the knowledge system. The various knowledge management models serve the following purposes:

- Provide holistic and comprehensive perspectives
- Provide conceptual background for knowledge management
- Can be considered a reliable, valid tool because it has been thoroughly tested by experts in the field

Knowledge management models can be classified according to their level of complexity and the nature of the work. Based on this approach, there are four categories: transaction model, cognitive model, network model, and community model. These models are shown in Figure 4.11.

■ 4.11.1 Transaction Model

The transaction model of knowledge management focuses on routine work done mainly at the individual level. These models are highly reliant on formal procedures, and are dependent on individual workers, bylaws, and training. The company that practices the knowledge management principles in the routine activities can consider this model when developing a knowledge management system. Call center knowledge management systems and consultancy providing systems are two examples that can employ this modeling strategy.

■ 4.11.2 Cognitive Model

Knowledge is a key element for any knowledge management system. The system must not change or disturb the knowledge during its development and use. Moreover, the knowledge must be extracted and used in the correct way. The models that emphasize conceptual strength, reuse, and standardization are called cognitive models.

■ 4.11.3 Network Model

The network model of knowledge management focuses on connections and relationships among elements of the knowledge management system. It considers how knowledge is acquired, shared, and transferred by the drivers of the system. Such models rely on multiple functions, with flexible teams and supporting technology using the system's knowledge.

■ 4.11.4 Community Model

The community model is used for collaborative and interactive types of knowledge management systems. This model recognizes the relationship between organizations, sees the need for a continuous exchange among knowledge roles, and helps circulate this knowledge.

Clearly, most organizations will incorporate more than one model when creating a knowledge management system, making use of the key components in each, such as knowledge, relationships, community, trust, and technology. In addition to well-defined models created by eminent researchers/practitioners and mixed-matched customized models based on the need of the organization, one may use the model for the knowledge-based system development discussed in Chapter 3. In a way, the knowledge management system is also a knowledge-based system.

■ 4.12 MODELS FOR CATEGORIZING KNOWLEDGE

The following is a summary of some existing models for knowledge management.

■ 4.12.1 Knowledge Spiral Model

The model by Nonaka and Takeuchi, who is also known as Takeuk [http://www.nwlink.com/~Donclark/history_knowledge/nonaka.html], focuses on creating and categorizing knowledge as either tacit or explicit. They have shown that the creation of knowledge is the result of a continuous cycle of four integrated processes: externalization, internalization, combination, and socialization.

■ 4.12.2 Knowledge Management Model

Ikujurio Nonaka (1991) articulated a model of "knowledge creation" in which he proposed four "knowledge-creating" processes: socialization, externalization, combination, and internalization.

Hedlund and Nonaka (1993) presented a framework for discussing knowledge management in which creating and exploiting knowledge within an organization revolves around the interaction of tacit and explicit knowledge. They provide a conceptual framework that looks at different aspects of knowledge management. This model reinforced an important idea—that the survival and success of organizations will depend on how well they create, transfer, and exploit their knowledge resources. This model also focuses on carriers and agents of knowledge, such as individuals, groups, organizations, and interorganization domains.

Karl Wiig, one of the pioneers in the field of knowledge management, presented a framework based on three pillars and a foundation. Wiig proposed that the foundation of knowledge management is comprised of the way knowledge is created; used in problem solving and decision making; and is manifested cognitively, as well as in culture, technology, and procedures. Upon this foundation he situates three pillars that categorize the exploration of knowledge, its value assessment, and its active management. This framework summarizes the main areas on which a knowledge management initiative should focus.

■ 4.12.3 Knowledge Category Model

Boisot [http://www.sussex.ac.uk/spru/documents/boisotslides.ppt] categorized knowledge into codified, uncodified, diffused, and undiffused categories. He emphasized structuring and sharing knowledge within an information space called I-space.

■ 4.13 MODELS FOR INTELLECTUAL CAPITAL MANAGEMENT

Chase's model of knowledge management emphasized the categorization of intellectual capital and knowledge assets into various classes. The major categories are human, customer, innovations, processes, and organization capital (Chase, 1997).

■ 4.14   SOCIALLY CONSTRUCTED KNOWLEDGE MANAGEMENT MODELS

Demerest's model for knowledge management considers knowledge construction, capture, interpretation, embodiment, dissemination, and use in a social context. Demarest (1997) identified some parameters for effective participation in knowledge management as follows:

• Culture, beliefs, and actions of managers about the value, purpose, and role of the knowledge
• Creation, dissemination, and use of knowledge within the firm
• The kind of expected strategic and commercial benefits of a firm
• Maturity of knowledge systems
• The way knowledge is organized
• The role of IT in the KM program

McAdam and McCreedy (2000) modified this model to incorporate scientific views of knowledge construction, acquisition, and interpretation. By adding the scientific aspect, the model has an increased scope.

■ 4.15   TECHNIQUES TO MODEL KNOWLEDGE

Models are used to capture the essential features of real systems by breaking them down into more manageable parts that are easy to understand and manipulate. Models are very much associated with the domain they represent. Real systems are large entities consisting of interrelated components working together in a complex manner. Models help people appreciate and understand such complexity by enabling them to look at each particular area of the system in turn. Models are used in systems development activities to draw the blueprints of the system and to facilitate communication between different people in the team at different levels of abstraction. People have different views of the system, and models can help them understand these views in a unified manner.

The modeling process constructs conceptual models of knowledge-intensive activities. During the knowledge acquisition stage, most of the knowledge is unstructured and often in tacit form. The knowledge engineer will try to understand both the tacit and the explicit part of the knowledge and then use simple visual diagrams to stimulate discussion among users and knowledge experts. This discussion process generates ideas and insights as to how the knowledge should be used, how decisions are made, the factors that motivate, and so on. The knowledge engineer then has to construct the conceptual model based on what has been discussed during the knowledge acquisition stage. This knowledge is then communicated to the information specialist, who will transform the model into workable computer programs or codes. This approach is similar to that of software engineering, where models are used to represent user requirements. The main difference here is that in knowledge engineering, it is the modeling of knowledge and its related flows, whereas software engineering models the information and process flow.

Among the many techniques used to model knowledge, the most common are CommonKADS and Protégé 2000.

■ 4.15.1 CommonKADS

CommonKADS has become the de facto standard for knowledge modeling and is used extensively in European research projects. It supports structured knowledge engineering techniques, provides tools for corporate knowledge management, and includes methods that perform a detailed analysis of knowledge-intensive tasks and processes. A suite of models is at the core of the CommonKADS knowledge engineering methodology (Schreiber et al., 1999). The suite supports the modeling of the organization, the tasks that are performed, the agents that are responsible for carrying out the tasks, the knowledge itself, the means by which that knowledge is communicated, and the design of the knowledge management system. CommonKADS incorporates an object-oriented development process and uses Unified Modeling Language (UML) notations, such as class diagrams, use-case diagrams, activity diagrams, and state diagrams. CommonKADS also has its own graphical notations for task decomposition, inference structures, and domain schema generation.

The benefit of using a CommonKADS structured approach to knowledge engineering includes improved communication, standardization, technology support, availability of reusable components, and better audit trails. Such benefits are vital in the manufacture of large-scale knowledge systems to support the knowledge wealth.

■ **FIGURE 4.12**
CommonKADS
Editor

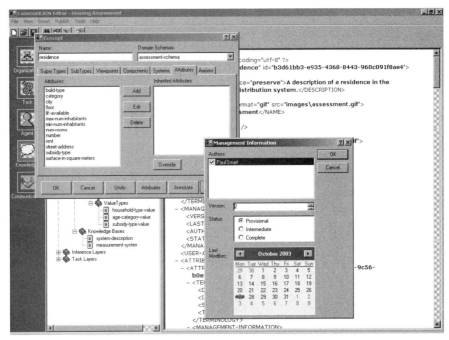

The CommonKADS Editor (Schreiber et al., 1999), shown in Figure 4.12, provides broad support for a range of CommonKADS models, including:

- *Organization model*: The organization model supports analysis of the key features of the organization in order to locate problems and opportunities for knowledge systems, establish their feasibility, and assess the impacts on the organization of the intended knowledge actions.
- *Task model*: The task model supports the analysis of tasks within an organization. Tasks are the pertinent elements of a business process. The task model analyzes the global task layout, its inputs and outputs, preconditions, and performance criteria, as well as needed resources and competencies.
- *Agent model*: The agent model supports the analysis of the agents responsible for performing the tasks analyzed in the task model. An agent can be a human, an information system, or any entity capable of carrying out a task. The agent model presents the characteristics of agents—in particular, their competencies, authority to act, and constraints in this respect. Furthermore, it lists the communication links that exist between agents in carrying out a task.

• *Knowledge model*: The knowledge model is designed to show in detail the types and structures of knowledge used in performing a task. It provides an implementation-independent description of the role that different knowledge components play in problem solving, in a way that is understandable for humans. This makes the knowledge model the principle means of communication with experts and end users about the problem-solving aspects of a knowledge system.

■ 4.15.2 Protégé 2000

The original Protégé was developed by the Stanford Center for Biomedical Informatics Research for domain-specific applications. Protégé 2000 (Noy et al., 2000) is a modeling technique developed by Musen and colleagues from Stanford Medical Informatics. The Protégé 2000 knowledge-modeling environment is a frame-based ontology editing tool with knowledge acquisition tools that are widely used for domain modeling. The frames are the main building blocks for a knowledge base. The Protégé ontology has classes, slots, facets, and axioms.

More importantly, Protégé 2000 is an open-source tool that assists users in the construction of large electronic knowledge bases. It has an intuitive user interface that enables developers to create and edit domain ontologies. Numerous plug-ins provide alternative visualization mechanisms, enable management of multiple ontologies, allow the use of inference engines and problem solvers with Protégé ontologies, and provide other functionalities. Figure 4.13 depicts the Protégé knowledge-acquisition tool, which you can use to acquire instances of the classes defined in your ontology.

The knowledge-acquisition process consists of three steps. First, a class and its template slot are defined. Second, the form to acquire the instances of the class is laid out. Finally, the class instances are acquired. Each class has an associated form and is used to get the instances of the class.

A knowledge base in Protégé is developed in the following sequence. First, concepts and their relationships are defined by an ontology. Second, the domain experts enter their knowledge of the domain area using the domain-specific knowledge-acquisition tool. Finally, problem-solving techniques are used to answer questions and solve problems of the domain using the knowledge base.

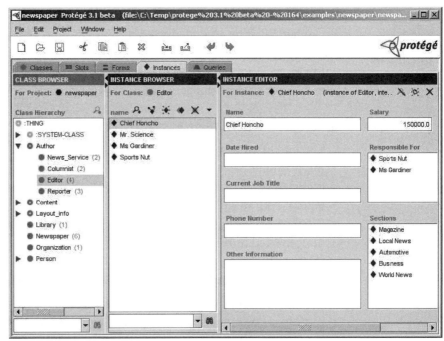

4.16   K-COMMERCE

K-commerce (knowledge commerce) is the trading of knowledge. A patent is the classic example of packaged and tradable knowledge. K-commerce deals with knowledge-intensive products and services for effective knowledge management. The information and communication technology (ICT) and AI techniques provide many solutions to make knowledge more portable and tradable. K-commerce may use the Internet as a low-cost global platform. Conceptually, k-commerce is a combination of e-commerce with a knowledge network. In the future, one may observe evolutionary hybrid and embedded systems for knowledge workers' support. The basic objective of such systems or devices is better knowledge management in a user-friendly way for wide use.

4.17   BENEFITS OF KNOWLEDGE MANAGEMENT

Knowledge is an important factor to achieving sustained competitive advantages in business. Capital, labor, land, or other resources do not have such capability. That is why knowledge is considered the driver of the world economy. Effective knowledge management offers benefits to the individuals and organizations in which it is employed and provides the platform for knowledge innovation. The following paragraphs describe the typical benefits of knowledge management in an organization.

■ 4.17.1 Knowledge-Related Benefits

- Documentation and safekeeping of knowledge
- High degree of availability and access to the latest organization-wide knowledge
- Reduces knowledge loss
- Provides background of innovation and new knowledge creation
- Controls redundancy of stored knowledge

■ 4.17.2 Organizational and Administrative Benefits

- Improved customer service in the most flexible way
- Improved customer relationships and brand image of the organization
- Reducing cost and increasing productivity and performance simultaneously
- Reducing process/product cycle time
- Faster problem solving
- Ease of administration and control
- Supporting best practices
- Useful as a tool for human resource development, training, and research and development (R&D)

■ 4.17.3 Individual Benefits

- High-quality decision within a given timeframe
- Job security and personal development
- Rewards and recognition

■ 4.18 CHALLENGES OF KNOWLEDGE MANAGEMENT

Many organizations overlook factors like work environment, interpersonal relationships, initiatives taken by the employees, and the overall attitude of the employees. A knowledge management system should consider an individual's knowledge, provide methods to reward it, and hence establish a culture that recognizes tacit knowledge and encourages employees. The need to promote the KM concept to employees shouldn't be taken lightly.

As with various physical resources, the significance of knowledge can erode over time. Since knowledge can get old quickly, the content in a KM program should be constantly updated, amended, and, if necessary, deleted. There is no endpoint to a KM program. Similar to product development and marketing, KM is a forever-evolving business practice.

Quantity rarely equals quality, and KM is no exception. Therefore, organizations carefully need to be on the lookout for information overload. Indeed, the purpose of a KM program is to recognize and disseminate knowledge from available information. Additionally, efforts required to develop KMSs and to manage the abstract nature of knowledge, the challenge of organizing the knowledge resources of an organization to generate a viable advantage becomes more critical due to the following:

- The marketplace is gradually more competitive and the rate of innovation is growing, so that knowledge must evolve and be incorporated at a rapid pace.
- Competitive pressures are reducing the size of the workforce that holds this knowledge.
- Employees are starting to retire earlier and are becoming increasingly mobile, leading to loss of knowledge.

■ 4.19 WARM-UP QUESTIONS, EXERCISES, AND PROJECTS

Warm-up Questions

1. Explain the difference between a knowledge engineer and a knowledge manager.
2. List any two real-life situations that would benefit from using a case-based reasoning approach to problem solving.
3. Draw a detailed diagram to show the case-based reasoning process, keeping in mind the steps involved.
4. A meta-search engine is a search tool that broadcasts user requests to various other search engines and databases and combines the results into a single list or displays them according to their source. AskJeeves, Google,

MetaCrawler, and Dogpile are examples of meta-search engines. Ask a question to interact with these search engines. Find interesting features of these engines.

5. Go to the Sevana ITsolutions website at http://www.sevana.fi/context_data_analysis.php. Here you will see a collection of data entered. This is available as a module for an online store. You can enter new data to analyze and click the "Submit" button at the bottom of the Web page. What type of predictions does this system produce?

6. Describe the various stages when constructing a knowledge model and the typical activities to be carried out during each stage.

7. The UML notations are typically imported into software development methodologies. CommonKADS follows a similar approach. There are activity diagrams, state diagrams, class diagrams, and use-case diagrams. Explore the basic elements of each diagram, their notation, and for what purposes each diagram can be used within CommonKADS.

8. Prepare a short note on each of the following assertions:

   a. Knowledge management is about making possible the sharing of knowledge among individuals.

   b. Knowledge sharing is nothing but knowledge re-creation and communication.

Exercises

1. Explain the following sentence with supportive examples: *Knowledge is a complex form of information.*

2. Compare and contrast knowledge engineering and knowledge systems.

3. Explain the knowledge management cycle by providing a specific example.

4. Why is knowledge management difficult?

5. What constitutes knowledge-based assets?

6. What technologies can support knowledge management?

7. List various challenges of knowledge management.

8. Besides using technology, how else can tacit knowledge be transferred?

9. What benefits can organizations expect from knowledge management?

10. What is social network analysis and how is it useful in knowledge management?

Projects

1. Investigate a business rule management system and a business rule engine. Prepare a survey of existing business management software. Why is the hybrid approach most suitable for such system development?

2. Knowledge automation pushes the boundaries of traditional knowledge management because it streamlines and automates the authoring and workflow process, helping to make service and support organizations more efficient. By means of knowledge automation, technology is applied to these critical processes to adapt to the way that people actually work. There is a need for such human expertise to become automated to help in-house staff as well as customers. Examples of such systems are provided. Select one of them and explore how the technology, based on case-based reasoning and expert systems, will convert tacit human expertise into explicit knowledge.

   a. Online help desk
   b. Recommendation system

References

Akerkar, R. & Lingras, P. *Building an Intelligent Web: Theory and Practice*, Sudbury, MA: Jones and Bartlett Publishers, 2008.

Chase, R. L. Knowledge management benchmarks, *Journal of Knowledge Management*, vol. 1, no. 1, pp. 83–92, 1997.

Demarest, M. Understanding knowledge management, *Long Range Planning*, vol.30, no.3, pp. 374–384, 1997.

Ford, J. M. & Wood, L. E. SNOWBALL: Representational issues in the design of a knowledge documentation system for expert system development in *Systems, Man, and Cybernetics, 'Decision Aiding for Complex Systems'*, IEEE International Conference, vol.2, pp.1183–1188, 1991.

Hedlund, G. & Nonaka, I. Models of Knowledge Management in the West and Japan, in *Implementing Strategic Process: Change, Learning and Cooperation,* Lorange, P. et al., editors, Oxford: Basil Blackwell, 1993.

McAdam, R. & McCreedy, S. A critique of knowledge management: Using a social constructionist model, *New Technology, Work and Employment*, vol. 15, no. 2, 2000.

Nonaka, I. The Knowledge Creating Company, *Harvard Business Review*, November–December, pp. 96–104, 1991.

Noy, N. F., Sintek, M., Decker, S., Crubezy, M., Fergerson, R.W., & Musen, M. A. Creating Semantic Web Contents with Protégé-2000, *SMI Technical Report* SMI-2001-0872, 2000.

Schreiber, G., Akkermans, H. et al. *Knowledge Engineering and Management*, Boston: MIT Press, 1999.

Skyrme, D. J. Knowledge management: Approaches and policies, DEEDS Policy Group Meeting, Brussels, 2002. Retrieved from http://www.providersedge.com/docs/km_articles/KM_-_Approaches_and_Policies.pdf

Wiig, K. *Knowledge Management Foundations: Thinking about Thinking—How Organizations Create, Represent and Use Knowledge,* Arlington, Texas: Schema Press, 1993.

CHAPTER 5

Fuzzy Logic

■ 5.1 INTRODUCTION

Fuzzy logic, a flexible machine-learning technique, is an attempt at mimicking the logic of human thoughts. Human logic is flexible and less rigid when compared to crisp logic. Crisp logic is a two-value logic representing two possible solution states, often represented by yes/no, 0/1, black/white, or true/false. Fuzzy logic is a multivalued logic introduced by Zadeh (1965) that allows intermediate values to be defined between the two aforementioned conventional evaluations. With crisp logic, it is difficult to represent notions like *rather warm* or *pretty cold* mathematically and have them processed by machines. Such linguistic terms help in applying a more human-like way of thinking to the programming of computers. Using fuzzy logic makes the system more flexible, transparent, and user-friendly.

A procedure embeds fuzzy logic in the form of fuzzy rules containing linguistic terms with multiple values. There are fuzzy membership functions that map the linguistic values to crisp values, which then can be understood by machines, which can then interpret and execute commands. The knowledge-based system that consists of such fuzzy rules is known as a fuzzy rule-based system. Fuzzy logic provides an inference mechanism that enables approximate human reasoning capabilities to be applied to knowledge-based systems. Many different types of uncertainties are common in expert domains. Some of them are uncertain knowledge, uncertain data, incomplete information, and random fluctuations/randomness. Fuzzy systems are suitable for uncertain or approximate reasoning, even with the uncertain information, especially for the system with a mathematical model that is difficult to derive. Fuzzy systems are widely applied in control and engineering fields.

■ 5.2 FUZZY LOGIC AND BIVALUED LOGIC

If somebody asks you if you are under 40 years of age, you may answer with a specific and definite value: yes or no. In a machine, this information can be represented as a Boolean value: 0/1 or T/F. But suppose you are asked if you are young; your answer is relative. You may answer "definitely," "why not," "not that much," and so on. "Definitely young" might be assigned a 1, "not young" would be assigned a 0, "why not" would be assigned a 0.6, and "not that much" would be assigned a 0.3. This demonstrates a kind of graded memberships where grades are between [0, 1]. Similarly, the truthfulness of the statement "6 is a large number" may take multiple values between 0 and 1 instead of only one of two values: 1/0 or yes/no. Bivalue logic is also referred to as crisp logic, and multivalue logic is referred to as fuzzy logic. These logic concepts are illustrated in Figure 5.1.

■ 5.2.1 Fuzzy Versus Probability

In probability theory, we deal with the chance of occurrence. The membership degree of fuzzy set theory is plausibility; that is, everything is a matter of degree. For instance, let us assume that someone's membership degree in a set of young women is 0.6. This means, in a fuzzy sense, that the woman is fairly young to the degree of 60% right now, all the time. This does not mean that this woman is young 60% of the time and old the remaining 40%. In a nutshell, probability theory deals with the likelihood of nondeterministic, stochastic events, whereas fuzzy theories deal with deterministic plausibility.

■ **FIGURE 5.1**
Fuzzy and crisp
concepts

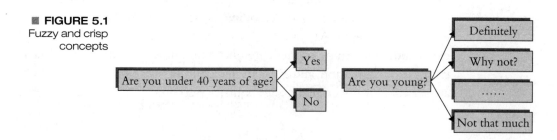

■ 5.3 FUZZY LOGIC AND FUZZY SETS

Fuzzy logic is based on the fuzzy set introduced by Zadeh (1965) to represent and manipulate data and information possessing nonstatistical uncertainties and vagueness. According to Zadeh (1965), some of the essential characteristics of fuzzy logic are as follows:

- Exact reasoning is viewed as a limiting case of approximate reasoning.
- Everything is a matter of degree.
- Knowledge is interpreted as a collection of elastic or, equivalently, fuzzy constraints on a collection of variables.
- Inference is viewed as a process of propagating elastic constraints.
- Any logical system can be fuzzified.

Humans routinely and subconsciously place things into classes whose meaning and significance are well understood but whose boundaries are not well defined. *Hot season, large car, young boy,* and *rich people* are a few such examples. The notion of fuzzy sets helps in defining and dealing with such entities with machines, and hence, makes the machine more user-friendly. As stated earlier, fuzzy logic is based on a fuzzy set. An element of a fuzzy set is a number, which defines the degree to which it is contained in a set.

Fuzzy sets offer an opportunity for a member to possess flexible belongingness into the set, which is measured in a degree. That means member A either belongs to crisp set C or does not. On other hand, member A can partially belong to the fuzzy set F, with a truth value (degree) of 0.6, which is between $[0, 1]$. Figure 5.2 represents the crisp and fuzzy sets.

Fuzzy logic was designed to represent a linguistic type of knowledge that offers both good readability and a base of reasoning process. It enables the expression of knowledge in verbal form and provides a means to manipulate this knowledge using a computer.

Definition of a Fuzzy Set: Let X be a nonempty set. A fuzzy set A in X is characterized by its membership function $\mu A: X \rightarrow [0, 1]$, where $\mu A(x)$ is the degree of membership of element x in fuzzy set A for each $x \in X$.

■ **FIGURE 5.2**
Fuzzy and crisp sets

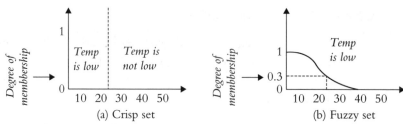

In this definition, X is treated as a universe of discourse, which is a set with a reference to a context that contains all possible elements of the set. It is obvious that all of the elements posses the same properties—examples are all integers, all books in a library, and all vehicles in the world.

Example: Consider a set of temperatures T, which consists of all temperature readings between 0°C to 40°C. That is, if $t = 27$°C, $t \in T$. But if it is claimed, "The temperature is very low," one cannot be sure that the low temperature t is a member of T. This example is illustrated in Figure 5.3.

■ 5.4   MEMBERSHIP FUNCTIONS

A membership function maps elements of a fuzzy set to real numbered values in the interval 0 to 1. The curve representing the mathematical function is nothing but a membership function that determines the degree of belonging of a member x to the fuzzy set T. If $x = 27$°C, a fuzzy membership function A defines from a set of possible temperatures to the interval [0, 1]. Mathematically, it is represented as follows:

$$\mu A: X \rightarrow [0, 1],$$

where X is the set of all possible temperatures and
μA is the fuzzy membership function

The membership function shown in Figure 5.3 yields value $\mu A(x) = \mu A(27 * c) = 0.3$.

Similarly, *high salary, old people, large car,* and *rich person* can be defined with the help of fuzzy logic. The *hot, cold, warm,* and *comfortable* functions for a typical air conditioner can be given as shown in Figure 5.4.

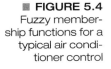

■ **FIGURE 5.4**
Fuzzy member-
ship functions for a
typical air condi-
tioner control

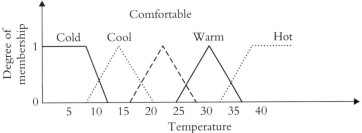

■ 5.4.1 Fuzzification

Definition: The process of transforming crisp input values into linguistic values is called "fuzzification." It has two major steps:

Step 1: Input values are translated into linguistic concepts, which are represented by fuzzy sets.

Step 2: Membership functions are applied to the measurements, and the degree of membership is determined.

In the example shown in Part (b) of Figure 5.3, the crisp value of temperature $t = 27 * c$ is to be converted to a "low" temperature, with the membership value 0.3.

■ 5.4.2 Defuzzification

Defuzzification converts the fuzzy value into a "crisp" value. It is the process of producing a quantifiable result from the fuzzy linguistic variable used. Defuzzification is necessary because a fuzzy set might not translate the fuzzy values directly into crisp values. Some example methods of defuzzification are:

• Max-membership method: This method chooses the element with the maximum value.
• Centroid method: The centroid defuzzification method finds the "center" point of the targeted fuzzy region by calculating the weighted mean of the output fuzzy region.
• Weighted average method: The weighted average method assigns weights to each membership function in the output by its respective maximum membership value.

■ 5.5 OPERATIONS ON FUZZY SETS

On the crisp sets, operations like intersection, union, and complement are well defined. Such operations are possible on fuzzy sets as well. Zadeh (1965) suggested the minimum operator for the intersection between two fuzzy sets and the maximum operator for the union of two fuzzy sets. These operators coincide with crisp unification and intersection only if we consider the membership degrees 0 and 1.

■ 5.5.1 Intersection of Fuzzy Sets

The intersection of A and B is defined as $(A \cap B)(x) = \min\{A(x), B(x)\} = A(x) \cap B(x)$, for $\forall \, x \in X$, as demonstrated in Figure 5.5.

FIGURE 5.5 Intersection of fuzzy sets

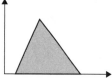  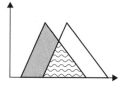

■ 5.5.2 Union of Fuzzy Sets

The union of A and B is defined as $(A \cup B)(x) = \max\{A(x), B(x)\} = A(x) \cup B(x)$, for $\forall \, x \in X$, as shown in Figure 5.6.

FIGURE 5.6 Union of fuzzy sets

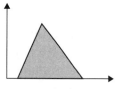 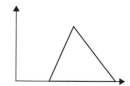 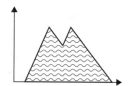

■ 5.5.3 Complements of Fuzzy Sets

The complement of a fuzzy set A is defined as $(\sim A)(x) = 1 - A(x)$, as shown in Figure 5.7.

FIGURE 5.7 Negation of fuzzy sets

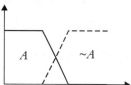

■ 5.5.4   Equality of Fuzzy Sets

Let A and B be fuzzy sets on a classical set X. A and B are said to be equal, denoted $A = B$, if $A \subset B$ and $B \subset A$. That is $A = B$ if and only if $A(x) = B(x)$ for $\forall\ x \in X$.

■ 5.6   TYPES OF FUZZY FUNCTIONS

■ 5.6.1   Quasi-Fuzzy Membership Functions

With this type, the membership function follows a quasi-curve. A quasi-curve is a real line with a normal fuzzy convex and a continuous membership function satisfying the limit conditions, as demonstrated in Figure 5.8.

$$\lim_{x \to \infty} A(x) = 0, \qquad \lim_{x \to -\infty} A(x) = 0,$$

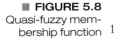

■ FIGURE 5.8
Quasi-fuzzy membership function

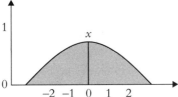

■ 5.6.2   Triangular Fuzzy Membership Functions

If the membership curve follows a triangular shape, it is called a triangular membership function. Fuzzy function A is called triangular fuzzy function $(A = (a, \alpha, \beta))$ with peak (or center) a, left width $\alpha > 0$, and right width $\beta > 0$, if its membership function has the following form (see Figure 5.9):

$$A(x) = 1 - (a - x)/\alpha \text{ is if } a - \alpha \leq x \leq a$$
$$= 1 - (x - a)/\beta \text{ if } a \leq x \leq a + \beta$$
$$= 0 \text{ otherwise.}$$

■ FIGURE 5.9
Triangular fuzzy membership function

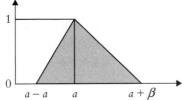

■ 5.6.3 Trapezoidal Fuzzy Membership Function

This membership function follows a trapezoidal curve. A trapezoidal curve is a function of $(A = (a, b, \alpha, \beta))$ with tolerance interval $[a, b]$, left width α, and right width β, if its membership function has the following form (see Figure 5.10):

$$A(x) = 1 - (a - x)/\alpha \text{ if } a - \alpha \leq x \leq a$$
$$= 1 \text{ if } a \leq x \leq b$$
$$= 1 - (x - b)/\beta \text{ if } a \leq x \leq b + \beta$$
$$= 0 \text{ otherwise.}$$

■ **FIGURE 5.10**
Trapezoidal fuzzy membership function

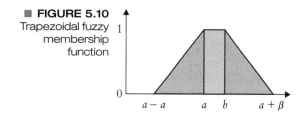

■ 5.7 LINGUISTIC VARIABLES

The power and strength of fuzzy logic comes from its ability to deal with vague linguistic variables. A linguistic variable is a variable whose values are words or sentences in a natural language. For example, temperature is a linguistic variable if it takes values such as *hot, cool, warm,* and *comfortable* instead of 20°C, 24°C, 30°C, and so on. The framework of a linguistic variable is given as $(X, Lx, \chi, \mu x)$, where:

- X denotes the symbolic name of a linguistic variable (e.g., age, height, speed, temperature, etc.).
- Lx is a set of linguistic values that X can take, such as hot, cool, warm, and comfortable for temperature. Lx is also called a term set or reference set of X.
- χ is the physical domain that defines crisp values. In the case of the linguistic variable temperature, it can be the interval $[-10, 35]$.
- μx is a fuzzy function that maps linguistic terms of the variable to the equivalent crisp values.

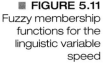

FIGURE 5.11

Fuzzy membership functions for the linguistic variable speed

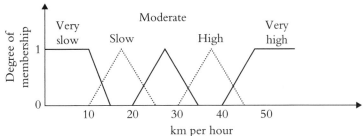

km per hour

In the following example, speed is interpreted as a linguistic variable. For this example, components of $(X, Lx, \chi, \mu x)$ are given as follows:

- X is the name of the linguistic variable, that is, speed.
- Lx is the set of linguistic values that X can take; here, it is the set {fast, moderate, slow, very slow}.
- χ is the physical domain that defines crisp values. With regard to the linguistic variable speed, χ is the interval [0, 100], with a unit of km/hour.
- μx is a fuzzy function that maps linguistic terms of the variable to the equivalent crisp values.

The membership function can be defined as shown in Figure 5.11.

5.7.1 Linguistic Hedges

Hedges are modifiers of fuzzy values, and they allow multiple generations of fuzzy statements through mathematical calculations. These are nothing but adverbs and adjectives used with a linguistic variable to modify the fuzzy function. Hedges are classified as concentrators, dilators, or contrast hedges, according to their definition and use. That is, for the linguistic variable temperature "warm," terms like "very warm" and "rather warm" are used as hedges of the variable. A concentrator hedge intensifies the fuzzy region, whereas a dilator hedge dilutes the force of the fuzzy set membership function. The contrast hedge changes the nature of the fuzzy region by making it either less fuzzy (through intensification) or more fuzzy (through diffusion)—see Figure 5.12.

FIGURE 5.12
Linguistic hedges

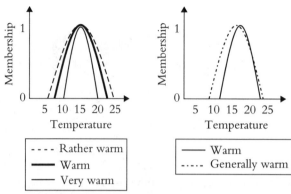

5.8   FUZZY RELATIONSHIPS

Consider the set of machines, M, and the set of people, P, defined as follows:

M = {set of all machines in a domain}

e.g., $M = \{m_1, m_2, m_3, \ldots, m_n\}$ where n is a finite small number

P = {set of people}

e.g., $P = \{p_1, p_2, p_3, \ldots, p_k\}$ where k is a finite small number

If the machines of set M are used by the people of set P, the relationship, R, can be defined as a relationship of $M*P$ and identified with the "used by" phrase. Here, R is a subset of $M*P$ and denoted as $R \subset M*P$. The individual relationship can be presented as follows:

$(p_1, m_1), (p_2, m_2), (p_3, m_3), \ldots$.

Such relationships are crisp in nature and easy to handle mathematically. Relationships like "comfort of a person while working with a machine" is really a fuzzy relationship and comparatively difficult to handle with crisp logic. The fuzzy relationship "generally comfortable" can be defined as follows:

	m_1	m_2	m_3
p_1	1.0	0.4	0.7
p_2	0.8	1.0	0.6
p_3	0.7	0.6	1.0

This table shows that a person is comfortable with the machine allotted to him or her, but not very comfortable with machines allotted to other persons.

Definition:
If U and V are sets and μ is a function from $U*V$ to $[0, 1]$, then the set of all tuples of the form (u,v) with $\mu(u,v)$ defines a fuzzy relationship on $U*V$.

Example:
Consider $U = V = \{1,2,3\}$. The relationship of $U*V$, defined as "approximately equal," is a binary fuzzy relationship given by $1/(1,1)$, $1/(2,2)$, $1/(3,3)$, $0.8/(1,2)$, $0.8/(2,3)$, $0.8/(2,1)$, $0.4/(1,3)$, and $0.4/(3,1)$. The following table presents the situation in matrix form.

X/Y	1	2	3
1	1.0	0.8	0.4
2	0.8	1.0	0.8
3	0.4	0.8	1.0

The membership functions can be defined as:

$$\mu R(x) = \begin{cases} 1.0 & \text{for } x = y \\ 0.8 & \text{for } |x-y| = 1 \\ 0.4 & \text{for } |x-y| = 2 \end{cases}$$

The intersection and union operators are also applicable to fuzzy relationships. They are defined as follows:

$$\mu_{R \cap S}(x,y) = \min(\mu_R(x,y), \mu_S(x,y))$$
$$\mu_{R \cup S}(x,y) = \max(\mu_R(x,y), \mu_S(x,y))$$

Example:
Consider $U = V = \{1,2,3\}$. Relationship R of $U*V$ was defined earlier as "approximately equal" and given as follows:

X/Y	1	2	3
1	1.0	0.8	0.4
2	0.8	1.0	0.8
3	0.4	0.8	1.0

Consider another relationship, S, of $U*V$ in which x is considerably larger than y for $\forall x \in U$ and $\forall y \in V$. The relationship S can be given as follows:

X/Y	1	2	3
1	0	0.6	0.8
2	0	0	0.6
3	0	0	0

Then, $R \cap S$ can be given as follows:

X/Y	1	2	3
1	Min(1,0)	Min(0.8,0.6)	Min(0.4,0.8)
2	Min(0.8,0)	Min(1,0)	Min(0.8,0.6)
3	Min(0.4,0)	Min(0.8,0)	Min(1,0)

resulting in $R \cap S$, as shown:

X/Y	1	2	3
1	0	0.6	0.4
2	0	0	0.6
3	0	0	0

Then, $R \cup S$ can be given as follows:

X/Y	1	2	3
1	Max (1,0)	Max (0.8,0.6)	Max (0.4,0.8)
2	Max (0.8,0)	Max (1,0)	Max (0.8,0.6)
3	Max (0.4,0)	Max (0.8,0)	Max (1,0)

Hence, $R \cup S$ can be given as:

X/Y	1	2	3
1	1.0	0.8	0.8
2	0.8	1.0	0.8
3	0.4	0.8	1.0

Fuzzy relationships can be explained with the following simple, real-life example. Consider the relationship between the size of the information system project for development, X, and the effort required, Y, where $X =$ {Small, Medium, High} and $Y =$ {Low, Average, High}. The fuzzy relationship R of $X*Y$ is given as follows:

X/Y	Low	Average	High
Small	1.0	0.5	0
Medium	0.3	1.0	0.4
Large	0	0.2	1.0

The fuzzy relationship R helps form rules on the fuzzy rule base as follows:

If the project is small, then effort is low.
If the project is large, then effort is high.

Figure 5.13 shows the required membership functions and relationships for this example.

■ FIGURE 5.13
Membership functions and relationships between project size and effort required

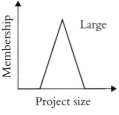

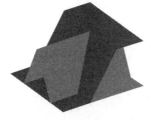

■ 5.9 FUZZY PROPOSITIONS

A fuzzy proposition is a statement that derives a fuzzy truth value. The truth value of the proposition can be given as $T(p)$, which lies between $[0, 1]$. For example, if p: Mr. Bond is honest, then $T(p) = 0.9$.

■ 5.9.1 Fuzzy Connectives

Fuzzy connectives are used to join simple fuzzy propositions to make compound propositions. Negations ($\sim$), disjunctions ($\cup$), conjunctions ($\cap$), and implications ($\Rightarrow$) are used as fuzzy connectives. The operations are defined in the following sections.

5.9.1.1 Disjunctions

The meaning of a disjunction is given by a union function:

X is either A or B

Then X is $A \cup B$

The meaning of "X is $_A\cup_B$" is given by $\mu_A\cup_B$. The maximum operator, as discussed earlier, can be used for disjunctions.

Example:
Consider p and q as follows:

p: Mr. Bond is honest.

q: Mr. Bond is efficient.

Then $p \cup q$: Mr. Bond is either honest or efficient.

5.9.1.2 Conjunctions

The meaning of a conjunction is given by an intersection function:

X is A

X is B

Then X is $A \cap B$

The meaning of "X is $_A\cap_B$" is given by $\mu_A\cap_B$. The minimum operator, as discussed earlier, can be used for conjunctions.

Example:

If p: pressure is not very high and
     q: pressure is not low

Then the proposition produced by the conjunction will be

$p \cap q$: pressure is not very high and not low

5.9.1.3   Negations

A negation is a complementary function, defined as: $1 - \mu_{A \cap B}$.

Example:

If p: pressure is not very high
Then $\sim p$: pressure is very high

5.9.1.4   Implications

Implications are obtained by combining negation and intersection functions.

If X is A and Y is B
Then X is B

The meaning of "$A \Rightarrow B$" is given by max $(1 - (\mu_A) (\mu_B))$.

Example:
Consider p and q as follows:

p: Mr. Bond is honest.

q: Mr. Bond is efficient.

Then $p \Rightarrow q$: If Mr. Bond is honest, then he is efficient.
Compound fuzzy propositions are also possible—for example:

X is A and X is B
X is A or X is B
X is not A
If X is A, then X is B

and so on.

Example:

Let A = "x is bigger than 5" and let B = "x is bigger than 4." It is easy to see that $A \rightarrow B$ is true, because it can never happen that x is bigger than 5 and not bigger than 4.

■ 5.10 FUZZY INFERENCE

Fuzzy inference provides a powerful framework for reasoning with imprecise and uncertain information. The inference procedures are known as generalized modus ponens (GMP) and generalized modus tollens (GMT).

GMP is described as follows:

Given: X is A, then Y is B

X is A'

One may conclude that Y is B'.

GMT is described as follows:

Given: X is A, then Y is B

Y is B'

One may conclude that X is A'.

Example:

The tomato is very red.

If the tomato is red, then the tomato is ripe.

Then the conclusion can be "the tomato is very ripe."

■ 5.11 FUZZY RULES

The power and flexibility of simple if-then-else logic rules are enhanced by adding the linguistic parameter. Fuzzy rules are usually expressed in the form:

IF variable IS set THEN action

Some examples are as follows:

IF temperature IS very cold THEN stop air conditioner

IF temperature IS normal THEN adjust air conditioner

IF temperature IS hot THEN start air conditioner

The AND, OR, and NOT operators (also known as Zadeh's operators) are defined in the earlier section are applicable to these rules.

FIGURE 5.14
Fuzzy rules and relationships

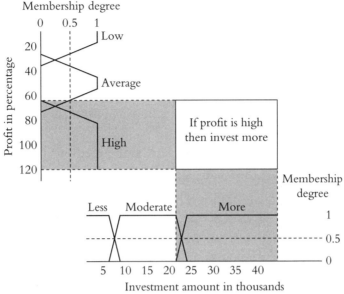

Figure 5.14 shows fuzzy rules and their relationship in the portfolio management for a financial application (Sajja, 2006).

■ 5.12 FUZZY CONTROL SYSTEM

A fuzzy control system is based on fuzzy logic. Given membership functions that map crisp values to fuzzy values and vice versa, the machine can interact with the human being in friendlier way. Fuzzy logic systems address the imprecision of the input and output variables by defining fuzzy numbers and fuzzy sets, which can be expressed in linguistic variables (e.g., high, low, and average). Fuzzy controllers are the most important applications of fuzzy theory. They work rather differently from conventional controllers because the experts' knowledge is used for more effective and human-like control instead of a pure, crisp, mathematical approach (like differential equations) to describe a system.

This knowledge can be expressed in a natural way using linguistic variables, which are described by fuzzy sets. Fuzzy logic-based control systems are also useful for some of the control applications where a systematic mathematical model does not exist. Instead of describing control strategy as mathematical equations, control is expressed as a set of linguistic rules. A control system can be abstracted as a box with inputs flowing into it and outputs emerging from it. The process of designing a fuzzy control system can be described using following steps:

Step 1: Identify the principal input, output, and process tasks.

Step 2: Identify linguistic variables used, and define fuzzy sets and membership accordingly.

Step 3: Use these fuzzy sets and linguistic variables to form procedural rules.

Step 4: Determine the defuzzification method.

Step 5: Test the system and modify if necessary.

The components of a typical control system are shown in Figure 5.15.

Mamdani and Assilian (1975) designed a fuzzy control system for a steam engine. The purpose was to maintain a constant speed by controlling the pressure on pistons by adjusting the heat supplied to a boiler. After that, fuzzy controllers were developed for air conditioners, video cameras, washing machines, and so on. The fuzzy control system can be considered a nonlinear static function that maps controller inputs on controller outputs. Fuzzy controllers are used for systems where a preferred response must be maintained based on whatever inputs are received. Naturally, inputs to the system can alter the state of the system, which causes a change in response. Thus, the duty of the controller is to take appropriate action by providing a set of inputs to ensure the preferred response.

A fuzzy controller consists of four main components:

1. Fuzzy knowledge base: The knowledge base consists of fuzzy rules for the system that represent the knowledge and experience of a human expert. For example, "If the temperature is fairly high and the pressure is very low, then the output is medium."

FIGURE 5.15
A fuzzy controller

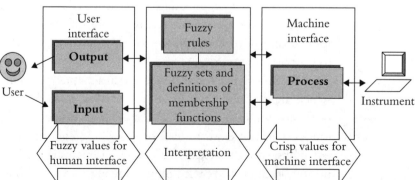

2. Fuzzifier: The fuzzifier receives the actual output of the system and transforms the nonfuzzy values into membership degrees based on the corresponding fuzzy sets.

3. Action interface: This interface defuzzifies the outcome of the inference engine to produce a nonfuzzy value, which represents the actual control function to be applied to the system.

4. Inference engine: It performs inferencing upon fuzzified inputs to produce a fuzzy output.

Many real-world control systems use rules that are described in descriptive expressions because this is the way experts perform their operations. Membership functions can be defined for the fuzzy variables. Furthermore, fuzzy inference can be performed, and output can be generated.

■ 5.13   FUZZY RULE-BASED SYSTEM

A fuzzy rule-based system (FRBS) is an application of fuzzy logic to rule-based systems. Generally, two models are available: the Mamdani model (Mamdani, 1974) and the Takagi-Sugeno-Kang model (Takagi & Sugeno, 1985). Mamdani (1974) was the first to model Zadeh's (1965) fuzzy logic concept in a structure, resulting in a fuzzy rule-based system for a control problem. That is, the fuzzy controller discussed in Section 5.12, is a modified case of Mamdani's FRBS.

■ 5.13.1   Models of Fuzzy Rule-Based Systems

The basic structures of the Mamdani and Takagi-Sugeno-Kang (TSK) models are presented in Figure 5.16.

The Takagi-Sugeno-Kang model calculates the output with a simple formula (*weighted average*). The Mamdani fuzzy model requires the values to be fuzzified and defuzzified, which makes this model more complicated. One of the basic differences between the Mamdani and TSK fuzzy models is the fact that the results are, respectively, fuzzy and crisp sets. Hence, the procedures involved in the computation of the output signals are distinct.

■ 5.14   TYPE-1 AND TYPE-2 FUZZY RULE-BASED SYSTEMS

Most of the systems considered so far are typical fuzzy logic-based systems mapping fuzzy to crisp and vice versa. These systems are called Type-1 fuzzy systems (T1 FS) and have no specific, customized mechanisms to deal with

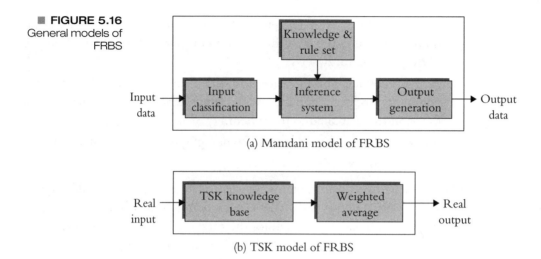

(a) Mamdani model of FRBS

(b) TSK model of FRBS

vague parameters. Type-2 fuzzy systems (T2 FS) take us one more step toward the goal of "computing with words," or using computers to represent human perception. Zadeh (1999) presents that perceptions of size, health, and comfort cannot be modeled by traditional mathematical techniques and that fuzzy logic is more suitable. Since T2 FS are based on fuzzy sets whose membership grades are noncrisp, fuzzy membership functions, they can model perceptions more effectively than the T1 FS (John & Coupland 2007; Mendal 2007). That is, a T1 FS has a grade of membership that is crisp, whereas a T2 FS has grades of membership that are fuzzy. Such sets are useful when it is difficult to model the exact membership function. For more imprecise data, T2 FS offers a significant improvement on T1 FS. A view of the relationships between levels of imprecision, data, and techniques is shown in Figure 5.17 (John & Coupland, 2007).

■ 5.14.1 T2 FS Membership Functions

To improve an understanding of perceptions in more human-friendly way, a fuzzy system needs a measure of dispersion to capture more information about linguistic uncertainties than just a single membership function (MF). T1 FS can only deal with a single MF. A T2 FS, however, provides these measures of dispersion (Mendal, 2007). For example, suppose a variable of interest is "assistance required" to complete a course, denoted by x, where $x \in [0, 10]$, 0 means no assistance required, and 10 means maximum assistance required. Now, "some assistance required" can be interpreted in different ways

■ **FIGURE 5.17**
T1 FS and T2 FS
relationships

Precision: Precise   Imprecise

Data: Numbers   Words   Perceptions

Technique: Math. Modeling   T1 FS   T2 FS

for different people, which is denoted in Figure 5.18. From the figure, it is clear that, if all uncertainty disappears, the T2 FS reduces to a T1 FS.

■ 5.15   MODELING FUZZY SYSTEMS

Fuzzy system modeling can be pursued using the following steps:

- Choose the relevant input and output variables.
- Determine the number of linguistic terms associated with each input/output variable. Also, pick the appropriate family of membership functions, fuzzy operators, reasoning mechanisms, and so on.
- Select a specific type of fuzzy system, such as Mamdani's system. Most of the time, the inference of the fuzzy rules is carried out using the "min" and "max" operators for fuzzy intersections and unions.
- Design a collection of fuzzy if-then rules (the knowledge base). To formulate the initial rule base, the input space is divided into multidimensional partitions and then actions are assigned to each of the partitions.

■ **FIGURE 5.18**
Triangular MFs for
T2 FS when base
points (l) and (r)
have uncertainty
associated with
them for the variable "some assistance required"

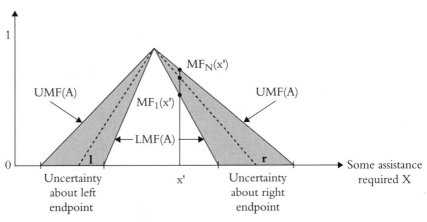

In most applications, partitioning is achieved using one-dimensional membership functions using fuzzy if-then rules.

■ 5.16 LIMITATIONS OF FUZZY SYSTEMS

- Fuzzy systems lack the capabilities of machine learning, as well as a neural network-type memory and pattern recognition. Therefore, hybrid systems (e.g., neurofuzzy systems) are becoming more popular for specific applications.
- Verification and validation of a fuzzy knowledge-based system typically requires extensive testing with hardware in the loop. This is an expensive affair.
- Determining exact fuzzy rules and membership functions is a hard task. One cannot predict how many membership functions are required even after wide testing.
- Stability is an important concern for fuzzy control.

■ 5.17 APPLICATIONS AND RESEARCH TRENDS IN FUZZY LOGIC-BASED SYSTEMS

Fuzzy logic becomes trivial for complex procedures that are nonlinear by nature, lack a mathematical model, and require expert knowledge. The following are some recent application areas:

- Automatic control (power plants; robots; industrial control; manufacturing; machines like air conditioners, automobiles, etc.)
- Prediction, diagnostic, and advisory systems
- User interface and Natural Language Processing (NLP)
- Domestic appliances and embedded systems
- Software engineering
- Soft computing and hybrid systems with Artificial Neural Network (ANN) and Genetic Algorithm (GA) (e.g., fuzzy interface with the ANN and rule extraction to autodevelop a fuzzy system)
- Very Large Scale Integrated circuits (VLSI) microcontroller
- Fuzzy expert system and fuzzy inference
- Automatic-type reducing techniques for T2 FS from T1 FS
- Fuzzy operations, propositions, and inference for T2 FS

- Applications in medicine, management science, and economics that involve fuzzy information processing

Fuzzy logic is beneficial for handling imprecise data. This is convenient when a problem can be described linguistically or, as with neural networks, where there is data and you are looking for relationships or patterns within that data. Thus, fuzzy logic applications include a wide range of applications—robotics, washing machine control, nuclear reactors, focusing a camcorder, information retrieval, train scheduling, system modeling, and tracking stock performance.

Communications and networking have been able to use fuzzy logic for network traffic modeling, management, and data transfer rate control, as well as nonlinear channel equalization, telecommunication ranking, and network admission control. Communication systems are real-time, deterministic, well-defined systems that reliably transport voice and data signals from point A to point B. However, the transmitted signal is subject to considerable distortion by a harsh environment, the medium, and the system itself. As the signal departs from point A, it is subject to the algorithmic manipulations (equalization, digital signal processing, analog-to-digital conversions) and transformations (sound to electronic, to photonic, to electromagnetic waves) it endures from external influences (electromagnetic, environmental). The result is a distorted or fuzzy signal. Therefore, fuzzy logic can be useful in reproducing the initial transmitted signal at the receiver end (Akerkar, 2008).

Fuzzy logic control can play an important role in the development of intelligent systems for space applications. Lee and Berenji (1989) pointed out that the basic difficulty in the design of fuzzy logic systems is fine-tuning the membership functions for the labels used in the rules. Berenji and Khedkar (1992) proposed reinforcement learning for the fine-tuning of membership functions, and developed two architectures: Approximate reasoning-based intelligent control (ARIC) and generalized ARIC (GARIC). GARIC is a hybrid architecture for fuzzy logic control and reinforcement learning of control rules. In reinforcement learning, it is not assumed that a supervisor critically judges the chosen control action at each step. Rather, the learning system is told indirectly about the effect of the control action. GARIC uses reinforcements from the environment to refine globally all of the rules for its definitions of fuzzy labels. Berenji et al. employed GARIC to develop a controller for tether control on board the Space Shuttle. The problem was complicated due to a number of considerations, such as the need to operate in a vacuum, gravitational and magnetic forces, and lack of an external gravitational field. The time-varying dynamics of the long, flexible, variable-length tether and those of the orbiter and satellite made tether control an even more difficult task. The attitude and translational control are key elements of the Space Shuttle in-orbit operations. The attitude controller executes a variety of tasks. One of the tasks is maintaining the preferred attitude within a tiny region of the preferred value. It is called a dead-band. GARIC learned to maintain the dead-band in a small number of trials.

The reasons why the fuzzy logic approach is superior to traditional control techniques are as follows:

- Fuzzy systems are easy to implement, even if the designer has little knowledge of formal fuzzy logic theory.
- Fuzzy systems can deal with crucial parameter changes and broadly unstable load conditions.
- Fuzzy logic is appropriate for industrial processes where the control cycle time may operate over an extended period.
- Fuzzy systems help in reducing complexity and increasing user friendliness.
- Fuzzy systems manage imprecise data and information used.

A number of software packages are available to help with the development of fuzzy systems, especially fuzzy control systems. They include MATLAB Fuzzy Logic Toolbox™, Mathematica Fuzzy Logic™, SieFuzzy™, fuzzyTech™, TILShell™, FIDE™, RT/Fuzzy™, Fuzzy Knowledge Builder™, and Fuzz-C™. These packages provide user-friendly, graphical interfaces, which make the development process simple and efficient.

■ 5.18 WARM-UP QUESTIONS, EXERCISES, AND PROJECTS

Warm-up Questions

1. Discuss the four steps of fuzzy inference.
2. Explain the difference between Boolean logic and fuzzy logic.
3. Visit the following website: http://www.nrlmry.navy.mil/~medex/. Explore the features of this fuzzy rule-based system and explain the benefits it offers.

4. Download a free trial of the FLINT toolkit at http://www.lpa.co.uk/
   fln.htm. It has a fuzzy editor that will help you to define and edit membership functions.
5. Compare and contrast linguistic variables and hedges.
6. In defuzzification, how is the max-min used to find an approximate
   scalar value to represent the action to be taken?
7. Search the Web for more information about the following fuzzy control
   systems:
   a. Table-based control systems
   b. Takagi-Sugeno control systems

Exercises

1. Implement the membership function for the fuzzy set of values that are
   close to a, where a is a real number.
2. In a class of 10 students (the universal set), 3 students speak Hindi to
   some degree—namely, Rita to degree 0.7, Nita to degree 1.0, and Amit
   to degree 0.4. What is the size of the subset A of Hindi-speaking students in the class?
3. Give three natural-language examples where fuzzy sets may be applied
   to model certain concepts.
4. Characterize graphically reasonable membership functions for the following fuzzy sets. What is the universal set in each case? The fuzzy subset
   is emphasized in italics:
   - n is a *large number*
   - these persons are *very old*
   - *about 10* persons attended the seminar
   - x is *between -7 and 4*
   - x is *greater than 5*
   - x is *greater than, or equal to, 5*
   - x is *almost equal to y*
5. What is the difference between the membership function of an ordinary
   set and a fuzzy set?
6. Investigate the essential steps for designing Mamdani-type controllers.
7. What are the components of a fuzzy system?

8. Use the MATLAB Fuzzy Logic Toolbox to model the following gas equation for a confined gas

$$pV = nRT$$

where p is the pressure, V is the volume, and T is the temperature of the gas. n and R are constants. Assume further that we have a way of keeping the temperature constant, such that the entire right side is constant. Use rules such as

IF(V IS large) THEN (p IS low)

What types of membership functions would be good to use here?

9. Use MATLAB to plot the original function for a range of pressures, with $nRT = 0.8$. Then implement your rule base and see if you can adjust your fuzzy inference system to show the same behavior.

10. Use the MATLAB Fuzzy Logic Toolbox to model the tip after a visit to a forest by two friends, where the visit can be *interesting, not good, satisfying,* or *refreshing*; and the forest can be *dense, not so dense,* or *not at all dense.*

11. Describe the fuzzy logic control system of a washing machine.

Projects

1. Design a fuzzy control system to control a set of four elevators for an 18-floor office building in order to maximize utilization and minimize delays.

2. You are expected to solve a practical problem using fuzzy logic. The problem can be an actual industrial application suggested by your instructor, but interesting practical problems out of recent literature also may be used.

References

Akerkar, R. Soft computing approaches to applications in communication systems, *Journal of Hybrid Computing Research*, vol.1, no. 2, pp. 1–7, 2008.

Berenji, H., & Khedkar, P. Learning and tuning fuzzy logic controllers through reinforcements, *IEEE Transactions on Neural Networks*, vol. 3, no. 5, 1992.

John, R. I., & Coupland, S. Type-2 fuzzy logic: a historical view. *IEEE Computational Intelligence Magazine*, vol.2, pp. 57–62, 2007.

Lea, R., Villarreal, J., Jani Y., & Copeland, C. Learning characteristics of a space time neural network as a tether skiprope observer, *North American Fuzzy Information Processing Society*, pp. 154–165, Puerto Vallarta, Mexico, December 1992.

Lee, C. C. & Berenji, H. *An intelligent controller based on approximate reasoning and reinforcement learning*, Procedures of IEEE International Symposium on Intelligent Control, Albany, NY, 1989.

Mamdani, E. H. Applications of fuzzy algorithm for control a simple dynamic plant, *Proceedings of the IEEE*, vol.121, no.12, pp.1585–1588, 1974.

Mendal, J. M. Type-2 fuzzy sets and systems: An overview, *IEEE Computational Intelligence Magazine*, vol.2, pp. 20–29, 2007.

Sajja, P. S. A fuzzy agent to input vague parameters into a multilayer connectionist expert system: an application for the stock market, *ADIT Journal of Engineering*, vol.3, no.1, pp. 30–32, 2006.

Takagi, T. & Sugeno, M. Fuzzy identification of systems and its applications to modeling and control, *IEEE Transactions on Systems, Man and Cybernetics*, vol.15, no.1, pp.116–132, 1985.

Zadeh, L. A. From computing with numbers to computing with words—from manipulation of measurement to manipulation of perceptions. *IEEE Transactions on Circuits and Systems-I: Fundamental Theory and Applications, vol.45*, pp.105–119, 1999.

Zadeh, L. A. Fuzzy sets, *Information and Control*, vol.8, pp. 338–353, 1965.

CHAPTER 6

Agent-Based Systems

■ 6.1 INTRODUCTION

The word "agent" is widely used, not only in computer science, but also in the "real world." In general terms, an agent is a person authorized to act on behalf of another person. In day-to-day activities, we come across many agents while handling transactions relating to education, sports, real estate, investment, traveling, marketing, advertising, and more. These agents help facilitate transactions for people who do not have the expertise, time, and resources.

A robot acting in a real-world environment is nothing but an agent. Intelligent agents are artificial intelligence (AI) tools, which are autonomous robots or programs that interact with their environment and make intelligent decisions according to the need and situation. In order to achieve this, they are enriched with necessary skills and motivations, and can communicate with other entities in the environment in which they are situated. Various application areas, ranging from simple extensions of existing software (such as an extension to a word processor or spreadsheet) to complex workflow management systems, are candidates for the agent technology.

From a historical point of view, agents and multiagent systems have their roots in AI. The notion of a multiagent system began to emerge in the 1980s. Interestingly, research into individual agents progressed largely separate from research into multiagent systems until the 1990s. Agents and multiagent systems are now a well-established research field, with a number of potential applications. The discipline of agents is a fusion of ideas and concepts from other areas as diverse as biology, mathematics, sociology, philosophy, computer science, and ethology.

The term "agent" is loosely defined in computer terminology. This chapter presents a general definition of an agent and discusses its characteristics. In the next section, the architecture of a typical agent is shown. The advantages agent technology offers are then discussed. Agents are classified into various groups, according to their characteristics (like mobility) or by the role they play. A few types of agents are discussed, along with their architectural diagrams and applications. Agents must communicate with their users and with other agents in order to perform their intended tasks. For this, a means of communication is necessary. This chapter also presents formal communication language through the use of examples. At the end, the concept of the multiagent system is presented, along with the typical architecture. The chapter concludes with examples of research directions in which agent-based technology can go.

■ 6.2   WHAT IS AN AGENT?

An agent refers to a component of software and/or hardware that is capable of acting in a certain way to accomplish tasks on behalf of its user. That is, an agent is a computational entity capable of autonomous decision-making when it comes to its area of interest. Agents generally look for complete automation of complex processes through artificial intelligent techniques acting on behalf of human users. For such problem-solving assistance, agents are supposed to have knowledge of an application domain and target users. The level of knowledge required is directly related to the complexity of the tasks intended for the agents.

Definition 1: An agent is a computational entity that:

- Acts on behalf of other entities in an autonomous fashion
- Performs its actions with some level of proactivity and/or reactiveness
- Exhibits properties like learning, cooperation, and mobility to a certain extent

Software agents (often simply termed agents) are software systems that freely fit the aforementioned criteria and can principally be described as inhabiting computers and networks, assisting users with computer-based tasks.

But are knowledge-based systems agents? A knowledge-based system can be characterized as being intelligent, similar to an agent. However, knowledge-based systems have no control over their actions. They provide domain-specific information and usually do not adapt. Their ability to interact is rather limited. That means knowledge-based systems do not interact with the environment or other knowledge-based systems. Thus, they do not possess true social ability.

■ 6.3 CHARACTERISTICS OF AGENTS

Agents are expected to work on behalf of users; hence, they must be capable of working autonomously without human intervention. For this purpose, they are supposed to possess necessary skills and be enriched with required resources. In case resources are not directly available due to certain constraints, a reference (path) to resources must be made available to the agents. That is, agents should "know" how to meet the expectations within the environment. This leads to another important characteristic of cooperation and learning. Agents need to work in cooperation with users and other entities (including other agents) in order to learn and complete their tasks. Such learning and cooperation is driven by a set of tendencies, which may be derived from a list of objectives or functionalities expected of agents. In short, agents are the entities working towards satisfying predefined objectives with the help of their resources and skills, and depending on their perception and the communications they receive. Another important characteristic that agents may have is mobility. The intelligence of an agent is related to its associated mobility.

Agents perceive their environment and respond in a timely fashion to the changes enforced by the environment. By nature, agents are proactive or reactive. Agents that act in response to their environment when provoked (triggered) by prespecified events are called reactive agents. Agents that can exhibit goal-oriented behavior by taking initiative are proactive agents. Table 6.1 outlines the characteristics of both types of agents.

There are many other characteristics of agents which are worth considering. Some of them are mobility, veracity, benevolence, and rationality (Jeffrey, 2002). Mobility refers to the ability of an agent to move around within

■ Table 6.1 Characteristics of Agents

Characteristic	Description
Autonomy	Agents must have the capability to work autonomously without human intervention. For this purpose, they are supposed to possess necessary skills and be enriched with required resources.
Cooperation	In order to complete their tasks, agents must interact with users, the environment, and other agents.
Learning	Agents should be able to learn from the entities with which they interact to complete their tasks.
Reactivity	Agents perceive their environment and respond in a timely fashion to changes enforced by the environment.

a distributed network to perform the expected tasks. An agent must not knowingly communicate false information, which refers to the property of veracity. The goal must be known to the agent, and in case there are multiple goals, obviously, they must not be contradictory. An agent can perform its duties without any confusion whenever it is expected to do so. This property is known as benevolence. Rationality helps agents to act in order to achieve their goals, and they will not act in such a way as to prevent their goals from being achieved. Above all, there is a characteristic called social ability, which refers to the ability to interface and interact with other agents via a communication language.

Figure 6.1 represents the typical architecture of an agent, along with its general characteristics.

■ FIGURE 6.1
Architecture of an
agent

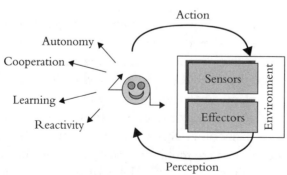

■ 6.4 ADVANTAGES OF AGENT TECHNOLOGY

The modern business systems and problem-solving requirements are becoming more complex day by day. The systems we need to analyze span different application areas (such as the interdependencies of physical and economical infrastructures) and are increased in their scope. Several new tools, modeling approaches, and design methodologies are making the tasks more confusing instead of solving problems. This leads to the need for agents that can be asked to frequently carry out their intended tasks. The intended application can be divided into multiple subtasks. These tasks can be independently entertained by one or more agents to achieve advantages of parallel processing. After completing the job, the agents may interact with each other in a cooperative fashion for resources or feedback. This saves time and offers a multidisciplinary solution, which would not have been possible with a stand-alone system.

The main advantages of agent technologies are as follows:

- They can be used to solve large, complex problems.
- They allow for the interconnection and interoperation of multiple existing legacy systems.
- They provide solutions to problems where information resources, expertise, and the problem itself are widely distributed.
- They enhance modularity, speed, reliability, flexibility, and reusability in problem solving.
- They lead to research into other issues—for example, understanding interactions among human societies (Hyacinth, 1996).

So what is it that makes agents different, above and beyond other software? Whereas traditional software applications need to be told explicitly what it is that they need to accomplish and the exact steps that they have to perform, agents only need to be told what the goal is, but not how to achieve it. They will actively seek ways to satisfy this goal, with less intervention from the user. Agents will figure out what needs to be done to achieve the goal, but also will react to any changes in the environment as they occur that may affect their plans and goal accomplishment, and then subsequently will modify their course of action.

Agents can solve problems that are beyond the scope of other methodologies or programming paradigms, such as open systems. In open systems, the components are not known in advance, their structure and topology may change, and the individual components are inherently heterogeneous because they may be implemented by different developers using different languages and technologies. One such example is the Internet. In short, agents are suitable for dynamic, uncertain, information-rich, and process-rich environments.

Moreover, agents can also be used for problems that can be solved using other methodologies, but in a significantly better and more natural way. For example, problems where data, control, and expertise are inherently distributed will be appropriate for agent-based solutions. Agents with different expertise and computational recourses, which may be distributed over a network, can come together and coordinate to solve a complex task. The agent metaphor is a natural abstraction for such problems, and therefore, a collection of agents can be viewed as a society of sorts. Agents can be used further as a means to incorporate and interact with legacy components or systems. Legacy components are technologically obsolete pieces of software that are a part of organizations and are essential for their functionality but are difficult to replace.

■ 6.5   AGENT TYPOLOGIES

Agents can be classified according to several different parameters—dividing them into proactive and reactive groups is a broad classification. Agents may also be classified according to the role they play. Another, better way to classify agents is according to their mobility and nature. This section describes different classifications of agents according to their nature and the role they play.

■ 6.5.1   Collaborative Agent

This type of agent emphasizes autonomy and cooperation with entities like users and other agents of the environment in order to perform tasks. These agents are quite useful when the problem domain is large. As their name denotes, collaborative agents interconnect different standalone legacy systems to define the problem and acquire resources and expertise from distributed areas. This enhances the structure and modularity of the system. An example of this system is a Visitor Hosting System for a temple. The basic objective

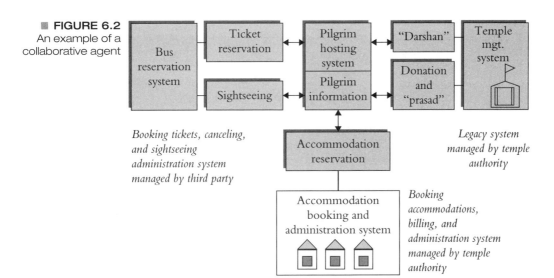

of such a system is to facilitate pilgrims of the temple by providing various services, such as "darshan" (vision of the divine), meal coupons, donations, accommodations, purchase of religious items and "prasad" (gracious gifts), booking return tickets, sightseeing, and so on. Figure 6.2 presents this scenario as an example of a collaborative agent.

Collaborative agents are used in situations where the problem is too large and/or resources are widely distributed.

■ 6.5.2 Interface Agent

Interface agents are the ideal means for providing a user-friendly environment to work with a highly technical application. This type of agent is like a personal assistant, helping users to interact with the system. Their ability to learn about users can be enhanced to identify user level and interact according to the user's need and style (see Figure 6.3).

Examples of applications that use interface agents include personal assistants/organizers, preferential information filters, financial decision systems, and entertainment and tutorial systems.

■ 6.5.3 Mobile Agent

The mobile agent offers an alternative for network and distributed computing that contrasts sharply with the predominant methodologies currently

■ **FIGURE 6.3**
An example of an
interface agent

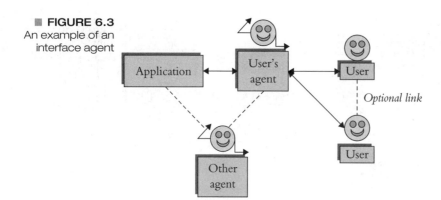

available: the client-server model, code-on-demand, and more recent Web services approach.

An agent's mobility refers to its ability to move around an electronic network. For this purpose, such agents encompass techniques to interact with a wide area network, such as the World Wide Web (WWW). The typical tasks they can perform are searching and collecting information on behalf of their owners and interacting with the remote systems. Mobile agents exhibit sophisticated social ability, proactiveness, and autonomy (Moraitakis, 1997). Figure 6.4 presents a workflow for a typical mobile agent. Mobile agents can be integrated and embedded with the office automation system in order to manage communication through fax, email, and telephone calls.

Mobile agents are used in situations where the information must be retrieved from various remote resources.

■ **FIGURE 6.4**
Workflow for a
mobile agent

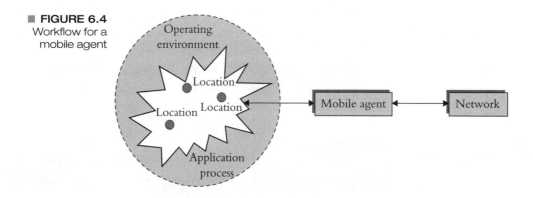

A number of mobile agent systems have emerged in the last decade. The rapid development of mobile agents has been facilitated by the development and adoption of the Java language. However, not all mobile agent systems use Java as their underlying platform.

Example 1: *Aglet—Java-based mobile agent system*

This is the most well-known Java-based mobile agent system. Aglet is a combination of the words "agent" and "applets." It was developed at the IBM Tokyo Research Lab (Nakamura & Yamamoto, 1997). Environments are provided on hosts by specialized servers, which understand the Aglet Transfer Protocol (ATP) and provide security and other services. The aglet distribution is provided with a server, called Tahiti. The design of aglets is modeled on that of Java applets. The basic abstractions in the aglet framework are:

- **Aglet:** An aglet is a mobile Java object that visits aglet-enabled hosts in a computer network. It is autonomous because it runs in its own thread of execution after arriving at a host, and it is reactive because of its ability to respond to incoming messages.
- **Proxy:** A proxy is a representative of an aglet. It serves as a shield for the aglet, protecting it from direct access to its public methods. The proxy also provides location transparency for the aglet; that is, it can hide the aglet's real location.
- **Context:** A context is an aglet's workplace. It is a stationary object that provides a means for maintaining and managing running aglets in a uniform execution environment where the host system is secured against malicious aglets. One node in a computer network may run multiple servers, and each server may host multiple contexts. Contexts are named and can thus be located by the combination of their server's address and their name.
- **Message:** A message is an object exchanged between aglets. It allows for synchronous as well as asynchronous message passing between aglets. Aglets can use message passing to collaborate and exchange information in a loosely coupled fashion.
- **Future reply:** A future reply is used in asynchronous message sending as a handler to receive a result later.
- **Identifier:** An identifier is bound to each aglet. This identifier is globally unique and immutable throughout the aglet's lifetime.

These abstractions provide an aglet with the environment in which it can carry out its tasks. The aglet uses a simple proxy object to relay messages and has a message class to encapsulate message exchange between agents. However, group-oriented communication is not available, and the choice of using a proxy to relay a message may not be a scalable solution in a high-frequency transport situation. The designers of aglets leverage the existing Java infrastructure to take care of platform-dependent issues and to use the existing mobile code facility of Java.

■ 6.5.4 Information Agent

Due to advances in information and communication technology (ICT), a vast amount of information is available at users' fingertips. However, this available information has to be checked for its reliability and usability. Such an explosion of information in an unstructured and redundant format makes the task of problem solving difficult. Thus, information agents help by searching for and managing information on users' behalf. Such agents are enriched with techniques for information searching, ranking, extracting, and filtering according to need. Figure 6.5 demonstrates how this type of agent works. Information agents can also be utilized in conjunction with one or more large databases to serve users' information needs. An information agent working in a distributed network area, like the Internet, is known as an Internet agent. *Softbot* (www.cs.washington.edu, 2008) is a well-known example of an information agent.

■ 6.5.5 Hybrid Agent

A hybrid agent combines two or more agent categories. For example, an agent facilitating effective information searching from large databases and providing communication through a well-designed, natural-language interface is a hybrid agent because it encompasses the methodologies of an infor-

■ **FIGURE 6.5**
Workflow for an
information agent

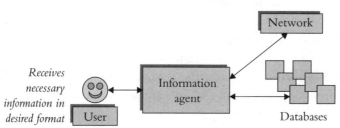

mation agent as well as an interface agent. Such hybrid agents can be placed at the upper level of the agent hierarchy and hence, become application-specific.

■ 6.6 AGENT COMMUNICATION LANGUAGES

An agent communication language consists of three parts:

- An inner language, known as the Knowledge Interchange Format (KIF)
- An outer language, known as Knowledge Query and Manipulation Language (KQML)
- Common vocabularies (i.e., ontologies)

Knowledge Interchange Format (KIF) is an interlingua represented in first-order predicate calculus. It is a generic, formal representation of the expression of the internal knowledge base of an agent. An executable agent can apply a specific formal representation of the knowledge, translate it into KIF, and communicate it to other agents.

To complete the specified tasks, an agent must interact with users and other agents. Interaction is easy if the agents communicate in the same language. KQML was one of the earliest attempts to construct an agent communication language based on speech act theory. Figure 6.6 shows a sample KQML block.

KQML is a general purpose, high-level, message-oriented communication language. As Figure 6.6 shows, it facilitates interoperability and communication between software agents. In short, it is a protocol for information

■ **FIGURE 6.6**
KQML block
for agent
communication

A query about the price of a share

```
(ask-one
:content "price (Infosys, [?price])"
:receiver stock-server
:language LPROLOG
:ontology NYSE-TICKS)

(ask-all
:content "price(Infosys, [?price, ?time])"
:receiver stock-server
:language standard_prolog
:ontology NYSE-TICKS)
```

exchange, independent of content syntax and ontology. There are three layers in a KQML message:

1. Content Layer: This layer yields the actual content in the program's own representation language.
2. Communication Layer: This layer encodes a set of features to the message that describes the lower-level communication parameters.
3. Message Layer: This layer identifies the network protocol with which to deliver the message and supplies a speech act, or *performative,* that the sender attaches to the content.

More information and references can be found at the website: http://www.cs.umbc.edu/kqml/.

Other tools facilitating agent communications are the Agent Communication Language (ACL) and eXtensible Markup Language (XML). The ACL is based on KQML and represents the world standard for agent communication by enabling a library of permissible tasks for the agents. Quite a few agent systems "speak" ACL.

XML is used to define tags related to certain actions and access rights. This is one of the more popular tools for agent communication. However, this requires a Document Type Definition (DTD) and Cascading Style Sheet (CSS) for tag definition, verification, and presentation. There is a standard version of ACL written in XML.

Ontologies are controlled vocabularies providing the basic terminology necessary for representation of a domain of discourse. They are considered fundamental elements of knowledge media.

There have been a number of attempts to develop logical approaches to agent programming. Concurrent METATEM is a multiagent programming language based on linear temporal logic. A multiagent system based on Concurrent METATEM consists of concurrently executing agents whose behavior is implemented using executable temporal logic and which can communicate via asynchronous broadcast message passing.

APRIL is a symbolic programming language designed by Skarmeas and his colleagues in 1999. It is specially designed for writing mobile, distributed, and agent-based systems suited for the Internet. Its features include code mobility, pattern matching, higher-order functions, and asynchronous message sending and receiving. The language is compiled into byte-code, which is then interpreted by the APRIL runtime engine.

While the agent-oriented programming (AOP) paradigm was introduced more than ten years ago by Yoav Shoam, there are still no AO languages used in practice for developing a multiagent system. Some tools have been developed in recent years to support the implementation of agents and multiagent systems, but none are based on a proper agent-oriented language. An inspiring list of agent tools is available at the AgentLink website (http://www.agentlink.org). Current agent development tools are mainly built on top of Java and use the object-oriented paradigm for implementing software. The most used developing tools are JACK and JADE.

JACK is a commercial agent-oriented development environment built on top of and fully integrated with Java. It includes all components of the Java development environment and offers specific extensions to implement agent behavior. JACK provides agent-oriented extensions to the Java programming language, whereby source code is first compiled into regular Java code before being executed. In JACK, a system is modeled in terms of agents defined by capabilities, which in turn, are defined in terms of plans (sets of actions), events, beliefs, and other capabilities.

JADE (Java Agent DEvelopment Framework) is a free software framework fully implemented in the Java language. It allows for the implementation of multiagent systems through middleware that complies with The Foundation for Intelligent Physical Agents (FIPA) specifications and through a set of graphical tools that supports the debugging and deployment phases. More information on JADE is available at the website http://jade.tilab.com/

■ 6.7   STANDARD COMMUNICATIVE ACTIONS

Some communicative actions are more common than others, regardless of the agents' type and application—examples include inform, request, and query-reference. Table 6.2 briefly describes standard communicative actions.

■ 6.8   AGENTS AND OBJECTS

Objects are the executable software entities representing real-world concepts. They have been utilized to achieve modularity and reusability, which

■ **Table 6.2 Example Communicative Actions**

Communicative Action	Description

Inform	This action is sent along with the message content, with propositions to be checked. The sender informs that the given proposition is either true or false.
	Example:
	(inform
	  : sender (agent identifier :Agent A)
	  : receiver (set (agent identifier B))
	  : content (message file name)
	  : language (language name))

Request	The sender requests the receiver agent to perform the action written in the content file. The receiving agent must be passed with the supporting documents (here, data. txt file) and printer resources to print.
	Example:
	(request
	  : sender (agent identifier :Agent A)
	  : receiver (set (agent identifier B))
	  : content (open \\.data.txt to print)
	  : language (language name))

Query-ref	With this action, sender agents can ask for the reference of unknown entities from the receiver agent. If the receiver agent "knows" anything, it may return the requested information or perform suggested actions on these entities.
	Example:
	(query-ref
	  : sender (agent identifier :Agent A)
	  : receiver (set (agent identifier B))
	  : content (select services from B; print all;)
	  : language (Structured Query Language))

increases the cost-effectiveness of the solution. On the other hand, agents are autonomous and independent. Objects are reusable, lower-level components of a system. Agents are smart, capable of flexible (reactive, proactive, and social behavior), and possess an ability to learn.

The object-oriented approach views a software system as a collection of interacting entities called *objects*. Each object has an identity, state, and behavior. The state of an object is described by the member variables and its behavior by a set of methods that can be invoked. Objects interact with each other by sending messages. As we know, a message is a procedure call that is executed in the context of the receiving object. Objects that share common characteristics are grouped into classes and implemented as class objects. A number of different relationships may be present among classes of objects.

In the agent-oriented approach, the system is viewed as a collection of loosely coupled and interacting agents. Similar to objects, agents have an identity, a state, and behavior, but these are much more complex than with simple objects. For instance, an agent's state may be described in terms of knowledge, beliefs, desires, intentions, goals, and obligations. Its behavior may be described in terms of plans to achieve goals, actions, and reactions to events and roles. Consequently, the behavior of an agent is not characterized by a direct mapping of input to output.

There are other distinctions as well:

- Agents exhibit autonomy. They have control over their state, execution, and behavior. Objects have control over their internal states; however, they have no control over their execution and behavior.
- Agents exhibit goal seeking, reactive, and social behavior. They communicate in complex conversational ways, and they can assume different roles in different contexts. They may also be persistent, self-aware, and able to learn and adapt to new environments. However, the object-oriented paradigm in itself has nothing to say about goal-seeking, reactive, social, or adaptive behavior.
- Agents have their own thread of (distributed) control within a multiagent system, whereas in the object-oriented system, there is a single thread of control. Even though Java language offers multithreaded programming, the object-oriented model does not provide multithreaded control.

Nevertheless, the most common way of building agents is through the use of object-oriented languages. The important thing is that although we can build agents using objects, objects by themselves are not agents. An active object is somewhat closer to the concept of an agent because it has some degree of autonomy in which it can exhibit control over its behavior without being operated upon by another object.

■ 6.9   AGENTS, AI, AND INTELLIGENT AGENTS

Agents have many expectations. The most important of them are being autonomous and able to learn. Agents are supposed to "know" the objectives of their intended tasks and can perform independently on behalf of their users. For this, they must have AI techniques, which help them make the "right" decisions when completing tasks and learning.

An intelligent agent is a software system that can send information to and receive it from other agents using appropriate protocols (sensing and communication) (Farhoodi & Fingar, 1997). According to Wooldridge (2002) and Rudowsky (2004), intelligent agents are defined as agents capable of flexible autonomous action to meet their design objectives. Such intelligent agents learn multiple objectives, create action plans, process the information received, and perform reasoning (e.g., inferencing, synthesis, and analysis) through AI techniques. In order to achieve full functionality of a multiagent system (MAS), agents must include the following features (Bobek & Perko, 2006; Padghan & Winikopff, 2004):

- Events and tasks list: Tasks that the agent can perform within the environment
- Controller: Controlling and communication activities
- Goals: Objectives to be accomplished
- Knowledge base: Consists of facts, beliefs, rules, and so on

Complete information may not be required for an intelligent agent to work. It uses its own internal knowledge architecture, inference mechanisms, and user interface for explanation and reasoning. To manage all these activities, an agent has a controller function. The controller manages the agent's interaction with the environment and selects the task to be performed according to the agent's goals and capabilities. The main components of an intelligent agent are controller, interface-managing I/O queue, knowledge base of executable tasks, objectives, and inference engine.

Figure 6.7 describes the typical structure of an intelligent agent. The key components of the agent are a knowledge base and the inference engine. Knowledge about the agent, users, environment, and domain is incorporated here in different knowledge structures. The inference mechanism infers the content stored in the knowledge base. Because users tend to set the goals and objectives to the agents dynamically, there is a separate component possessing a matching ontology. With time, an agent may learn to solve new tasks; hence, there is a dynamic tasks list containing executable tasks. The control-

■ **FIGURE 6.7**
Structure of an
intelligent agent

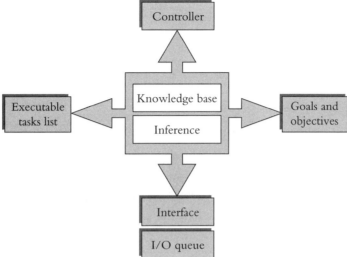

ler manages the overall framework with the stored prototype architectural behavior.

■ 6.10   MULTIAGENT SYSTEMS

A multiagent system is comprised of several intelligent agents working together toward a goal or completion of a task. It is a loosely coupled network of problem-solving entities that work together to find answers to problems that are beyond the capacity of any individual problem-solving entity. This system is called for when complex problems require the services of multiple agents with diverse capabilities and needs. Multiagent system development is challenging, in that it has to address all of the problems of a distributed and concurrent system in addition to the difficulties that arise with flexibility requirements and sophisticated interactions within a multiagent framework (Wood & DeLoach, 2000).

If a problem domain is particularly complex, large, or unpredictable, the only way it can reasonably be addressed is to develop a number of functionally specific and (nearly) modular components (agents) that are specialized at solving a particular problem aspect. This decomposition allows each agent to use the most appropriate paradigm for solving its particular problem (Capuano et al., 2000).

Besides multiple agents, a multiagent system (MAS) does the following:

- Provides an environment for the agents
- Sets the relationships between the entities
- Provides a platform for a set of operations that can be performed by the agents

Researchers have discovered that multiagent systems can accomplish tasks as well as or even better than their centralized single-program counterparts (Ferber, 1999). Multiagent systems can support distributed collaborative problem solving through agent collections that dynamically organize themselves (Honavar, 1999). MAS can manifest self-organization and complex behaviors, even when the individual strategies of all their agents are simple. The multiagent model differs from the single-agent-based system in that the multiple agents embedded in it make the application too specific and dynamic. To accommodate the objectives and goals of the different agents in a given multiagent system, the environment-providing framework to them must be dynamic. In other words, the dynamics of the multiagent system are defined by its agents. Multiagent systems can be classified into two categories: homogeneous or heterogeneous. When the agents within the system follow a similar topology, it is called a *homogeneous multiagent system*; otherwise, it is called a *heterogeneous multiagent system*.

According to Jennings et al. (1998), the term multiagent system has been given a more general meaning, and it is now used for all types of application systems composed of multiple autonomous components with certain characteristics. Table 6.3 briefly explains a few desired characteristics of multiagent systems.

■ 6.10.1 Layered Architecture of a Generic Multiagent System

Here we propose a layered architecture for a generic multiagent system (see Figure 6.8). The system is supposed to complete a user's tasks independently by employing a knowledge-based approach through the multiple agents encompassed within it. Since the system has to complete its tasks autonomously, it needs at least one intelligent (or knowledge-based) agent in it.

■ **Table 6.3 Characteristics of a Multiagent System**

Characteristic	Description
Reliability	Dynamic coordination of various agents and efficient recovery of component failures with controlled redundancy of the agents.
Extensibility	Number and capabilities of agents working on a problem can be altered easily from a structured framework without disturbing other agents.
Quality	Multiple objects working for a common goal increases the computational efficiency, resulting in a significant increase in quality. Ability to isolate an agent leads to easy repair and testing.
Reusability	Once developed, the agents can be reused in many similar applications.
Ease of development and maintainability	A modular, "divide and conquer" approach helps in maintenance and development.

■ **FIGURE 6.8**
Layered architecture of generic multiagent system

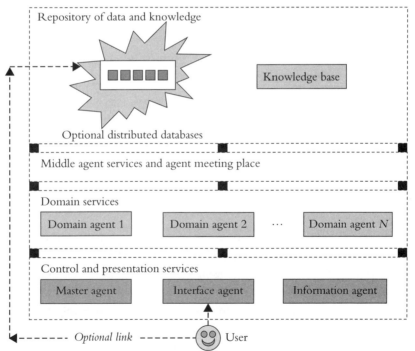

The master agent in the control and presentation services in the architecture interacts with other agents of the system, as well as with the repository layer containing the knowledge base and databases. The master agent plays a key role in managing the knowledge base (and databases, if needed) and facilitating different agent actions and communications. If the domain knowledge and/or the databases required are available on a distributed environment, like the World Wide Web, the multiagent platform requires middle agent services. This middle layer also serves as the meeting place for agents, facilitating communication between them with the added workspace. Above these are agents working in the domain services layer. Along with the master agent, to facilitate users' interaction with the system, an *interface agent* is required in the control and presentation service layer. This layer can be used to manage local documents, storing users' profiles and history for effective presentation.

Multiagent systems are successful due to several causes (we only mention the more relevant ones here):

- They are able to solve large problems, especially those where classical systems are not successful.
- They allow different systems to work together in an interconnected fashion.
- They provide efficient solutions where information is distributed among different places.
- They allow software reusability; therefore, there is more flexibility in adopting different agent capabilities to solve problems.

Example 2: *TravelPlan* is a distributed and cooperative multiagent approach to problem solving in dynamic environments (for instance, the Web), applied to the e-tourism domain (Akerkar, 2005; Camacho, 2003). TravelPlan integrates different types of agents such as:

- **UserAgent**: This agent pays attention to the user's queries and shows the solution. It analyzes the problem and obtains an abstract representation. Subsequently, it presents a solution to the problems to the PlannerAgent. The UserAgent has various skills, such as communication with PlannerAgents and users, or learning the users' profiles so as to customize the answers offered.
- **PlannerAgent**: PlannerAgents are designed to work with UserAgents and determine a set of possible solutions to a problem. PlannerAgents

have different skills, such as communicating with different agents in the system, planning (its main reasoning module), and learning (using CBR techniques to index and categorize each stored plan).

- **WebBot**: These agents fill in the details (requested by PlannerAgents), obtaining the required information from the Internet. Different partial solutions given by the WebAgents are combined by the PlannerAgents to obtain a detailed solution (or solutions) to the UserAgent queries.

In Figure 6.9, a graphic representation of TravelPlan is shown. The system consists of a set of agents that can communicate and cooperate with each another to reach the solution.

TravelPlan has a cooperative architecture whereby different agents need to cooperate to reach solutions. Different agents need to share knowledge and skills to carry out the abstract solutions obtained by the PlannerAgent.

Agents in TravelPlan use a common representation for the knowledge. This characteristic allows simplified sharing and reasoning with the knowledge. Communication among agents uses *performatives*. Any performative stores an implicit order to other agents. For two system agents to communicate, a subset of the KQML format is used.

TravelPlan agents need to implement a communication language. Figure 6.10 shows an example of that protocol. A UserAgent (UA) initiates the process, sending to a PlannerAgent (PA) a description of the user's problem. The PlannerAgent solves the problem using its reasoning module and the

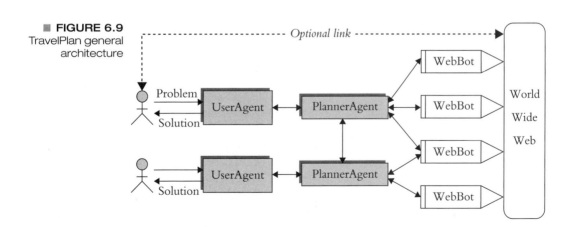

■ **FIGURE 6.9**
TravelPlan general architecture

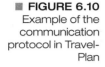

■ **FIGURE 6.10**
Example of the
communication
protocol in Travel-
Plan

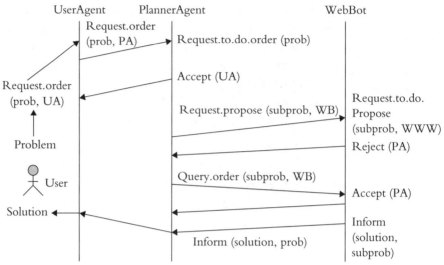

cooperation of other agents like WebBots (WB). The example shows different types of performatives, such as request, inform, and accept.

In the communication process, each agent acknowledges the messages sent by any other agent generating the performative accept (agent). When processed, the receiver agent sends an answer message to the sender agent, and the task starts. If the agent is not ready to perform the task, it generates the performative reject (agent). When a request performative is sent, the receiver agent may generate different types of acts (actions performed by the agent). Using request.order (prob, agent), the sender orders the execution of a task (without negotiation). In Figure 6.10, the PlannerAgent sent a proposal for cooperation to the WebBot, and this agent rejected the request. When the PlannerAgent really needs the information sent, a new request.order finally obtains the desired information. When the WebBot information has been processed, the PlannerAgent can complete the solution and send it to the UserAgent, which will show it to the user.

■ 6.11 KNOWLEDGE ENGINEERING-BASED METHODOLOGIES

In this section, we will present current popular agent-based software engineering methodologies. If we want to realize the full potential of the agent as a software engineering paradigm, establishing a systematic methodology for the analysis and design of agent-based applications is imperative. The available methodologies for agent-based and multiagent systems can be divided into three categories:

1. Agent-oriented methodologies
2. Object-oriented-based methodologies
3. Knowledge engineering-based methodologies

We will limit our discussion to knowledge engineering-based methodologies. Adopting these methodologies for the design of agent-based systems has some advantages. Such methodologies provide techniques for modeling the agents' knowledge and knowledge acquisition processes. Most importantly, any existing tools, ontologies, and problem-solving method libraries can be reused. The basic disadvantage of such methodologies is that they cannot address the distributed aspects of agents and their goal-oriented attitudes due to the fact that the knowledge-based system is conceived as a centralized system. There are two popular approaches: MAS-CommonKADS and DESIRE.

■ 6.11.1 MAS-CommonKADS

MAS-CommonKADS extends the CommonKADS methodology for knowledge-based systems by employing techniques from object-oriented methodologies as well as protocol engineering. There are three important phases. The first phase is conceptualization. This deals with extracting the fundamental system requirements from the user. The second phase is the analysis phase. The following models are developed in this phase:

- Task and expertise model: Specify the agent characteristics, tasks that the agents can carry out, and knowledge that they acquire in order to achieve their goals
- Coordination model: Describes interactions among agents
- Organization model: Describes the social organization of the system
- Communication model: Identifies the human software agent interactions and the human factors for developing user interfaces

The last phase is the design phase, which is based on the previously developed models. The architecture of the system and the individual agents are defined using the design model.

■ 6.11.2 DESIRE

The DEsign and Specification of Interacting REasoning (DESIRE) components framework supports the specification and implementation of compositional systems that consist of autonomous interacting agents. This approach supports the conceptual design and specification of both dynamic and static aspects of agent behavior.

■ 6.12 CASE STUDY

In this section, we will describe the application of agent-based technology in advanced condition monitoring to interpret a large volume of data from a gas insulated substation (GIS), which has been a successful case study for agent-based data interpretation and monitoring (Mangina, 2005). Interpretation of the parameters is complex but essential to assess possible performance deficiencies. By measuring these parameters online, the data can be gathered in a form that is ideal for the application of an intelligent agent-based monitoring system, which will select the most appropriate interpretation technique under varying operational conditions.

The analysis of recorded signals could be simplified and automated through the application of classification tools and the use of intelligent agents, which apply artificial neural networks, k-means clustering, and C5.0 rule-induction methods. This software system enhances the capability of the partial discharge detection system by adding new intelligent tools specializing in the recognition of partial discharge sources.

■ 6.12.1 Partial Discharge Diagnosis Within a GIS

Partial discharge (PD) is the electrical phenomenon where small voltage and current pulses are generated by fast electrons and ions in electrical insulated systems. In extra high-voltage gas insulated equipment, PD occurs when a defect (i.e., small protrusion on the inner conductor or a free metallic particle) enhances the local electrical field. The electrical and chemical activity associated with the presence of such defects may lead to significant degradation of the insulation and sometimes to complete breakdown. Various types of defects can cause partial discharge. Commonly found defects fall into the following six categories:

- Free particles: When detached metallic particles are accountable to the alternating current (AC) voltage cycles, they hop at the bottom of the chamber and emit very fast current pulses.
- Busbar protrusion: Sharp needles on the high-voltage electrode cause partial discharge with a corona effect.
- Chamber protrusion: Same as busbar protrusion, but the needle is on the enclosure.
- Floating electrode: This is particular to situations where one of the electrodes has a part that is not directly connected to the main body. Sparks cross the gap between the two components.
- Surface contamination on insulating barrier: Metallic particles that are glued on to the surface of the spacer may cause surface discharge.
- Cavities in insulating barrier: Internal voids trapped in the insulating material can initiate partial discharge.

Not only do the standard defects need to be monitored, but also external sources that can be detected by the actual system, such as communications noise, radar signals and motor noise, and any other external source whose signal can be detected.

■ 6.12.2 Intelligent Agents for GIS Monitoring

Following the data preparation and the evaluation of different classification techniques, there could be identified cases for the GIS, where one individual method could not classify the type of defect accurately, or could identify only certain types of defects. As a result, a number of software entities have been developed and form a hybrid solution, called COMMAS-GIS (COndition Monitoring Multiagent System for GIS), the generic framework of which is given in Figure 6.11. The different software agents, which interact in a dynamic way to support the required data interpretation functions, include the following:

- Kohonen-map agent: Classifies data using Kohonen maps
- K-means agent: Classifies data using a k-means clustering algorithm
- C5.0_rule_induction agent: Classifies data using rule induction
- Case-based reasoning (CBR) agent: Reasons based on past cases dealing with the same type of defect

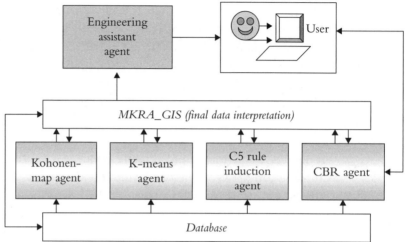

- Metaknowledge reasoning agent: Gathers information on the data processes from the previous agents and informs the EAA
- Engineering assistant agent (EAA): Informs the user of the final result, with details based on the user's profile

For this case study, five different types of intelligent software agents have been developed, while the number of EAAs depends on the number of users. Monitoring the PD signals and interpreting the parameters is complex but essential to assess possible performance deficiencies. The coupler within the GIS detects the signal, which is then sent to the diagnostic monitoring system. The "fingerprint" representation of the partial discharge record, as described, is based upon statistical analysis of the raw data. This reduces the amount of data to be stored and picks out the salient features within the data. Within this application, there were approximately 600 different cases in the database, covering seven distinct classes (types) of defects. The data provided to the software system are in the form of text files to be read and processed from the intelligent agents:

<Casename, Feature 1, Feature 2, ..., Feature 30>

COMMAS-GIS will identify new cases based on the most appropriate classification technique by calling the different classification agents. The software system has been implemented using agent technology, where each agent individually interprets and classifies the data using its embedded technique and communicates its results using KQML messages. The training of each algorithm has been implemented offline, and the accuracy of each method has been evaluated from the agents, which call the external programs responsible for testing. For each unidentified new case, the agents execute each method, and the final result is the outcome of their combined interpretation (based on the "majority voting system"). Within each type of classification agent (Kohonen_map, k-means, C5.0_rule_induction), each clustering algorithm has been implemented to classify the data based on the classification role model.

Although each classification agent is using a different method (by calling different external programs), they all belong to the same role model because the database has to be accessed and after (offline) training, the accuracy is calculated. For the identification of each case, the results are sent to the MKRA_GIS to be processed and the EAA informs the user of the procedure in detail. Each type of agent embodies the final vector of weights or rules from the training executed offline. The testing and the accuracy evaluation are accomplished online through each classification agent.

There are certain characteristics of each type of defect that could be seen from the 3-D display provided by the existing monitoring system. Specific defects tend to appear at certain times, or phases. The expert would, therefore, look at parameters like time and phase dependency. Any symmetry that existed within the pattern on both the negative and positive cycle would provide information about the physical reality of the defect. To emulate the experts' reasoning, representative cases of each defect could be identified, which would then be provided to the user through the case-based reasoning (CBR) software agent within the COMMAS-GIS. Along with the "fingerprints" for each case, the 3-D display from the raw data is stored for use by the CBR agent to display it to the user.

Based on the given images, the user will select which one is the most similar and will give feedback to the CBR agent, along with the confidence factor representing the user's belief in the new case being a certain type of defect. The result will be sent to the MKRA_GIS, and the new case will be stored in the case memory of the agent and will be used for testing another new case in the future. Here, the influence of the CBR agent on the overall multiagent system is of great importance, especially for cases the software system cannot identify and there is the need for the experts' input. The feedback from the experts is then stored in the case memory as new cases, and the knowledge can be reused.

■ 6.13 DIRECTIONS FOR FURTHER RESEARCH

In a multiagent system framework, once developed, the number of agents can be altered according to the need and nature of the application. The single-agent and multiagent technology needs to be verified against standards to ensure high quality. However, efforts are still required to give a standard set of development techniques, lifecycle model, and quality metrics to certify the system's quality. Multiagents are used for problem solving, simulation, linguistics, network management, data mining, control systems, virtual reality, construction of artificial synthetic worlds, robotics, and other business applications. A multiagent system provides a platform for true heterogeneous research. Some emerging trends in agent-based technology are as follows:

- Intelligent agent designs
- Learning in a multiagent system
- Analysis and design methodology for multiagent system development
- Agent communication, specification, and/or programming languages
- Agent protocols and standards
- Agents for a Semantic Web for automatic processing of data
- Agents for information retrieval and data mining
- Supporting agents for Web services and service-oriented computing
- Agents serving as middleware for grid computing
- Knowledge management agents for an organization
- Agents for e-commerce
- Query and interface agent for business applications
- Agents for a personal assistance system

■ 6.14 WARM-UP QUESTIONS, EXERCISES, AND PROJECTS

■ Warm-up Questions

1. Suppose you are designing a robot that carries out certain actions in the kitchen, such as cooking, washing, and serving. What benefits would there be in developing this as an intelligent agent?
2. Visit the website of AgentLand to search different agents at http://www.agentland.com/.
3. Distinguish between deterministic and nondeterministic environments.

4. What are the two approaches to the design of agent communication languages?

5. Search the Internet and prepare a survey report on the Knowledge Interchange Format (KIF).

6. Give examples of agents that you know of. Write down characteristic features of these agents.

7. Distinguish between agents and expert systems.

8. Give your own definition of the term multiagent system.

Exercises

1. Consider a software agent operating in a decision-making capacity for the military. What are the characteristics of this environment? List the agent's perceptions and actions.

2. Multiagent systems is a comprehensive research area, taking in input as well as providing output to a number of other disciplines. Can you think of any other areas that may be relevant to multiagent systems research and how?

3. Discuss the advantages and disadvantages of using mobile agents. Do you think that the disadvantages outweigh the potential benefits?

4. Examine the Amazon e-commerce toolkit, which can be downloaded from http://www.amazon.com. How could you use this toolkit to build a software agent that is able to obtain information on the price and other attributes of a product from Amazon?

5. The following are KQML messages representing a query about the price of a share of Infosys stock:

```
(ask-one
:content (PRICE Infosys ?price)
:receiver stock-server
:language LPROLOG
:ontology MSE)

(ask-all
:content "price(Infosys, [?price, ?time])"
:receiver stock-server
:language standard_prolog
```

```
:ontology MSE)

(stream-all
;;?VL is a large set of symbols
:content (PRICE ?VL ?price))
```

Give an interpretation of this message, making clear in your answer the role that the various components of the messages are playing.

6. Given an agent communication language, how best should these agents be organized to boost collaboration?

7. Explore a contract net approach. Describe it using KQML language.

Projects

1. Study the cybercrime laws of your own country. Investigate whether they express anything about online software agents. Why is such a law essential?

2. Design a simple multiagent solution to manage knowledge in the context of the software development process.

3. Experiment with one agent programming tool by developing an agent application with it.

4. Download the Aglets Software Development kit from http://www.trl. ibm.com/aglets/. Install it on your computer, and create a simple agent that can migrate from one context to another on the same computer. If you have access to a network of machines, you can create contexts on different machines and program your aglet to migrate to different contexts.

References

Akerkar, R. *Introduction to Artificial Intelligence*, Prentice-Hall of India, 2005.

Bobek, S. & Perko, I. Intelligent Agent-Based Business Intelligence, *Current Developments in Technology-Assisted Education*, FORMATEX, pp.1047–1051, 2006.

Camacho D., Molina J. M., & Borrajo D. Electronic tourism in the Web—An artificial intelligence approach, (Edited by R. Akerkar), *Proceedings of the Second*

International Conference on Applied Artificial Intelligence (ICAAI 2003). December, 2003. Kolhapur, India.

Capuano N., Marsella M., & Salerno S. ABITS: An agent-based intelligent tutoring system for distance learning, *Proceeding of ITS 2000*, Montreal, Canada. Retrieved from http://www.capuano.biz/Papers/ITS_2000.pdf

Farhoodi, F. & Fingar, P. Developing enterprise systems with intelligent agent technology, *Distributed Object Computing*, 1997. Retrieved from http://home1. gte.net/pfingar/docmag_part2.htm

Ferber, J. *Multiagent systems: An introduction to distributed artificial intelligence*, Reading, MA: Addison-Wesley, 1999.

Honavar, V. Intelligent agents and multiagent systems, Tutorial presented at IEEE CEC 1999.

http://www.cs.washington.edu/research/projects/WebWare1/www/softbots/softbots.html

Hyacinth, S. N. Software agents: An overview, *Knowledge Engineering Review*, vol.11, no.3, pp. 1–40, 1996. Retrieved from http://www.sce.carleton.ca/netmanage/docs/AgentsOverview/ao.html

Jeffrey, S. R. PowerPoint lecture slides for *An introduction to multiagent systems* by Michael, W. 2002. Retrieved from http://www.csc.liv.ac.uk/~mjw/pubs/imas/distrib/powerpoint-slides/

Jennings, N. R., Sycara, K., & Wooldridge, M. A roadmap of agent research and development, *Autonomous Agents and Multiagent Systems Journal*, vol.1, no.1, pp. 7–38, 1998.

Mangina, E. Intelligent agent based monitoring platform for applications in engineering, *International Journal of Computer Science & Applications*, Vol. 2, No. 1, pp. 38–48, 2005.

Moraitakis, N. Intelligent software agents: Application and Classification, 1997. Retrieved from http://www.doc.ic.ac.uk/~nd/surprise_97/journal/vol1/nm1/

Nakamura, Y. & G. Yamamoto (1997), An electronic marketplace framework based on mobile agents, Research Report, RT0224, IBM Research, Tokyo Research Laboratory, Japan.

Padghan, L. & Winikopff, M. Developing intelligent agent systems: A practical guide, New York: Wiley Publishers, 2004.

Rudowsky. S. Intelligent Agents, *Communications of the Association for Information Systems*, vol.14 pp. 275–290, 2004.

Sajja, P. S. Multiagent system for knowledge-based access to distributed databases, *Interdisciplinary Journal of Information, Knowledge, and Management*, vol.3, pp. 1–9, 2008.

Wood, F. M. & DeLoach, S. A. An overview of the multiagent systems engineering methodology, *Proceedings of the First International Workshop on Agent-Oriented Software Engineering*, 2000, Limerick, Ireland. Retrieved from http://people.cis.ksu.edu/~sdeloach/publications/Conference/mase-aose2000.pdf

Wooldridge, M. *An Introduction to Multiagent Systems*. New York, Wiley Publishers, 2002.

CHAPTER 7

Connectionist Models

■ 7.1   INTRODUCTION

While research into neural networks was initiated in 1942, the number of scientists involved was almost negligible for the first 40 years. In 1942, Norbert Weiner and his colleagues were formulating the ideas that were later called "cybernetics" and that he defined as "control and communication in the animal and the machine." The basic idea was to treat biological mechanisms from an engineering and mathematical perspective.

In the same year that Weiner was formulating cybernetics, McCulloch and Pitts published the first formal treatment of artificial neural networks (ANNs). One of the crucial attributes of neural networks is that they can learn from their experience in a training environment. In 1949, Donald Hebb pointed out a mechanism whereby this may come about in animal brains. Broadly, synaptic strengths change to reinforce any simultaneous correspondence of activity levels between the presynaptic and postsynaptic neurons. Translated into the language of artificial neural networks, the weight of an input should be augmented to reflect the correlation between the input and the unit's output. Learning schemes based on this "Hebb rule" have always played a prominent role. The next landmark was the invention of the perceptron by Frank Rosenblatt in 1957.

In 1983 the U.S. Defense Advanced Research Project Agency (DARPA) began funding neural network research. Later on, many other countries have taken initiatives and undertaken enormous global research. However, initially, this area produced many theoretical research papers but few practical applications. This situation changed in the 1990s.

An artificial neural network is connectionist model of programming using computers. An ANN attempts to give computers human-like abilities by mimicking the human brain's functionality. The human brain consists of a network of more than a hundred billion interconnected neurons. Neurons are individual cells that can process small amounts of information and then activate other neurons to continue the process. If an ANN is successfully implemented, machines like personal computers can be used more effectively in various areas of problem solving and decision making. Typical artificial intelligence (AI) methodology deals with the symbolic representation of knowledge, whereas ANN models document knowledge in the connection of the network. That is why it is called a "network." ANNs are exceptionally good at performing pattern recognition and other tasks that are difficult to program using conventional techniques. The main advantage such models offer is the ability to learn on their own and adapt to changing conditions.

Although neural networks are modeled on the human brain, their present state is far from the realization of actual intelligence. In fact, we know less about the human brain—the model for neural networks that actually generates intelligence. There are noteworthy differences in the physical characteristics of the human brain and neural networks. The number of neurons in the brain is on the order of 10^{11}. The total number of neurons in a high-performance system is, at most, on the order of 10^5 when we allocate a processor to each artificial neuron. The typical neural network has fewer neurons—for example, order of 10s or 100s.

■ 7.1.1   Advantages and Disadvantages of Neural Networks

The major advantage of neural networks is that they are well suited for parallel implementation because every neuron can work independently. Neural networks can deal with new patterns that are similar to learning patterns, so they are suitable for generalization. Nonlinear problems are difficult to solve theoretically, whereas neural networks can tackle any problem that can be represented as a pattern. Moreover, neural networks can deal with a certain amount of "noise" in the input. They can perform even if part of the neural network is damaged to a certain extent. Neural networks are utterly complement symbolic artificial intelligence.

The major disadvantage of an artificial neural network is that it cannot fully mimic the human brain functionalities or intelligence. A neural network cannot offer facilities like explicit explanation and reasoning; as knowledge is stored implicitly in generalized connections between neurons. Moreover, scaling up a neural network is not a straightforward affair. Suppose we trained a neural network for, say, 200 input neurons and now we wish to extend this to a neural network of 201 input neurons. Typically, we have to begin again with an entire training session for the new network.

■ 7.1.2 Comparing Artificial Neural Networks with the von Neumann Model

In this subsection, we will look at some features of artificial neural networks with the von Neumann model. The authenticity of these properties should become clearer as the operation of specific neural networks is studied.

- The style of processing is more similar to signal processing than symbol processing. The combining of signals and producing new ones is to be contrasted with the execution of instructions stored in memory.
- Information is stored in a set of weights rather than a program. The weights are supposed to adapt when the neural network is shown examples from a training set.
- Neural networks are robust in the presence of noise, which means small changes in an input signal will not drastically affect a node's output.
- Neural networks are robust in the presence of hardware failure. So a change in a weight may only affect the output for a few of the likely input patterns.
- High-level concepts will be represented as a pattern of activity across many nodes rather than as the contents of a small fraction of computer memory.
- The neural networks can deal with "unseen" patterns and generalize from the training set.
- Neural networks are good at "perceptual" tasks and associative recall. These are just the tasks that the symbolic approach has difficulties with.

■ 7.2 BIOLOGICAL NEURONS

The human brain is made up of approximately 10 billion interconnected neurons. Each neuron is a cell that uses biochemical reactions to receive, process, and transmit information. Considering the human brain as a whole would be far too complex, a human neuron (a brain cell) is considered here. Figure 7.1 shows a single biological neuron (Fraser, 1998). Biological neurons are comparatively less efficient than the personal computer and they are constantly dying; however, these neurons work in parallel fashion. Each neuron calculates a local solution, which adds up to the global solution. Hence, even if a few neurons do not work properly, the network still works. The power of the human brain comes from the ability of such small neurons working in parallel fashion.

■ 7.3 ARTIFICIAL NEURONS

A neuron is the basic building block of the human brain. It accepts a signal and, after processing it, fires the output to other neurons to which it is connected. The working of a biological neuron can be modeled in an artificial neuron as shown in Figure 7.2.

The artificial neuron takes inputs as $X_1, X_2, X_3, \ldots, X_n$ through n different input nodes. These input nodes are connected to a processing node. Each

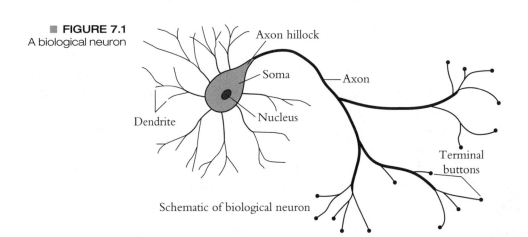

■ **FIGURE 7.1**
A biological neuron

Axon hillock

Soma

Axon

Dendrite

Nucleus

Terminal buttons

Schematic of biological neuron

■ **FIGURE 7.2**
An artificial neuron

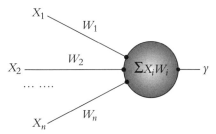

connection has some weight identifiers, noted as $W_1, W_2, W_3, \ldots, W_n$. The weighted average yields the activation level. That is:

$$\text{Activation} = X_1\, W_1 + X_2\, W_2 + X_3\, W_3 + \ldots + X_n\, W_n$$
$$= \sum X_i W_i \text{ for } i = 1, 2, 3, \ldots, n$$

This activation output is measured with a predefined threshold value. If it is greater than the threshold value, output is 1 (positive); otherwise, output is zero. This can be measured by a squashing function (generally mathematical sigma); hence, an output function "O" is defined by S (Activation) as follows:

Output $= S$ (Activation).

Figure 7.3 represents the different activation functions (Veloso, 2001).
Artificial neural systems can be considered simplified mathematical models of brainlike systems working as parallel distributed computing networks. However, in contrast to conventional computers, which are programmed

■ **FIGURE 7.3**
Different activation
functions

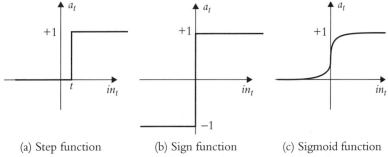

(a) Step function   (b) Sign function   (c) Sigmoid function

to perform a specific task, most neural networks must be taught, or trained. Such units learn by adjusting their weights and thresholds.

■ 7.4 NEURAL NETWORK ARCHITECTURES

Networks are categorized according to their structure and layers or learning mechanisms. Many architectures are available, such as radial basic function, feed forward, recurrent, and self-organizing networks.

- Single-layer feed-forward network: It has only one layer of computational nodes. It is a feed-forward network because the input fed to the network propagates in the forward direction only.
- Multilayer feed-forward network: It is feed-forward network with one or more hidden layers. The source node in the input layer supplies inputs to the neurons of the first hidden layer. The outputs of the first hidden-layer neurons are applied as inputs to the neurons of the second hidden layer, and so on. If every node in each layer of the network is connected to every other node in the adjacent forward layer, the network is called fully connected. If, however, some of the links are missing, the network is said to be partially connected.
- Recurrent neural networks: A recurrent neural network is one in which there is at least one feedback loop from output layer to input layer. There are different kinds of recurrent networks, depending on the way in which the feedback is used. In a typical case, it has a single layer of neurons, with each neuron feeding its output signal back to the inputs of all other neurons. Other kinds of recurrent networks may have self-feedback loops and hidden neurons.
- Lattice networks: A lattice network is a feed-forward network with the output neurons arranged in rows and columns. It can have one-dimensional, two-dimensional, or higher-dimensional arrays of neurons with a corresponding set of source nodes that supply the input signals to the array.

The following sections illustrate a few basic architectures of neural networks.

■ 7.4.1 Hopfield Model

The Hopfield model was proposed by John Hopfield (1982) of the California Institute of Technology. Hopfield introduced a neural network, which was proposed as a theory of memory. Its characteristics include distributed

■ FIGURE 7.4
Hopfield network

Connections
with weights

representation and control, fault tolerance, and content-addressable memory. Hopfield proposed a network where all the units are bi-state units—either "on" or "off." These states are also represented as "active" and "inactive." Here, the weight of the connections between the neurons has to be set in such a way that the network is stable. The Hopfield model consists of a single layer of processing elements, where each unit is connected to many other units in the network. If each unit is connected to every other unit, then the structure is said to be fully connected. It is also a symmetrically weighted network, as denoted in Figure 7.4.

All of the connections in the Hopfield model are weighted. The nodes take two-valued inputs, as stated earlier. These values can be binary (0 or 1) or bipolar (-1 or 1).

■ 7.4.2 Learning in a Hopfield Network Through Parallel Relaxation

The Hopfield model learns through the parallel relaxation of different neurons in it. The process can be demonstrated as follows:

```
procedure parallel relaxation
while not-stable network
pick a random unit
initiate sum as sum of the connections to all active neighbors
if sum is positive
then turn unit active else turn the inactive
end of procedure
```

If the connections are trained with a specific learning method, the Hopfield network can perform as robust content-addressable memory, resistant to connection alterations.

■ 7.4.3 Perceptrons

The most influential work on neural networks (nets) in the 1960s went under the heading of "perceptrons," a term coined by Frank Rosenblatt.

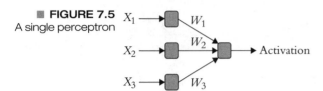

The perceptron was developed as a computational model simulating the human perception–human visual system. Figure 7.5 models a single perceptron.

Figure 7.5 shows three input nodes—X_1, X_2, and X_3—with the corresponding weights as W_1, W_2, and W_3. The activation function can be given as follows:

$$\text{Activation} = f(X,i)$$
$$= \sum X_i W_i \text{ for } i = 1,2,3$$
$$= X_1\, W_1 + X_2\, W_2 + X_3\, W_3$$

The output function O is defined as follows:

$$\text{Output } O = 1 \text{ if Activation} >= \theta$$
$$= 0 \text{ otherwise}$$
$$\text{Where } \theta \text{ is a threshold value}$$

The threshold value collects the outputs of the predicates through weighted edges and computes the final decision.

Definition
A simple perceptron is a computing unit with threshold θ that, when receiving the n real inputs X_1, X_2,..., X_n through edges with the associated weights $W_1, W_2,...,W_n$, outputs 1 if the inequality $\sum w_i x_i >= \theta$ holds, and 0 otherwise.

Example
Suppose we have two Boolean inputs X_1, $X_2 \in \{0, 1\}$ and one Boolean output $O \in \{0, 1\}$. The training set is given by the following input/output pairs:

X_1	X_2	$O(X_1, X_2)$
1	1	1
1	0	0
0	1	0
0	0	0

Find the output function O.

Solution

The neural network adjusts the weights and threshold to get the desired output that matches every training dataset. This yields an understanding that the output neuron fires if and only if both inputs are on. A straightforward solution to this equation can be given as $W_1 = W_2 = ½$ and $\theta = 0.6$. Hence, the output function O is given as follows:

$$O(X_1, X_2) = 1 \text{ if } X_1/2 + X_2/2 \geq 0.6$$
$$= 0 \text{ otherwise}$$

This example shows a neural network simulation of a simple Boolean function AND, which is shown in part (a) of Figure 7.6. Similarly, another Boolean function, OR, can be simulated with a perceptron. See part (b) of Figure 7.6.

From Figure 7.6, it is obvious that the Boolean functions AND and OR are linearly separable functions. Part (c) of Figure 7.6 shows a general picture of a linearly separable function.

■ FIGURE 7.6
Linearly separable
functions

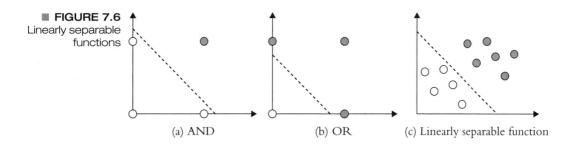

(a) AND   (b) OR   (c) Linearly separable function

Definition

Two sets of points A and B in an n-dimensional space are linearly separable if $n + 1$ real numbers $W_1, \ldots, W_{n+1}$ exist such that every point $(X_1, X_2, \ldots, X_n)$ $\in$ A satisfies $\sum W_i X_i >= W_{n+1}$ and every point $(X_1, X_2, \ldots, X_n) \in B$ satisfies $\sum W_i X_i < W_{n+1}$.

■ 7.4.4 Perceptron Learning Rule

Perceptron output (assuming a single output unit) is determined by separating a hyperplane defined by $W_1 {}^* X_1 + W_2 {}^* X_2 + \ldots + W_n {}^* X_n = t$; hence, a perceptron can only learn functions that are linearly separable. A perceptron learns by using the update-weights function given by the formula:

$$W_i = W_i + \delta W_i$$

Where $\delta W_i = \alpha \, (T - O) \, X_i$

Xi is the input associated with the ith input unit. T is the desired output. α is a constant between 0 and 1 known as the learning rate.

This learning rule is also known as the Delta Rule or the Widrow–Hoff Rule. This rule performs a gradient descent in "weight space." That is, this rule will be used to iteratively adjust all the weights in such a way that with every iteration, the error is decreasing (more correctly, the error is monotonically nonincreasing).

The problem of learning is one of locating an appropriate decision surface. That is, informally we can say that if the perceptron fires when it should not fire, make each W_i smaller by an amount proportional to X_i. If the perceptron fails to fire when it should fire, make each W_i larger by a similar amount.

■ 7.4.5 Fixed-Increment Perceptron Learning Algorithms

The fixed-increment perceptron learning algorithm is a classification algorithm with n input features $(X_1, X_2, X_3, \ldots, X_n)$ and two output classes. The objective of this algorithm is to compute a set of weights $(W_1, W_2, \ldots, W_n)$ that will cause a perceptron to fire whenever input falls into the first output class.

1. Create a perceptron with $n + 1$ inputs and $n + 1$ weights, where extra input X_0 is set to 1.

2. Initialize weights $(W_0, W_1, W_2, \ldots, W_n)$ to random real values.

3. Iterate through the training set, collecting all examples misclassified by the current set of weights.

4. If all of the examples are classified correctly, output the weights and quit.

5. Otherwise, compute the vector sum S of the misclassified input vectors, where each vector has the form $(X_1, X_2, X_3, \ldots, X_n)$. In creating the sum, add to S a vector X if X is an input for which the perceptron incorrectly fails to fire, but add vector $-X$ if X is an input for which the perceptron incorrectly fires. Multiply the sum by a scale factor.

6. Modify the $(W_0, W_1, W_2, \ldots, W_n)$ by adding the elements of the vector S to them. Go to Step 3.

A function like XOR cannot be computed with one perceptron. Figure 7.7 shows that the XOR problem is not linearly separable.

It is clearly observed from Figure 7.7 that there is no single line that can separate the two classes. Hence, XOR is not a linearly separable function and cannot be solved by one perceptron. Figure 7.8 shows two perceptrons identifying two equations of the lines shown in Figure 7.7.

■ FIGURE 7.7
XOR as a non-linearly separable function

■ FIGURE 7.8
Perceptron solving XOR problem

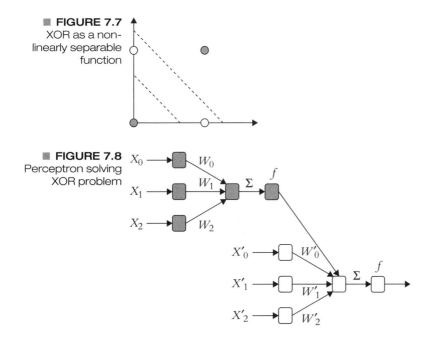

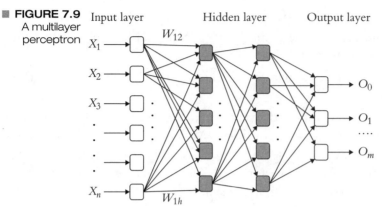

■ FIGURE 7.9
A multilayer
perceptron

With the perceptron learning rule, the network is unable to determine the scale by which weights have to be adjusted. The second perceptron shown in Figure 7.8 does not know the actual inputs, as they are masked by the first perceptron. Thus, it is difficult for the second perceptron to learn correctly. Assigning a nonlinear threshold function (like a sigmoid function instead of a bi-state on/off or 0/1) helps a bit in this situation. This leads to the need for a multilayer network, which is an important step in building intelligent machines from neuronlike components. Figure 7.9 shows the architecture of a multilayer perceptron.

■ 7.4.6 Multilayer Perceptrons

A perceptron may contain more than one layer to solve complex real-world applications. The multilayer perceptron in Figure 7.9 has n input nodes, h hidden nodes in its (one or more) hidden layers, and m output nodes in its output layer. In this figure, two hidden layers are shown; however, there may be several more, depending on the application's nature and complexity. There may be multiple input and output layers if required. The W_{ij} is the weight associated with the ith node of the input layer to the jth node of the next layer. In a similar fashion, each node of a given layer is connected to every node in its adjacent layer. All of the connections are in a forward direction only. That is why such a structure is known as fully connected, feed-forward, multilayer network.

The network receives inputs from neurons in the input layer, and the output of the network is given by the neurons on an output layer. In such a network, the artificial neurons, which are organized in layers, send their signals "forward," and then the errors are propagated backwards. The idea of such back-propagation is to reduce this error until the ANN *learns* the training data in a supervised fashion. The training begins with random weights, and the goal is to adjust them so that the error will be minimal.

The training procedure for a multilayer perceptron encompasses the following phases:

Step 1: Create a structure of an artificial neural network with at least one input layer and one output layer.

Step 2: For the input layer, consider the major parameters that affect the decision to be taken and take that many neurons as input nodes.

Step 3: For the output layer, consider all the opportunities and let each neuron represent an opportunity.

Step 4: Create two to three hidden layers and create neurons in each layer using the following generalized heuristics: The total number of neurons in the hidden layer = ½ (number of neurons in the input layer + number of neurons in the output layer).

Step 5: Initialize random weights and thresholds.

Step 6: Apply a training pattern consisting of the desired input with the output.

Step 7: Calculate the actual output, compute the output error, and adjust weights accordingly.

Step 8: If the training set is exhausted, evaluate the average system error; otherwise, go to Step 2.

Step 9: If the evaluated error is acceptable, stop; otherwise, go to Step 2.

■ 7.4.7 Back-Propagation Algorithms

The back-propagation algorithm has become the most widely used for training the multilayer perceptron. The back-propagation algorithm (Rumelhart & McClelland, 1986) is a gradient-descent algorithm. The basic idea behind gradient descent is to consistently decrease the output error by adjusting weights. This is done by propagating errors backward through the network, starting at the output units and working toward the input units.

The algorithm provides a compositionally efficient method for the training of a multilayer perceptron. The systematic back-propagation algorithm is as follows (Gershenson, 2003). The activation function of the artificial neurons in ANNs implementing the back-propagation algorithm is the sum of the inputs x_i multiplied by their respective weights W_{ji} :

$$A_j\left(\overline{x},\overline{w}\right)=\sum_{i=0}^{n}x_i w_{ji} \tag{1}$$

Here summing over i means summing over the n inputs to node j. This is nothing but the sum of weighted outputs of all of j's suppliers. If the activation (output) function is the identity, the neuron would be called linear. Here we use the most common form of activation function, sigmoid with threshold.

$$O_j=\left(\overline{x},\overline{w}\right)=\frac{1}{1+e^{A_j\left(\overline{x},\overline{w}\right)}} \tag{2}$$

The sigmoid function performs similarly to a step function, but it is entirely differentiable. In Equation (2), the sigmoid function is 0.5 if the sum (i.e., $A_j=\left(\overline{x},\overline{w}\right)$) is 0. This is contrary to the perceptron, where the sum should be either 0 or 1. As the sum gets larger, the sigmoid function approaches 1. Moreover, as the sum gets smaller, the sigmoid function approaches 0. Here, the output depends only on the activation, which in turn depends on the values of the inputs and their respective weights.

A back-propagation network (Akerkar, 2003) usually starts out with a random set of weights. The network updates its weights every time it sees an input–output pair. Every input–output pair requires two passes, namely a forward pass and a backward pass. The forward pass takes the inputs to the network and allows activations to run until they reach the output. In the backward pass, the actual output of the network is compared with the desired output and error estimates are calculated for the output nodes. Because of this backward changing process of the weights, the model is called "back-propagation." It is also known as the generalized delta rule since it is a systematic generalization of the delta rule procedure. The error function can be given as follows:

$$E_j = \left(\overline{x}, \overline{w}, d \right) = \left(O_j \left(\overline{x}, \overline{w} \right) - d_j \right)^2 \tag{3}$$

In order to consider the difference between the output and the desired target, we take the square of the error. It is also considered as the distance of the output and desired target. The error of the network will simply be the sum of the errors of all of the neurons in the output layer:

$$E \left(\overline{x}, \overline{w}, \overline{d} \right) = \sum_j \left(O_j \left(\overline{x}, w \right) - d_j \right)^2 \tag{4}$$

Taking the square of the difference is a well-known approach for minimization problems. Another popular technique for minimization problems, the *gradient-descendent method*, is used to adjust weights:

$$\Delta w_{ji} = -\eta \frac{\partial E}{\partial w_{ji}} \tag{5}$$

Equation (5) basically represents the distance times the direction of change. The distance, η, is a typical parameter in neural networks and is often called the learning rate. In more advanced algorithms, this rate may steadily decrease during the epochs (outer loop iteration) of the training phase. If we update all the weights using this same formula, then this amounts to moving in the path of steepest descent along the error surface—hence the name, gradient descent. Equation (5) is used until the error is minimal or acceptable. But, computing $\frac{\partial E}{\partial w_{ji}}$ is not trivial.

With reference to Equation (3), the dependencies of the error on the output, which is the derivative of E with respect to O_j, can be calculated as follows:

$$\frac{\partial E}{\partial O_j} = 2 \left(O_j - d_j \right) \tag{6}$$

And then, how much the output depends on the activation, which in turn, depends on the weights [from Equations (1) and (2)]:

$$\frac{\partial O_j}{\partial w_{ji}} = \frac{\partial O_j}{\partial A_j}\frac{\partial A_j}{\partial w_{ji}} = O_j\left(1-O_j\right)x_i \tag{7}$$

We can compute $\dfrac{\partial E}{\partial w_{ji}}$ for neural networks using sigmoid functions [from Equations (6) and (7)] as:

$$\frac{\partial E}{\partial w_{ji}} = \frac{\partial E}{\partial O_j}\frac{\partial O_j}{\partial w_{ji}} = 2\left(O_j-d_j\right)O_j\left(1-O_j\right)x_i \tag{8}$$

So, the weight update for networks using sigmoid (transfer) functions is [from Equations (5) and (8)]:

$$\Delta w_{ji} = -2\eta\left(O_j d_j\right)O_j\left(1-O_j\right)x_i \tag{9}$$

We can use Equation (9) as it is for training an ANN with two layers.

It is interesting to note that the preceding update rules for w_{ji}, for both the identity and sigmoid functions, involve batch processing. In batch processing, we compute the total error for all training instances before we update the weights.

Moreover, one should choose a much lower value of the learning rate, η, for incremental updating than for batch processing. The major weakness of such incremental updating is that the final weight values can be dependent upon the order of presentation of the examples.

The next step is to compute $\dfrac{\partial E}{\partial v_{ik}}$. To adjust the weights (say, v_{ik}) of a previous layer, one has to calculate how the error depends not on the weight, but on the input from the previous layer. By using the calculus chain rule in Equations (7), (8), and (9), we observe the error of the network depends on the adjustment of v_{ik}:

$$\Delta v_{ik} = -\eta\frac{\partial E}{\partial v_{ik}} = -\eta\frac{\partial E}{\partial x_i}\frac{\partial x_i}{\partial v_{ik}} \tag{10}$$

Where:

$$\frac{\partial E}{\partial w_{ji}} = 2\left(O_j - d_j\right)O_j\left(1 - O_j\right)w_{ji} \tag{11}$$

Furthermore, using Equation (7), we suppose that there are inputs u_k into the neuron with v_{ik}:

$$\frac{\partial x_i}{\partial v_{ik}} = x_i\left(1 - x_i\right)v_{ik} \tag{12}$$

Similarly, more layers can be added. For practical reasons, ANNs implementing the back-propagation algorithm do not have too many layers, since the time for training the networks grows exponentially.

The back-propagation algorithm suffers from a typical problem whenever the gradient method is employed to minimize a target function. Normally, the error E starts with the large value and slowly decreases as iterations proceed. If E is a smooth function, that means it has a smooth monotonically decreasing curve, then E will ultimately reach the global minimum. In other words, E may be trapped in a *local minimum*. There are two issues associated to the local minimum problem. One is how to detect the local minimum and the other is how to escape it once it is found. The best way to escape the local minimum is to change the movement of E, by applying higher values of w_{ji}.

The back-propagation algorithm has many modifications and improvements. They differ in the following points: error calculation, activation function, number of epochs for updating the weights, the weights updating formula, and other parameters.

■ 7.5   LEARNING PARADIGMS

There are three major learning paradigms—namely, supervised learning, unsupervised learning, and reinforcement learning.

In supervised learning, a training data set, including input and corresponding output for every pattern, is given to the network. A teacher is assumed to be always available and supervising when a comparison is made between the computed output and the correct output to determine errors. The algorithm works in the following fashion:

Step 1:   Consider a training set containing input and output for every pattern.

Step 2:   The network calculates the actual output.

Step 3:   Each output unit is supplied with its desired (ideal) response to the given input signals.

Step 4:   The difference between the desired output and the actual one is represented as an error.

Step 5:   The error can be used to change the network parameters, which results in improved performance of the network.

An important issue concerning supervised learning is the problem of error convergence—that is, the minimization of error between the desired and computed unit values.

Reinforcement learning is nothing but training the network by giving punishments and rewards. The aim is to discover a policy for selecting actions that minimizes some measure of a long-term cost—that is, the expected cumulative cost. The environment's dynamics and the long-term cost for each policy are usually unknown, but can be estimated. With reinforcement learning, a network learns as follows:

Step 1:   Sample input is given to the network.

Step 2:   The network computes and presents a sample answer.

Step 3:   The network is supplied with an actual valued judgment (punishment or reward) by the teacher/developer.

Step 4:   The network adjusts its weights.

In unsupervised learning, the network is not provided with feedback for its output, not even an actual valued reinforcement. One popular unsupervised learning scheme is known as competitive learning. Competitive learning works in the following way:

Step 1:   Competitive learning considers an input vector and calculates the initial activation for each output unit.

Step 2: It allows the output units to "fight" until only one is active.

Step 3: The weights are adjusted for the connections between the active output unit and active input units. This makes it more likely that the output unit will be active the next time the pattern is repeated.

■ 7.6 OTHER NEURAL NETWORK MODELS

■ 7.6.1 Kohonen Maps

Kohonen maps are feed-forward networks that use an unsupervised training algorithm. Through a process called self-organization, they configure the output units into a topological or spatial map. Kohonen's work was reevaluated during the late 1980s, and the utility of the self-organizing feature map was recognized. Kohonen has presented several enhancements to this model, including a supervised learning variant known as *Learning Vector Quantization* (LVQ). A Kohonen-map neural network consists of two layers of processing units: an input layer fully connected to a competitive output layer. There are no hidden units. When an input pattern is presented to the feature map, the units in the output layer compete with each other, and the winning output unit is typically the one whose incoming connection weights are closest to the input pattern (in terms of Euclidean distance). Thus, the input is presented, and each output unit computes its closeness or match score to the input pattern. The output that is deemed closest to the input pattern "wins" and earns the right to have its connection weights adjusted. The connection weights are moved in the direction of the input pattern by a factor determined by a learning rate parameter. This is the basic nature of competitive neural networks.

The Kohonen map creates a topological mapping by adjusting not only the winner's weights, but also adjusting the weights of the adjacent output units in close proximity to the winner. So not only is the winner adjusted, but the whole neighborhood of output units is moved closer to the input pattern. Starting from randomized weight values, the output units slowly align themselves such that when an input pattern is presented, a neighborhood of units responds. As training progresses, the size of the neighborhood radiating out from the winning unit is decreased. Initially, large numbers of output units will be updated; later on, smaller and smaller numbers are updated until at the

■ **FIGURE 7.10**
Kohonen self-
organizing map

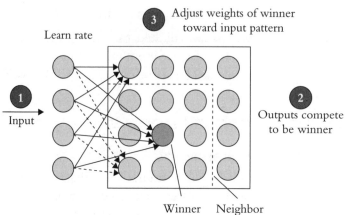

end of training, only the winning unit is adjusted. Similarly, the learning rate will decrease as training progresses, and in some implementations, the learning rate decays with the distance from the winning output unit.

A basic Kohonen algorithm can be given as follows:

```
begin
  randomize weights for all neurons
  for (i = 1 to iteration_number) do
    begin
    take one random input pattern
    find the winning neuron
    find neighbors of the winner
    modify synaptic weights of these neurons
    reduce the η (learning rate) and λ (neighborhood radius)
  end
end.
```

Figure 7.10 represents the basic structure and steps of Kohonen self-organizing maps.

A Kohonen neural network can be used to compress and quantize data, such as images and speech, before storage or transmission to condense the quantity of information to be stored or sent.

■ 7.6.2 Probabilistic Neural Networks

Probabilistic neural networks (PNNs) include a feed-forward architecture and supervised training algorithm similar to back propagation. Instead of adjusting the input-layer weights using the generalized delta rule, each training input pattern is used as the connection weights to a new hidden unit. Actually, each input pattern is integrated into the PNN architecture. This technique is extremely fast, because only one pass through the network is required to set the input connection weights. Additional passes might be used to adjust the output weights to fine-tune the network outputs.

Many researchers have claimed that adding a hidden unit for each input pattern might be overkill. Several clustering schemes have been proposed to cut down on the number of hidden units when input patterns are close in input space and can be represented by a single hidden unit. Probabilistic neural networks offer several advantages over back-propagation networks. Training is much faster—usually a single pass. Given enough input data, the PNN will converge to a Bayesian (optimum) classifier. Probabilistic neural networks allow true incremental learning, where new training data can be added at any time without needing to retrain the entire network. Due to the statistical root for the PNN, it can give an indication of the amount of evidence it has on which to base its decision.

■ 7.7 INTEGRATING NEURAL NETWORKS AND KNOWLEDGE-BASED SYSTEMS

A knowledge-based system (KBS) frequently fails to handle inconsistent and noisy data. It is also difficult to formalize knowledge in domains where a priori rules are unknown. Normally, the performance in learning from examples and dealing with atypical situations is insufficient. The rules used by conventional knowledge-based systems are able to represent complex concepts only approximately. Knowledge acquisition is another problem in a KBS. It is impractical for an expert to describe his or her domain-specific knowledge entirely in form of rules or other knowledge representation schemes. Moreover, it is difficult to describe expertise acquired by experience.

Artificial neural networks handle knowledge in a subsymbolic form. They can solve nonlinear problems frequently better than conventional methods and are able to approximate nonlinear relations in data. Moreover, incomplete and imprecise data can be processed. Neural networks learn in a particularly parallel and self-organizing manner. Ability to generalize and an elegant degradation of error are the major characteristics of the connectionist system. Besides having the ability to process inconsistent and noisy data, neural networks compute the most plausible output to each input.

Knowledge-based systems do not deal with uncertainty to any level approaching human abilities. These uncertainties occur within the inputs of a system or within the knowledge base of the system. Conventional knowledge-based systems require that special account be made of any uncertainty. Neural networks offer an ability to deal with uncertainty as an implicit part of their operation. This is enhanced by their ability to learn from example, exhibit fault-tolerant behavior, and their inherent parallelism.

■ 7.8 APPLICATIONS FOR NEURAL NETWORKS

Connectionist systems are popular for many reasons. A few of them are parallel processing, the ability to handle distributed representations, the ability to learn without documenting the knowledge, and remaining robust with respect to noisy data. However, learning with such systems takes time. Another disadvantage of an ANN-based system is that it stores knowledge implicitly; hence, direct (explicit) explanation and reasoning, like the kind symbolic AI systems provide, are not available. An ANN system is comparatively less interpretable and hard to debug.

These limitations of the connectionist approach can be overcome with the integration of the symbolic AI techniques, such as genetic algorithms and fuzzy logic and neuro-fuzzy hybridization (Sajja, 2007; 2008; 2009). Above all, ANN systems have a wide scope, mainly because of their robust mechanism and self-learning capabilities.

Some of the application areas are as follows:

• Optimization, function approximation, time series prediction, and modeling
• Classification, pattern matching and recognition (three-dimensional object recognition), novelty detection, and sequential decision making
• Data processing (including filtering, clustering, blind source separation, and compression), data mining, data compression (speech signals or image—for example, faces), and data validations
• System identification and control (vehicle control or process control) and signal processing

- Game playing and decision making (backgammon, chess, or racing)
- Sequence recognition (gestures or handwritten text recognition)
- Medical diagnosis (for example, disease diagnosis or storing medical records based on case information)
- Financial applications (automated trading systems, time series analysis, or stock market prediction) and customer research
- Cognitive science, neurobiology, and the study of models of how the brain works
- Biological neural networks, which communicate through pulses and use the timing of the pulses to transmit information and perform computations
- Integration of fuzzy logic and neural networks for applications in automotive engineering, screening applicants for jobs, controlling a crane, or monitoring a medical condition like glaucoma
- Robotics (navigation and vision recognition)
- Speech production and recognition
- Vision (face recognition, edge detection, and visual search engines)
- New topologies and hardware implementations
- New learning algorithms
- In hybrid systems and soft computing—for example, rule extraction for fuzzy systems, self-evolving ANNs, and neuro-fuzzy systems

All neural network technologies will be greatly improved upon in the future. All of the previously mentioned applications will become more sophisticated as researchers develop better training methods and network architectures.

■ 7.8.1 Applications for the Back-Propagation Model

There are many well-known applications for the back-propagation model, and reasons for this versatility are, namely, the input and output can have many origins than only visual images and application types can be other than recognition.

The major application categories of the back-propagation model are:

- Classification
- Prediction
- Control

For example, in character recognition, to verify whether a given pattern is character "X" or some other character is an easy classification problem. The basic principle is to recognize and classify given patterns to much fewer groups of patterns. The latter will be the output of the network for this type of application. The network can be trained using sample patterns and their correct answers. When the network is well trained, it gives correct answers for not only the sample patterns, but also for new similar patterns. As mentioned, the input can be of any form, not just a visual image.

We have to consider time as one of the factors while using neural networks for prediction problems. For instance, assume that a neural network is given several patterns under various circumstances over a specific length of time. Given patterns in its earlier stage, the neural network may be able to predict the most likely pattern to follow.

The control problem can be deemed as a mapping problem from input, which may include feed-in attributes and possible feedback, to output of control parameters. Here, the mapping of diverse input/output values can be viewed as patterns and further, they can be learned by the neural network. This idea can be used for various components of transportation such as a car, airplane, and mechanical controls such as the action interface in robots.

■ 7.9   WARM-UP QUESTIONS, EXERCISES, AND PROJECTS

Warm-up Questions

1. What is a perceptron?
2. What are network layers?
3. What does the transfer function do?
4. Biological neurons have a cell body, axons, dendrites, and synapses.

   a. Draw a diagram and label these terms on it.

   b. Draw the computational equivalent and label it.

5. How can you graphically represent the input/output behavior of a simple perceptron?
6. What are the advantages of having a multilayer perceptron over a single-layer perceptron?

7. Compare connectionist and symbolic systems.

8. Build a network consisting of four artificial neurons. Two neurons receive inputs to the network, and the other two give outputs from the network.

9. Visit the Nenet Software website to see the use of a self-organizing map at http://koti.mbnet.fi/~phodju/nenet/Nenet/InteractiveDemo.html. Open the demonstration by clicking the "demonstration" link. Proceed through the demonstration.

10. To observe how self-organizing maps work, go to the website http://davis.wpi.edu/~matt/courses/soms/applet.html. You can try diverse iterations and evaluate the variations in accuracy of color grouping.

Exercises

1. List the main differences between the artificial neural network model and the biological equivalent.

2. What is the purpose of the back-propagation algorithm in neural networks?

3. Derive expressions for the weights and threshold of a perceptron that computes the logical functions NOR and OR.

4. What is the fundamental concept of the Hopfield network?

5. Explain how a gradient-descent algorithm can be used to train multi-layer perceptrons.

6. Is it necessary to add noise to the training data when training a neural network?

7. If a two-dimensional self-organizing map has a map of dimension $w \times d$ and p input neurons, how many weights does it have?

8. Study basic neuron models and learning algorithms by using MATLAB's Neural Network Toolbox.

9. Implement a Kohonen one-dimensional neural network.

Projects

1. The Java Object-Oriented Neural Network (JOONE) is an open-source project that offers a highly adaptable neural network for Java

programmers. The JOONE project source code is covered by a Lesser GNU Public License (LGPL). In a nutshell, this means that the source code is freely available. JOONE can be downloaded from http://www. jooneworld.com/. It allows you to create neural networks easily from a Java program. You can create and test your own neural networks using the GUI Editor provided by the engine.

2. A variety of methods and technologies can be utilized in knowledge modeling. Explore how neural networks are beneficial in this respect. Prepare an article with appropriate example cases.

References

Akerkar, R. & Joshi, M., *Neural Networks: Bringing Dynamism to AI*, Artificial Intelligence—New Trends, Allied Publishers, pp. 217–227, 2003.

Fraser, N. Introduction to neural networks, 1998. Retrieved from http://www. virtualventures.ca/~neil/neural/neuron.html

Gershenson, C. Artificial neural networks for beginners, 2003. Retrieved from http://uk.arxiv.org/abs/cs.NE/0308031

Haykin, S. *Neural Networks: A Comprehensive Foundation*, 2nd edition, Prentice Hall International, Inc., 1999.

Hopfield, J. J. Neural networks and physical systems with emergent collective computational abilities, *Proceedings of the National Academy of Sciences of the USA*, vol. 79, no. 8, pp. 2554–2558, 1982.

Rumelhart, D. E. & McClelland, J. L. *Parallel Distributed Processing*, vol. 1, Cambridge, MA: MIT Press, 1986.

Sajja, P. S. An evolutionary computing approach for a multilayer connectionist system, *Journal of Computer Science*, vol.2, no.4, pp. 325–331, 2007.

Sajja, P. S. Type-2 fuzzy user interface for artificial neural network based decision support system for course selection. *International Journal of Computing and ICT Research*, vol.2, no.2, pp. 96–102, 2008.

Sajja, P. S. An evolutionary fuzzy rule based system for knowledge based diagnosis. *Journal of Hybrid Computing Research*, vol.2, no.1, 2009.

Takefuji, Y. *Neural Network Parallel Computing*, Norwell, MA: Kluwer Academic, 1992.

Veloso, M. Perceptrons and neural networks, 2001. Retrieved from http://www.cs.cmu.edu/afs/cs.cmu.edu/academic/class/15381-f01/www/handouts/110601.pdf

CHAPTER 8

Genetic Algorithms

■ 8.1 INTRODUCTION

The basic purpose of a genetic algorithm (GA) is to mimic Mother Nature's evolutionary approach in science and engineering fields, including computer science. The algorithm is based on the process of natural selection—Charles Darwin's "survival of the fittest." A GA provides a natural alternative to other solution strategies, outperforming them in certain situations. For example, many of the real-world problems that involve finding optimal parameters can prove difficult for traditional methods but are ideal for GAs (Obitko, 1998). GAs can be used in problem solving, function optimizing, machine learning, and in innovative systems.

According to Hales (2006), instead of just accepting a random testing strategy to arrive at a solution, one may choose a strategy like:

- Generate a set of random solutions
- Repeat

  Test each solution in the set (rank them)

  Remove any bad solutions from the set (bad solutions refer to solutions that are less likely to provide effective answers according to fitness criteria given by experts)

  Duplicate any good solutions or make small changes to some of them
- Repeat test until an appropriate solution is achieved

It is smart to choose a quick solution from potentially huge search spaces and navigating them, looking for optimal combinations of things. Genetic algorithms are considered directed-search algorithms based on the mechanics of biological evolution. Historically, GAs were first conceived and used by John Holland (1975) at the University of Michigan. The basic objective of his work was to understand the adaptive processes of natural systems and hence, to design artificial systems software that retains the robustness of natural systems.

In one way, genetic algorithms are adaptive heuristic search algorithms based on the evolutionary ideas of natural selection (Obitko, 1998). The appeal of genetic algorithms comes from their simplicity and elegance as robust search algorithms. These are powerful tools to rapidly discover appropriate solutions for difficult high-dimensional problems. Genetic algorithms are useful and efficient when:

- The search space is large, complex, or poorly understood
- Domain knowledge is scarce or expert knowledge is difficult to encode to narrow the search space
- No mathematical analysis is available

GA is a type of evolutionary algorithm (EA). Other types of evolutionary algorithms are evolutionary strategies, evolutionary programming, and genetic programming. Each shares the basic EA design philosophy of domain-independent hypothesis generation followed by domain-specific selection. However, they differ in primary representations, the relative importance of mutation vs. crossover, and preferred selection strategies.

Evolutionary strategy is a strongly engineering-driven approach to evolutionary computation. Therefore, researchers who use it are interested in finding optimal solutions to technical problems, not in testing theories of evolution or intelligence. The philosophical difference between evolutionary programming and the other EAs lies in the view of each phenotype as representing an entire species. Since, by definition, members of one species cannot mate with members of another, the concept of genotype recombination has no place in evolutionary programming. Hence, it is the only EA in which crossover is forbidden. Genetic programming is clearly the most drastic of the EAs. Genetic programming applications run the gauntlet from musical composition and artistic design to state-of-the-art inventions of electrical circuits, antennas, and factory controllers.

■ 8.2 BASIC TERMINOLOGY

Each biological cell of every living thing contains *chromosomes,* which are nothing but strings of DNA. DNA is the building block of cells. Chromosomes can be bit strings, real numbers, permutations of elements, lists of rules, and data structures. On each DNA string, there is a set of *genes* responsible for some property of a human (or living thing) to which it belongs. Such properties, to name a few, are height, skin color, hair color, and eye color.

A *genotype* is a collection of such genes representing possible solutions in a domain space. This space, referred to as a search space, comprises all possible solutions to the problem at hand. These solutions can be encoded with strategies, such as character-based encodings, real-valued encodings, and tree representations. With every evolutionary step, known as a *generation,* the individuals in the current population are *decoded* and *evaluated* according to some predefined quality criterion, referred to as the *fitness* or *fitness function.* The degree of *fitness* is related to the strength of the genes in an individual. When a new child is born, the parents' genes are inherited sometimes directly, without any modification, if they are strong enough. This process is known as duplication (exact resemblance of the child to its parent) in the new generation. Strong genes are normally represented in the new generation. Genes that are not strong are combined with their mates and used to generate new individuals in a process known as recombination. *Mutation* and *crossover* are such recombining operators. If no such operation is performed, the offspring is an exact copy of one of the parents.

An initial population is considered to have a fixed number of individuals (also known as offspring) containing building blocks or chromosomes on which genes are set. These individuals are evaluated for their ability to survive in critical situations. This test is known as a fitness function. A fit individual with strong genes can reproduce itself. Otherwise, in the next generation, the strong genes from one or more individuals can be combined, resulting in a stronger individual. Over time, the individuals in the population become better adapted to their environment. This process is shown in Figure 8.1.

■ **FIGURE 8.1**
Operations in the process of natural selection

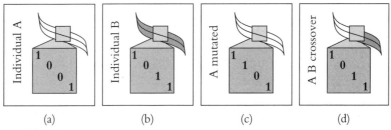

(a)   (b)   (c)   (d)

In Figure 8.1, two individuals are shown, named A and B in parts (a) and (b), respectively. Parts (a) and (b) show how genes are stored on chromosome A as well as on B. In real life, genes are not sequences of binary numbers. A mutation on A results in a change in the sequence on the chromosome, resulting in a new individual, which is known as mutated A. The mutated A is shown in part (c). In this case, only a single bit is altered. In part (c), two chromosomes that come into contact can "cross over" and exchange parts of themselves with each other. Part (d) shows the resultant individual with half of the gene sequence moved from one chromosome to another.

■ 8.3 GENETIC ALGORITHMS

The genetic algorithm discussed in the previous section can be documented as shown in Table 8.1.

A genetic algorithm is based on independent sampling provided by large populations, which are initialized randomly. Among these populations, high-fitness individuals are preserved through selection, and this biases the sampling process toward a region of high fitness. Operators like crossover, mutation, and selection combine partial solutions, called building blocks,

■ **Table 8.1 The Genetic Algorithm**

Step		Action
1		The algorithm considers the initial population generated randomly with a population of N chromosomes.
2		Calculate the fitness $f(x)$, where x is a valid individual of the population.
3		Create a new population by repeating the following steps until the new population has the required number of fit individuals.
	3.1	Select two parent individuals from the population with better fitness.
	3.2	Form a new individual by applying an operation such as crossover, mutation, or selection.
4		Evaluate the new population for the fitness of its individuals.
5		Test the new population for the solution; if the solution is achieved, stop.
6		Repeat Steps 2 through 5 until a desirable solution is achieved.

from different strings onto the same string, thus exploiting the parallelism provided by the population of candidate solutions. The performance of any GA depends on parameters like a suitable encoding scheme (as it works on the encoded parameters set) and proper fitness function. The GA's power comes from its ability to conduct parallel searches in a population.

■ 8.4   GENETIC CYCLES

Figure 8.2 represents a genetic cycle based on the genetic algorithm described previously.

■ 8.5   BASIC OPERATORS OF A GENETIC ALGORITHM

The performance of any genetic algorithm is influenced by its operators. Mutation and crossover are two basic operators that significantly contribute to increasing the performance of the algorithm. However, before these operations can be applied on the selected individuals, it is necessary to encode the individuals. The most common method of encoding is with a binary string. Each individual represents one binary string. Each bit in this string can represent some characteristic of the solution. Then the individual (or chromosome) can be represented as shown in Figure 8.3.

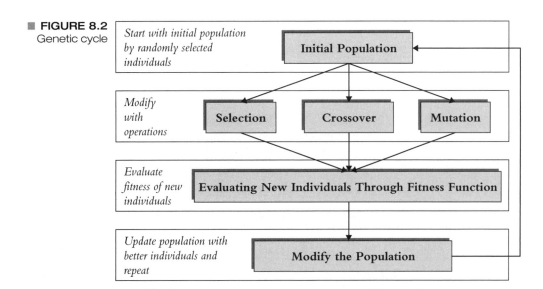

■ **FIGURE 8.2**
Genetic cycle

Start with initial population by randomly selected individuals

Initial Population

Modify with operations

Selection   **Crossover**   **Mutation**

Evaluate fitness of new individuals

Evaluating New Individuals Through Fitness Function

Update population with better individuals and repeat

Modify the Population

| Individual 1 | 0 | 1 | 0 | 1 | 0 | 1 | 0 | 0 | 1 | 0 | 0 | 1 | 0 | 1 | 1 | 1 |
| Individual 2 | 1 | 1 | 0 | 0 | 0 | 1 | 1 | 0 | 0 | 0 | 0 | 1 | 0 | 0 | 1 | 0 |

Depending on the nature of the problem, one can adopt other ways of encoding individuals, such as numbers and alphabets.

■ 8.5.1 Mutation

Mutating a bit involves flipping it, changing a gene with another one with the help of a small mutation probability $P_{mutation}$. A number between 0 and 1 is chosen at random. If the random number is smaller than $P_{mutation}$, the outcome of flipping is true; otherwise, the outcome is false. If, at any bit, the outcome is true, the bit is altered; otherwise, the bit is kept unchanged. For binary encoding, a mutation means to flip one or more randomly chosen bits from 1 to 0 or from 0 to 1. Using mutation alone induces a random walk through the search space. Figure 8.4 shows two original individuals and the mutation operation on them.

The mutation depends on the encoding. If encoding using permutation of alphabets is considered, the mutation could be exchanging two genes from given individuals.

■ 8.5.2 Crossover

Crossover selects substrings of genes of the same length from parent individuals (often called offspring) from the same point, replaces them, and generates a new individual. The crossover point can be selected randomly. This reproduction operator proceeds in three steps, as follows (see Figure 8.5):

Step 1: The reproduction operator selects at random a pair of two individual strings for mating.

Individual 1	0	1	0	1	**0**	1	0	**0**	1	0	0	1	0	**1**	1	1
New Individual 1	0	1	0	1	**1**	1	0	**1**	1	0	0	1	0	**0**	1	1
Individual 2	1	**1**	0	**0**	0	1	1	0	0	**0**	0	1	0	0	1	0
New Individual 2	0	**0**	0	**1**	0	1	1	0	0	**1**	0	1	0	0	1	0

FIGURE 8.5
Crossover of individuals

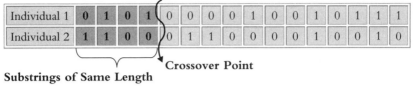

Step 2: A cross-site is selected at random within the string length.

Step 3: The position values are swapped between two strings following the cross-site.

Crossover can be done at multiple sites, as Figure 8.6 shows.

A GA often encodes solutions as fixed-length bit strings. Other alternative encoding strategies are symbols, alphabets, and tree structures, as stated earlier. Figure 8.7 presents mutation and crossover operations on Trees A and B, respectively.

Such tree representations are helpful in encoding while working with evolving programs. The syntax of the instructions can be represented in the form of trees (generally using a prefix notation), and operations like selection, mutation, and crossover are carried out. The resulting offspring are evaluated against a fitness function. This is known as genetic programming.

FIGURE 8.6
Multisite crossover of individuals

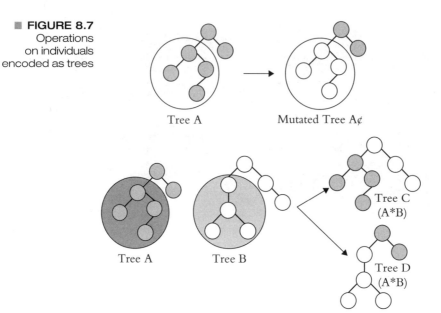

Tree A   Mutated Tree A¢

Tree A   Tree B

Tree C
(A*B)

Tree D
(A*B)

■ 8.5.3 Selection

This operator is also considered a reproduction operator. It makes clones of good strings, but does not create new ones. Individual solutions are selected through a fitness-based process, where fit solutions (as measured by a fitness function) are more likely to be selected. Many selection procedures are currently in use, one of the simplest being Holland's (1975) original *fitness-proportionate selection,* where individuals are selected with a probability proportional to their relative fitness.

Fitness-proportionate selection, also known as roulette-wheel selection, is a genetic operator used in genetic algorithms for selecting potentially useful solutions for recombination. In fitness-proportionate selection, as in all selection methods, the fitness function assigns fitness levels to possible solutions or chromosomes. These fitness levels are used to associate a probability of selection with each individual chromosome. If f_i is the fitness of individual i in the population, its probability of being selected is $Pi = f_i / \sum f_i$, where i takes values from 1 to N, where N is the number of individuals in the population.

While candidate solutions with higher fitness levels tend to be preserved, there is still a chance that they may be deselected. Contrast this with a less sophisticated selection algorithm, such as truncation selection, which will eliminate a fixed percentage of the weakest candidates. With fitness-proportionate selection, there is a chance that some weaker solutions may survive the selection process. This is an advantage because even though a complete solution is weak, it may include some components that could prove useful following the recombination process.

The name "roulette-wheel solution" comes from the analogy to a roulette wheel. Each candidate solution represents a pocket on the wheel; the size of the pockets is proportionate to the probability of the solution being selected. Selecting N chromosomes from the population is equivalent to playing N games on the roulette wheel, as each candidate is drawn independently.

Other selection techniques, such as stochastic universal sampling or tournament selection, are often used in practice. This is because they have less stochastic noise and have a constant selection pressure. Figure 8.8 presents a typical roulette-wheel selection.

Using selection alone will tend to fill the population with copies of the best individual from the population. Hence, it is not the selection but the crossover and mutation that can introduce new individuals into the population.

■ 8.6 FUNCTION OPTIMIZATION

A genetic algorithm is a technique for optimization; that is, it can be used to find the minimum or maximum of some arbitrary function. This technique is unique in that it has a stochastic method and it finds a global minimum.

Example 1

Consider the function $f(x) = x*x$ for maximization in the interval of $[0, 30]$. This function can be solved analytically, but if it could not, a genetic algorithm could be used to search for values of x that produce high values

■ FIGURE 8.8
Roulette wheel
selection

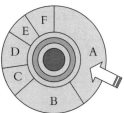

■ Table 8.2: First Generation of f(x) = x*x

Sr. No. of Individual	Value of x	Decimal Value of x	Fitness $f(x) = x*x$ (value in decimal)	Roulette Wheel Selection Count
1	01101	13	169	1
2	11000	24	576	2
3	01000	08	064	0
4	10011	19	361	1

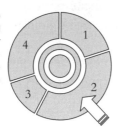

■ **FIGURE 8.9**
Roulette wheel presentation for the first generation shown in the $f(x) = x*x$ example

of $f(x)$ in a particular interval of [0, 30]. The simplest encoding strategy for the same is to follow a binary bit pattern. The population consists of four individuals, which are binary-encoded strings (genomes) of length 5. The initial population can be given as shown in Table 8.2. Figure 8.9 represents roulette-wheel presentation for the first generation shown in the Table 8.2.

Table 8.3 represents mutation and crossover to evolve the second generation of the example shown in Table 8.2.

Table 8.4 shows that the individuals have become stronger in the second generation.

■ Table 8.3: Mutation and Crossover After Reproduction for f(x) = x*x

Sr. No. of Selected Individual	Value of x	New Individual After Mutation and Crossover	Operation Site	Fitness $f(x) = x*x$ (value in decimal)
1	0110**1**	01100	5	12*12 = 144
2	1100**0**	11001	5	25*25 = 625
3	11**000**	11011	3	27*27 = 729
4	10**011**	10000	3	16*16 = 256

■ Table 8.4: Second Generation of the Function $f(x) = x*x$

Sr. No. of Individual	Value of x	Decimal Value of y	Fitness $f(x) = x*x$ (value in decimal)
1	01100	12	144
2	11001	25	625
3	11011	27	729
4	10000	16	256

Example 2

This example considers two variable functions $f(x,y) = x + y$ for maximization in the same interval of $[0, 30]$. The encoding strategy for the example is to follow a binary bit pattern of size 10, with the first 5 bits representing a value of the first variable x, and the remaining bits representing a value of the second variable y. The initial population with four individuals can be given as shown in Table 8.5.

Figure 8.10 shows the roulette-wheel presentation for the example shown in Table 8.5.

Table 8.6 demonstrates mutation and crossover after reproduction for the example shown in Table 8.5.

■ Table 8.5 First Generation of $f(x,y) = x + y$

Sr. No. of Individual	Value of x	Value of y	Bit String	Fitness $f(x) = x + y$ (value in decimal)	Roulette-Wheel Selection Count
1	01011	01010	0101101010	10 + 11 = 21	1
2	11000	01100	1100001100	24 + 12 = 36	2
3	01001	00101	0100100101	9 + 5 = 14	0
4	01011	00111	0101100111	11 + 7 = 18	1

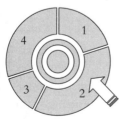

■ FIGURE 8.10
Roulette-wheel presentation for the generation shown in the $f(x,y) = x + y$ example

■ **Table 8.6: Mutation and Crossover After Reproduction for** $f(x,y) = x + y$

Sr. No. of Selected Individual	Value of x and y Bit Strings	New Individual After Mutation and Crossover	Operation Site	Fitness $f(x,y) = x + y$ (value in decimal)
1	**0101**101010	1100101010	1	25 + 10 = 35
2	**1100**001100	0101001100	1	10 = 12 = 22
3	110**0**001100	110**1**001100	4	26 + 12 = 38
4	010**1**100111	010**0**100111	4	9 + 7 = 16

Assignment

The maximum value of the function has reached 38 in two generations. Try to complete Example 2 to verify how many generations it may take.

■ 8.6.1 Stopping Criteria

GA gives "better" results as compared to traditional searching algorithms, especially in situations where there is no concept of an optimal solution. That is why, according to Frontline Systems (www.solver.com, 2008), evolutionary algorithms are best employed on problems where it is difficult or impossible to test for optimality. This also means that an evolutionary algorithm never knows for certain when to stop, aside from the length of time or the number of iterations or candidate solutions that you want it to explore. There are no clear and obvious termination criteria for a genetic algorithm. According to Weck (2004), some options are as follows:

- X number of generations completed—typically 100
- Mean deviation in performance of individuals in the population falls below a certain threshold
- Stagnation (marginal or no improvement from one generation to the next)
- A particular point in the search space is encountered

■ 8.7 SCHEMA

Holland (1975) introduced the notion of a schema to explain how genetic algorithms search for regions of high fitness. Schemas are theoretical constructs used to explain the behavior of genetic algorithms, and are not processed directly by the algorithm.

■ 8.7.1 Schema Defined

A *schema* is a template, defined over the alphabet {0,1,*}, which describes a pattern of bit strings in the search space {0,1}*l* (the set of bits strings of length *l*). For each of the *l* bit positions, the template either specifies the value at that position (1 or 0) or indicates by the symbol * (*referred to as don't care*) that either value is allowed.

The schema **1 1 * * 1 1 0 *** is a template for the following eight strings:

1 1 0 0 1 1 0 0
1 1 0 0 1 1 0 1
...
1 1 1 1 1 1 0 1

■ 8.7.2 Instance, Defined Bits, and Order of Schema

A bit string *x* that matches a schema's **S** pattern is said to be an instance of **S**. In a schema, ones and zeros are referred to as defined bits, the order of a schema is the number of defined bits in that schema, and the defining length of a schema is the distance between the leftmost and rightmost defined bits in the string.

The number of defined bits is the order $o(H)$ of the schema *H*:

1 1 * * 1 1 0 *	Order 5
* * * * 1 1 0 *	Order 3

The defining length is the distance $d(H)$ between the first and last bits of the schema:

1 1 * * 1 1 0 *	Defining Length 6
* * * * 1 1 0 *	Defining Length 2

■ 8.7.3 The Importance of Schema Results

Schemas capture important regularities in the search space and present them in a generalized fashion. One fitness evaluation of an individual comprising *l* bits schema (general pattern) implicitly gives information about the 2^l schemas, or hyperplanes, of which it is an instance.

A schema helps when searching for good regions of the search space corresponding to regularities in the problem domain. For example, a short, low-order, above-average schema receives exponentially increasing trials in subsequent generations of a genetic algorithm. During crossover, these "building blocks" become exchanged and combined. According to *Building Block Hypothesis* (Hayes, 2007), the genetic algorithm initially detects biases towards higher fitness in some low-order schemas (with a small number of defined bits) and over time, detects the same in high-order schemas. Holland (1975) determined that the observed best schemas will, on average, be allocated an exponentially increasing number of samples in the next generation.

■ 8.8 ORDERING PROBLEMS AND EDGE RECOMBINATION

■ 8.8.1 Traveling Salesperson Problem

The Traveling Salesperson Problem involves finding a path of a tour from a given set of cities so that each city is visited only once and the total distance traveled is minimized. One representation is an ordered list of city numbers/alphabets known as an *order-based* GA. Considering that there are five different cities to be traveled once with the minimum effort, the possible paths can be given as follows:

Plan 1: (3 5 2 1 4)

Plan 2: (2 5 1 3 4)

The standard mutation and crossover operators here create illegal/invalid solutions/plans. See the following example, in which Plan 1 undergoes a mutation operation at Location 1. City 3 can be replaced with one of the cities (1, 2, 4, or 5). This results in an illegal plan.

Original Plan 1: (3 5 2 1 4)

Mutated Plan 1: (**2** 5 **2** 1 4)

Similarly, a crossover also results in illegal solutions, as follows:

Plan 1: (3 5 <u>2 1 4</u>)

Plan 2: (2 5 <u>**1 3 4**</u>)

New Offspring Plan 3: (3 5 1 3 4)

New Offspring Plan 4: (2 5 2 1 4)

■ 8.8.2 Solutions to Prevent Production of Invalid Offspring

The following are possible solutions to the problem:

- Adopt a different representation
- Design a special crossover operator
- Penalize the illegal solution with the proper fitness function

■ 8.8.3 Edge Recombination Technique

With the help of the edge recombination technique, this problem can be solved. This technique considers the population of a finite number of legal tours as the initial generation. For every city, a list of adjacent cities has to be defined. With the initial population and the adjacency list, the following steps are performed:

Step 1: Select the parent at random and assign its first gene (element) as the first element in the new child.

Step 2: Select the second element for the child as follows: If there is an adjacency common to both parents, choose that element to be the next one in the child's permutation; if there is an unused adjacency available from one parent, choose it. If these two options fail, make a random selection.

Step 3: Select the remaining elements in order by repeating Step 2.

Consider five different cities labeled 1, 2, 3, 4, and 5 for a typical Traveling Salesperson Problem. The randomly generated two individuals are as follows:

Plan 1: (2, 3, 4, 1, 5)
Plan 2: (1, 2, 3, 5, 4)

The new adjacency list can be given as follows:

Key	Adjacency List
1	2, 4, 5
2	1, 3, 3
3	2, 2, 4, 5
4	1, 3, 5
5	1, 3, 4

With the previous algorithm, a new offspring can be generated, with City 3 as the random starting point. This member is (**3, 2, 1, 4, 5**), which is a legal plan. The fitness function is the cost or length of the path. When a minimum cost/shortest path state is achieved, further evolution can be terminated.

■ 8.9   ISLAND-BASED GENETIC ALGORITHMS

Because we can imagine a GA with a single population as a form of parallelization, more benefits can be obtained by evolving a number of subpopulations in tandem. This is called a cooperative model in which we have islands representing different populations. Naturally, selection, crossover, and mutation occur in every subpopulation independently from other subpopulations. Moreover, individuals are allowed to migrate to another subpopulation (i.e., island). Here, the important problem is how to initialize the subpopulations. One way is to use a random approach, but a better way would be to initialize subpopulations to cover different parts of the search space, further covering a larger search space and providing a sort of inching by individuals' islands. There can be random or tournament selection of individuals and the destination subpopulation during migration. Of course, individuals from a poor island may wish to migrate to a better place. However, these individuals may introduce bad genetic material into a good island. Therefore, acceptance of an immigrant may be based on the probability as a function of the immigrant's fitness value compared to that of the intended destination island.

There is another type of island model where instead of distributing entire individuals over several subpopulations, each subpopulation is given one gene to optimize. This is called coevolutionary process and was suggested by Mitchell Potter (1997).

■ 8.10   PROBLEM SOLVING USING GENETIC ALGORITHMS

The genetic algorithm approach to solving problems differs considerably from usual artificial intelligence and machine learning. Problem solving is often characterized as a search through a solution space, in which solutions/hypotheses are generated and then tested for feasibility, optimality, and so on. Usually, an efficient problem solver is one that exploits as much intelligence as possible to generate reasonably good solutions and thereby avoids wasting time testing bad hypotheses. Indeed, a measure of problem-solving improvement (i.e., learning) in knowledge-based systems was the degree to which test knowledge or constraints could be re-expressed in the generator.

Many knowledge-based systems can take a hypothesis and its test results as inputs and produce a new hypothesis that is more or less assured to be an improvement over the previous one. For instance, if a logic-based system uses disjunctions of primitive terms to produce classifications of input examples, and if the test results indicate that a hypothesis is too specific, the system will usually include an extra disjunction in order to generalize the hypothesis. The intelligence that the generator contains is simply a knowledge of logic.

On the other hand, if the representation form is an artificial neural network, the knowledge of the back-propagation algorithm leads it to increase and decrease connection weights in ways that decrease the network's output error. Here, the intelligence lies in a fundamental understanding of the effects of change in a system of interlinked equations. In either case, the intelligence is representation-dependent: The back propagation algorithm could not handle a logical disjunction written in standard propositional or predicate calculus, and a logical engine would be lost if given a neural network.

The generators associated with genetic algorithms have little intelligence, although this varies among the genetic algorithm types. The greater the effort required to convert genotypes to phenotypes, the less intelligent the genetic algorithm will appear in terms of its ability to generate good hypotheses. Interestingly enough, the fact that genetic algorithms permit a large representational gap between genotypes and phenotypes allows the genetic algorithm generator to operate relatively independently of the high-level phenotypic representation. For example, the same genetic algorithm can mutate and recombine bit-string genotypes that encode everything from logical expressions to neural networks to Bayesian probability tables at the phenotypic level. In this sense, genetic algorithms can be extremely representation-independent. However, the manipulations made to the genotypes have no assurance of creating improved phenotypes. Representation independence has a high price, but one that many are willing to pay when problems become so complex that the biases imposed by representation dependence prevent knowledge-based systems from finding a satisfactory solution.

Typical knowledge-based problem solvers include a great deal of information about how a good solution should be created and may possess metaknowledge about why it performs specific hypothesis manipulations. This bias helps avoid the generation of bad hypotheses. On the contrary, a genetic algorithm has little "how" or "why" information but a superior knowledge about what a good solution is.

■ 8.11 BAYESIAN NETWORKS AND GENETIC ALGORITHMS

A Bayesian network is a model representation based on reasoning with uncertainty. It is a well-known statistical approach. The Bayesian methodology is built upon the well-known Bayes' rule, which is itself derived from the fundamental rule for probability calculus:

$$P(a,b) = P(a|b) * P(b) \tag{1}$$

In Equation 1, $P(a,b)$ is the joint probability of both events a and b occurring, $P(a|b)$ is the conditional probability of event a occurring given that event b occurred, and $P(b)$ is the probability of event b occurring. This derivation further produces the following Bayes' rule:

$$P(b|a) = \frac{P(a|b) * P(b)}{P(a)} \tag{2}$$

Bayes' rule not only opens the door to systems that evolve probabilities as new evidence is acquired, but also provides the underpinning for the inferential mechanisms used in Bayesian belief networks.

A Bayesian belief network is a directed acyclic graph (DAG) that provides a compact representation or factorization of the joint probability distribution for a group of variables. Graphically, a Bayesian network contains nodes and directed edges between those nodes. Each node is a variable that can be in one of a finite number of states. The links or arrows between the nodes represent causal relationships between those nodes. Because the absence of an edge between two nodes implies conditional independence, the probability distribution of a node can be determined by considering the distributions of its parents. In this way, the joint probability distribution for the entire network can be specified. This relationship can be captured mathematically using the chain rule in Equation (3):

$$p(x) = \prod_{i=1}^{n} p\big(x_i \,\big|\, parents(x_i)\big) \tag{3}$$

In general terms, this equation states that the joint probability distribution for node x is equal to the product of the probability of each component x_i of x given the parents of x_i. Each node has an associated conditional probability table that provides the probability of it being in a particular state, given any combination of parent states. When evidence is entered for a node in the network, the fundamental rule for probability calculus and Bayes' rule can be used to propagate this evidence through the network, updating affected probability distributions. Evidence can be propagated from parents to children as well as from children to parents, making this method highly effective for both prediction and diagnosis.

The framework of Bayesian networks offers a compact and efficient graphical representation of dependence relations between the entities of a problem domain. Bayesian belief networks encode joint probability distribution functions and can be used as fitness functions in genetic algorithms. Individuals in the genetic algorithm's population then represent instantiations, or explanations, in the belief network. Computing the most probable explanations (belief revision) is, therefore, cast as a genetic algorithm search in the joint probability distribution space. The fittest individual in the genetic algorithm population is an estimate of the most probable explanation.

■ 8.12 APPLICATIONS AND RESEARCH TRENDS IN GA

The term *evolutionary algorithm* or *evolutionary computation* covers the domains of genetic algorithms, evolution strategies, evolutionary programming, and genetic programming (Sipper, 1996). GAs have been successfully applied to numerous problems from different domains, including optimization, automatic programming, machine learning, economics, operations research, ecology, population genetics, studies of evolution and learning, and social systems (Mitchell, 1996). However, according to Sipper (1996), the implementation of an evolutionary algorithm, an issue that usually remains in the background, is quite costly in many cases, since populations of solutions are involved, possibly coupled with computation-intensive fitness evaluations. One solution for reducing the cost can lead to the parallelization of the process. Other application and research areas where genetic algorithms can play an important role are as follows:

- Optimization, combinatorial, and scheduling problems
- Automatic programming
- Game playing
- Self-managing and sorting networks
- Machine and robot learning
- Evolving artificial neural networks, rule-based systems, and other hybrid architectures of soft computing
- Designing and controlling robots
- Modeling natural systems (to model processes of innovation)
- Emergence of economic markets
- Ecological phenomena
- Study of evolutionary aspects of social systems, such as the evolution of cooperation, evolution of communication, and trail-following behavior in ants
- Artificial life models (systems that model interactions between species evolution and individual learning)

We can illustrate an application of a genetic algorithm to one particular form of machine learning called a *classifier system*. In such a system, a knowledge base can be represented by a set of rules. Each rule produces the action based on the condition. A set of rules can be a solution of the genetic algorithm. Here, a fitness function is defined as imitating the goodness of each rule in terms of achieving the goal. The crossover breeding is performed to generate new progeny rules after selecting the mating pool for good rules. A mutation may generate suddenly novel ideas as new rules. In this fashion, the knowledge base will grow automatically.

Genetic algorithms can be computationally expensive, depending on a number of parameters, such as the size of the population, the complexity of the fitness function, the size of the chromosome, and the time to converge on an optimal solution. Therefore, it is necessary to consider the relative merits of advanced languages such as Java, C++, and C. For example, C is a relatively low-level language that has few operators for complex data manipulation, and C++ has a problem with standardization. Java is designed for developing highly reliable software. Java in particular is suitable for software that is capable of operating in distributed environments. Java's garbage collector relieves us from having to allocate and de-allocate memory for chromosomes in each generation. This allows us to concentrate explicitly on coding the problem at hand and not worry about memory management issues. Thus, Java has strong advantages as a development language for genetic algorithm systems. The advantages of Java are particularly evident in the area of distributed computing.

Many Java-based software packages are available that provide libraries of code for genetic algorithms. We will mention few names here, which will be useful for readers interested in further details.

1. GA Playground: This is a broad-purpose genetic algorithm toolkit available at http://www.aridolan.com/ga/gaa/gaa.html, where users can define and run their own optimization problems.

2. Eos: This is a platform for evolutionary algorithms (EAs) and ecosystem simulations developed by BT Futures Technologies Group (Bonsma, 2000). Eos provides an extensive library of algorithms and structures related to evolutionary algorithms and ecosystem simulations.

3. Java Genetic Algorithms Package (JGAP): This is a genetic algorithms and genetic programming component provided as a Java framework. It provides basic genetic mechanisms that can be easily used to apply evolutionary principles to problem solutions. Interested readers can learn more at http://jgap.sourceforge.net/

4. ECJ: This is an evolutionary computation research system written in Java. It was designed to be highly flexible, with almost all classes dynamically determined at runtime by a user-provided parameter file. All structures in the system are arranged to be easily modifiable. ECJ was developed at George Mason University's Evolutionary Computation Laboratory and is available at http://cs.gmu.edu/~eclab/projects/ecj/

5. JGProg: Groovy Java Genetic Programming (JGProg) is an open-source, pure-Java implementation of a strongly typed genetic programming experimentation platform. The link is http://jgprog.sourceforge.net/

The advantages and disadvantages of genetic algorithms are similar to those of artificial neural nets. The major disadvantages are the chance-dependent outcome and lengthy computation time.

■ 8.13 WARM-UP QUESTIONS, EXERCISES, AND PROJECTS

Warm-up Questions

1. What is evolutionary computing?
2. What is evolutionary strategy?
3. Illustrate the general computing flow in a genetic algorithm.
4. Why do genetic algorithms work?
5. Describe the various steps in designing a genetic programming solution.
6. What two conditions should a problem satisfy in order to solve it by a genetic algorithm?
7. Consider the problem of finding the shortest path through different towns, such that each town is visited only once and in the end return to the starting town. Let us assume that we use a genetic algorithm to solve this problem, in which genes represent links between pairs of towns. How many genes will be used in a chromosome in each individual if the number of towns is 20?
8. Visit the website http://www.obitko.com/tutorials/genetic-algorithms/tsp-example.php to see a genetic algorithm applet on the famous Traveling Salesperson Problem. Attempt to run the genetic algorithm with different crossovers and mutations. Study how the genetic algorithm performs.
9. Limitations with typical genetic algorithms have led researchers to look for a more powerful evolutionary system. Keeping this in mind, identify four weaknesses of genetic algorithms.
10. Use a freeware tool from the Microsoft research website at http://research.microsoft.com/en-us/um/redmond/groups/adapt/msbnx/ and experiment with Bayesian networks.

Exercises

1. Construct a genetic algorithm to train a feed-forward neural network.
2. Explore the use of a genetic algorithm to cluster data.
3. Develop sample programs from the genetic cycle shown in Figure 8.2.
4. How can genetic algorithms be employed to optimize the design of neural networks?
5. How are genetic algorithms used when searching for a solution to a problem? Consider the following problem: you are deciding what CDs to buy. There are six different ones that you are considering. Some are cheaper than others, and some are your favorites. How can a possible solution be represented as a bit string (sequence of zeros and ones)?
6. In Exercise 5, how could genetic algorithms be used to determine possible solutions?
7. Given the following data on insurance risk, explain how a suitable classification rule might be found using neural networks and genetic algorithms:

Example	City	Age	Gender	Risk
1	New York	Young	M	Low
2	New York	Young	F	Low
3	Boston	Old	M	Low
4	Boston	Young	M	High
5	Boston	Young	F	High

Projects

1. Search for material on List Processing (LISP), a high-level functional language, and write a report on how LISP is most suitable for genetic programming.
2. Design a genetic algorithm to build a simple neural network.

References

Bonsma, E., Shackleton, M., & Shipman, R. Eos—An Evolutionary and Ecosystem Research Platform, 2000, BT Technology Journal (2000) 18, pp. 24–31.

Hales, D. *Introduction to Genetic Algorithms*, 2006. Retrieved from http://cfpm.org/~david/talks/ga2006/ga-pres6.ppt

Hayes, G. *Genetic algorithm and genetic programming*, 2007. Retrieved from http://www.inf.ed.ac.uk/teaching/courses/gagp/slides07/gagplect6.pdf

Holland, J. H. *Adaptation in natural and artificial systems*, Ann Arbor, Michigan: The University of Michigan Press; 1975.

Jong, K. D. *Evolutionary Computation: A Unified Approach*, Cambridge, MA: MIT Press; 2006.

http://www.solver.com/

Mitchell, M. *An Introduction to Genetic Algorithms*. Cambridge, MA: MIT Press; 1996.

Obitko, M. *Introduction to Genetic Algorithms*, 1998. Retrieved from http://www.obitko.com/tutorials/genetic-algorithms/

Potter, M. *The Design and Analysis of a Computational Model of Cooperative Coevolution*, PhD Thesis, Fairfax, VA: George Mason University; 1997.

Sipper, M. *A brief introduction to genetic algorithms*, 1996. Retrieved from http://www.cs.bgu.ac.il/~sipper/

Weck, O. D. *Heuristic techniques: A basic introduction to genetic algorithms*, 2004. Retrieved from http://ocw.mit.edu/NR/rdonlyres/Aeronautics-and-Astronautics/16-888Spring-2004/D66C4396-90C8-49BE-BF4A-4EBE39CEAE6F/0/MSDO_L11_GA.pdf

CHAPTER 9

Soft Computing Systems

■ 9.1 INTRODUCTION TO SOFT COMPUTING

Soft computing is not a clearly defined field. Rather, it is a discipline that deals with hybrid intelligent systems. Soft computing is a consortium of computing methodologies that provides a foundation for the conception, design, and deployment of intelligent systems. The basic objective of soft computing is close to that of fuzzy systems—that is, to exploit the tolerance for imprecision and uncertainty to accomplish tractability, robustness, and low cost in practical applications. Soft computing systems aim to formalize the human ability to make rational decisions in an environment of uncertainty, imprecision, partial truth, and approximation.

The main constituents of soft computing involve disciplines like fuzzy logic; neuro-computing; evolutionary computing; machine learning; search and probabilistic reasoning; and their fusion in real, scientific, and industrial applications. Soft computing offers advantages in these fields by using a set of hybrid techniques in such a way that the major advantages of the candidate techniques are applied, and problem solving becomes more "human." Lofty Zadeh (1992) introduced soft computing as an emerging approach to computing that parallels the remarkable ability of the human mind to reason and learn in an environment of uncertainty and imprecision.

The world around us is imprecise, uncertain, and randomly changing. But we can cope with such an environment. The desire to mimic such coping into machines leads to the basic premises and the guiding principles of soft computing. Hard computing and symbolic problem solving deal with complete, precise, and full-truth-based systems. On the other hand, soft computing techniques exploit a given tolerance of imprecision, uncertainty, and reasoning to solve a particular problem.

In general, in soft computing, software is developed as a research solution for a specific problem or group of problems. At a high level, software can be regarded as a black box taking input data, performing some sort of processing, and returning output data. Uncertainty in one or more of these stages—in the input data, in the output data, or in the processing stage—is the primary concern.

A knowledge-based system imposes constraints on the processing involved. It must be understandable at some level by a human with expertise in the field addressed by the software. The program should be declarative in nature so that the processing can be understood without reference to the effect of a program on a computer. Naturally, it makes use of logic (or a logic-based approach) for knowledge representation; however, logic is too restrictive. Thus, the program needs to be augmented with a mechanism for handling uncertainty, such as soft computing constituents.

■ 9.2   CONSTITUENTS OF SOFT COMPUTING

In many cases, the problem can be solved in a better way by using a combination of different techniques rather than using one exclusively. As stated earlier, the techniques that can participate with each other are known as the constituents of soft computing. Figure 9.1 presents these constituents. Two or more technologies can be hybridized to get their advantages as shown in Application Layers 1 and 2.

As we have seen in the earlier chapters, the most popular intelligent techniques are *expert systems, neural networks, case-based reasoning, fuzzy-logic systems, and genetic algorithms.* The knowledge-based systems that make use of these techniques differ in the ways they *acquire, store, deal with,* and *apply* the knowledge. For instance, expert systems are useful when expertise is available and simple to extract from the human experts and various knowledge sources. Neural networks can learn and model complex relationships, and case-based reasoning helps to uncover the hidden knowledge in already solved problems and use that to solve new problems of a related type. Fuzzy systems deal with ambiguity and uncertainty in human decision making, while genetic algorithms are based on evolutionary principles and are suitable for applications involving searching best solutions and optimizing.

Each of these techniques has intrinsic limitations and strengths. Therefore, tackling problems with just one technique is not efficient. Combining

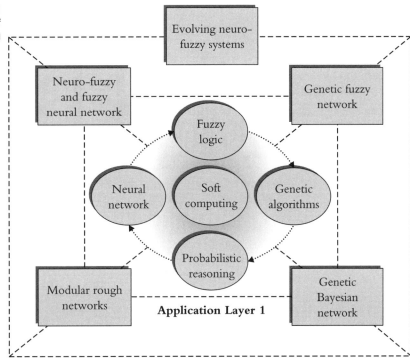

Application Layer 2

these techniques improves the total strengths and reduces weaknesses, thus helping to solve the overall problem in an efficient manner.

Table 9.1 describes the various fields and strengths they offer. Figure 9.1 illustrates the various constituents of soft computing.

Soft computing attempts to develop a hybrid intelligent system that offers the advantages of these techniques. Negnevitsky (2002) illustrated the individual strengths of the different constituents. Figure 9.2 demonstrates the rating of these strengths.

■ **Table 9.1 Strength of a Hybrid Soft Computing System**

Field	Strength Offered
Fuzzy logic	Approximate reasoning, impressions
Artificial neural network	Learning and implicit knowledge representation
Genetic algorithm	Natural evolution and optimization
Probabilistic reasoning	Uncertainty

FIGURE 9.2
Strength of constituents of soft computing

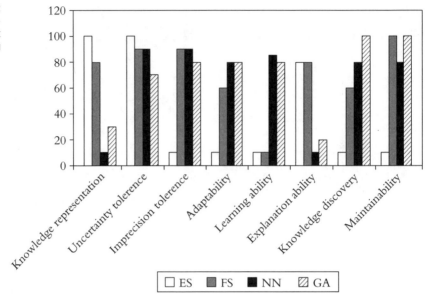

This classification scheme was suggested by McGarry and his colleagues to classify the hybrid systems into three major groups:

1. Unified hybrid systems: These systems have all processing activities implemented by neural network elements.

2. Transformational hybrid systems: In these systems, a symbolic representation is transferred into a neural one, and vice versa.

3. Modular hybrid systems: These hybrid systems are a composition of different modules/agents. Each module performs a given task using a specific technique.

Many hybrid systems are considered modular because they can be developed using existing commercial shells and do not comprise any changes to the conceptual operation of the previously mentioned techniques. Modular systems can be coupled in diverse configurations and can have different degrees of coupling and integration. In such systems, a control mechanism is required to coordinate the activities of the whole system. The complexity of modular hybrid systems depends on the number of modules and flow of control among them. The more complex the system, the more advanced the control mechanism must be. The complexity can further enhance systems that need multiple and concurrent access to the information as well as the modules.

■ 9.3   CHARACTERISTICS OF SOFT COMPUTING

The characteristics of soft computing systems are discussed in the following sections.

■ 9.3.1   Simulation of Human Expertise

Soft computing systems use fuzzy logic, which offers a flexible approach to dealing with the human-like classification of things into groups whose boundaries are vague, with the notion of fuzzy linguistic variables, such as large car, hot season, and rich person. Fuzzy inference also provides approximate reasoning and explanations.

Another important advantage that an artificial neural network offers is the ability to learn. These two main features—uncertainty handling through fuzzy logic and explanation/reasoning facility through fuzzy inference—make the soft computing paradigm more human-like in regard to problem solving and learning.

■ 9.3.2   Innovative Techniques

Soft computing systems provide innovative techniques for optimization, self-evolutionary solutions, machine learning, reasoning, and searching from various disciplines like genetic algorithms, neural networks, and fuzzy logic.

■ 9.3.3   Natural Evolution

The genetic algorithm, when hybridized within the soft computing system, helps in the natural evolution of a solution. An artificial neural network provides a means of self-learning and training itself, with or without training data. In this way, soft computing systems offer biologically inspired computing models for pattern recognition, nonlinear regression, and optimization.

■ 9.3.4   Model-Free Learning

Above all, the applications that cannot be solved by a specific model can be solved with a hybrid soft computing system. With the help of a genetic algorithm, for example, the model suitable for problem solving may itself evolve from the problem's characteristics. Similarly, just from the sample data sets given, the neural network computing system can develop a model that can solve a problem with the similar real data.

■ 9.3.5 Goal-Driven

Neural networks and genetic algorithms are goal-driven. That is, it is the solution that is important, not the path the network/algorighm follows. Similarly, the fitness function determines the strength of the solution and decides the existence of the solution as a candidate in the next generation.

■ 9.3.6 Extensive Numerical Computations

Soft computing systems rely on extensive computational algorithms offered by neural networks, fuzzy logic, and genetic algorithms, unlike traditional symbolic artificial intelligence (AI). This enhances the scope of the soft computing system beyond the typical AI applications. Examples where such extensive numerical computations are required include controlling signal processing and nonlinear regression.

■ 9.3.7 Dealing with Partial and Incomplete Information

Disciplines like fuzzy logic and artificial neural networks give soft computing systems the power to deal with incomplete, uncertain, and fuzzy information. Unlike a symbolic system, the soft computing system does not have to document knowledge specifically in the knowledge base.

■ 9.3.8 Fault Tolerance

Soft computing systems utilize an artificial neural network as one of its constituents. Neurons in an artificial neural network work in parallel fashion. Even if one of them were not working, the system would not fail. For example, in a large series of lights, even if a few bulbs are not working, the full pattern can be seen. So as with the fuzzy-logic-based system: If a rule is deleted, the fuzzy system still works. Thus, hybrid soft computing systems (e.g., neuro-fuzzy systems) are fault-tolerant in a true sense.

■ 9.4 NEURO-FUZZY SYSTEMS

The combination of fuzzy logic and neural networks constitutes a powerful means for designing a classical control scheme, analytical and diagnostic systems, image processing, forecasting and prediction systems, and so on, by harnessing the advantages of both technologies.

Fuzzy logic (FL) was formulated by Zadeh (1965) as multivalued logic between 0 and 1, and was developed as a response to the fact that humans routinely categorize items into classes that have no specific boundaries. FL is widely applicable, especially in system controls that are complex, uncertain, and cannot be modeled precisely even under various assumptions and approximations. FL systems provide a framework for approximate reasoning and allow qualitative knowledge about a problem to be implemented into systems using fuzzy rules. This makes the system more user-friendly, readable, easy to maintain, and effectively reduces the complexity by reducing the number of rules. The key benefit of FL is its ability to describe a system's behavior with simple "if-then" relationships, which leads to a simpler solution in less design time. However, the designer has to derive the "if-then" rules from the data sets manually, which requires a major effort with large data sets.

Knowledge stored in the form of generalized connections among artificial neural network (ANN) nodes makes ANN a structure with an implicit representation of knowledge. Since there is no explicit documentation of knowledge required for any ANN, it becomes difficult to provide an explanation and reasoning to justify the solution provided. In addition, the lack of an easy way to verify and optimize a neural net solution is another major limitation of the ANN technique.

ANN can learn from large data sets, but FL solutions are simple, easy to verify, and optimize. Clever combinations of these two technologies deliver the best of both worlds. Thus, the neuro-fuzzy system is a combination of ANN and FL technologies in which the ANN techniques are used to determine the parameters of FL systems. The basic objective of such a system is to improve one system by means of another. The more important aspect of the hybridization is that the system should always be interpretable in terms of fuzzy "if-then-else" rules (Nauck, 1995).

There are four major approaches to hybrid neuro-fuzzy computing, namely:

- Fuzzy neural network model
- Concurrent neuro-fuzzy model
- Cooperative neuro-fuzzy model
- Hybrid neuro-fuzzy model

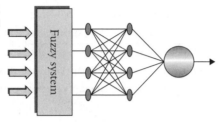

■ 9.4.1 Fuzzy Neural Networks

The fuzzy neural network is an example of enhancing the learning capabilities of a neural network with a fuzzy system. This approach is useful in creating a neural network that operates on fuzzy inputs and is utilized by Sajja (2006a, 2006b). It offers the dual advantages of FL and ANN technologies with utmost simplicity and ease of implementation in a distributed way. That is, both the FL and ANN agents can be developed and tested independently and integrated further. This approach is also useful in creating a neural network that operates on fuzzy inputs (Sajja, 2006a; Abraham, 2001; Halgamuge & Glesner, 1994), as shown in Figure 9.3.

■ 9.4.2 Cooperative Neuro-Fuzzy Model

The cooperative neuro-fuzzy model first uses the neural net to determine and enhance the parameters of the fuzzy system. Once parameters and rules are defined, the fuzzy system takes charge and solves problem more efficiently (Nauck, 1995; Abraham, 2001). This is demonstrated in Figure 9.4.

■ 9.4.3 Concurrent Neuro-Fuzzy Model

In the concurrent neuro-fuzzy model, ANN continuously assists the Fuzzy System (FS) to determine the required parameters, especially if the input variables of the controller cannot be measured directly. According to

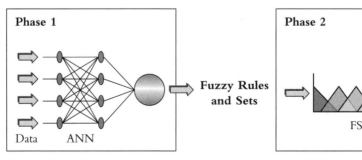

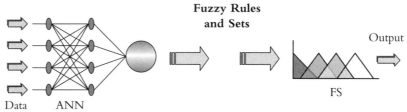

FIGURE 9.5
Concurrent neuro-fuzzy model

Abraham (2001), in some cases, the FS outputs might not be directly applicable to the process. In that case, ANN can act as a post-processor of FS outputs, as shown in Figure 9.5.

■ 9.4.4 Hybrid Neuro-Fuzzy Model

The hybrid neuro-fuzzy model supports a special neural network with fuzzy parameters. The neural network in a multilayer architecture can extract fuzzy rules. Alternatively, the fuzzy system can be implemented using a distributed approach in layers. The multipurpose models, such as ANFIS (Jang, 1992) NFECLASS (Nauck & Kruse, 1995), and Fuzzy Rule Net (Tschichold-Gurman, 1995), have been developed using this approach. Rutkowski and Cpalka (2003) designed a flexible neuro-fuzzy system using the same approach. Figure 9.6 shows the input and fuzzification layer, rule layer, output layer, and defuzzification layer in a general framework for a hybrid neuro-fuzzy model.

■ 9.5 GENETIC-FUZZY SYSTEMS

The genetic algorithm used in these systems helps in determining the optimum content of a fuzzy rule base or knowledge base of the fuzzy-logic-based system. Otherwise, it is comparatively difficult to optimize the content

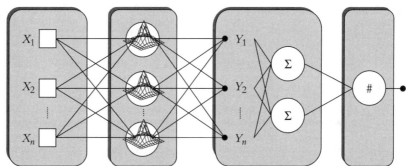

FIGURE 9.6
Hybrid neuro-fuzzy model

of the knowledge base. This is due to the nature of the knowledge: it is hard to characterize, voluminous, and continuously changing. Above all, the knowledge base is an unstructured entity encompassing the facts, rules, and heuristics in different ontologies.

Evolutionary algorithms have been successfully applied to many search, combinatorial, and optimization problems. They offer the advantages of parallel development and modification of multiple solutions in diverse areas of the solution space. Fuzzy-logic-based systems offer user-friendly ways to deal with imprecise or inexact knowledge for many real-world applications. Fuzzy and genetic systems are hybridized in the following ways:

- Genetic algorithms controlled by fuzzy logic, where genetic operators and functions use fuzzy linguistic terms
- Fuzzy evolutionary systems, where fuzzy rule sets are evolved
- Fuzzy controllers tuned by an evolutionary approach

■ 9.5.1 Genetic Algorithms Controlled by Fuzzy Logic

The fitness function of a genetic algorithm may employ fuzzy variables to determine suitable candidates within a population and the effective size of the population. Xu and Vukovich (1993) have categorized the size of populations as small, medium, and large. Another example is a fitness function to determine the "good-sized" project, which can be represented as a fuzzy decision tree, as shown in Figure 9.7.

■ 9.5.2 Fuzzy Evolutionary Systems

The parameters of fuzzy systems are also tuned by the genetic systems to get naturally selected ideal parameters. A fuzzy-logic-based system has the char-

■ FIGURE 9.7
Fuzzy decision tree for project size

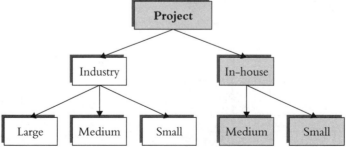

acteristic of representing human knowledge or experiences as fuzzy rules. However, in most of the existing systems, shapes and internal parameters of membership functions and fuzzy rules are determined and tuned through trial and error by operators. A genetic algorithm helps in designing, optimizing, and tuning the parameters of the fuzzy system and increases its effectiveness. Figure 9.8 shows an example of an iterative hybrid system in which the fuzzy structure is built and the parameters are constructed and tuned by the genetic learning algorithm. The working of the system is comprised of two fundamental phases based on cross-validation as follows:

Phase 1: Determination of optimum parameters using genetic learning process: learning from training and fitness evaluation with validation data

Phase 2: Inference with testing data using optimum model parameters

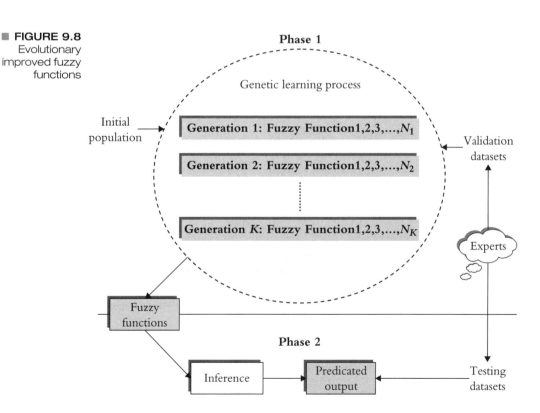

FIGURE 9.8
Evolutionary improved fuzzy functions

The simplest way of encoding the rules is to use a binary encoding strategy, which is a bi-state strategy and easy for a machine to deal with. The condition and action parts are encoded as a group of genes using bits of zeros and ones. The whole group together is known as a chromosome. There may be number of conditions in the condition part of a rule. Every variable within the condition part is further divided into three parts: the weight of the condition variable used, the operator, and the value. The action part represents the binary representation of a related action. It can be an encoded version of a reference/path to the file containing an action sequence. Weight is the real value between [0, 1] to identify the fuzzy existence of the variable in the rule. Value 0 of a weight of the given variable indicates the absence/insignificance of the variable in the rule. Sometimes a threshold value of weight is used to determine the significance of the condition variable. The operator value is an index value to a list of relation operators stored in memory to determine the operator that goes with the condition variable and values. This encoding strategy is shown in Figure 9.9.

■ 9.5.3 Evolving Knowledge Bases and Rule Sets

Besides the creation of new lower-level rules, one may want to generate populations considering full-fledged knowledge bases, among which the "most suitable" knowledge base can be considered. Figure 9.10 presents the generic architecture of the fuzzy system based on the Mamdani model, using an evolutionary approach to evolve the knowledge base and rule set.

■ **FIGURE 9.9**
Encoding chromosomes

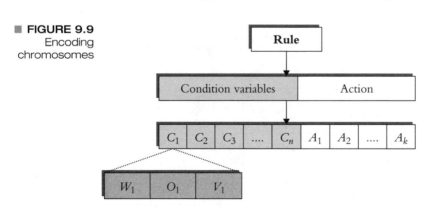

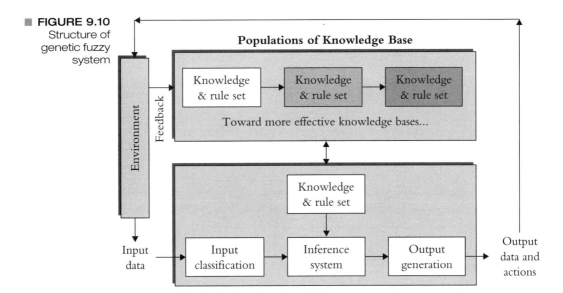

Populations of Knowledge Base

Knowledge & rule set

Knowledge & rule set

Knowledge & rule set

Toward more effective knowledge bases...

Environment

Feedback

Knowledge & rule set

Input data

Input classification

Inference system

Output generation

Output data and actions

■ 9.6 NEURO-GENETIC SYSTEMS

Neuro-genetic systems are able to learn and evolve simultaneously. The neural network constituent enables the system to store knowledge in the connections and evolve its structure. Such connectionist-based systems evolve their structure and functionality in a continuous, self-organized, online, adaptive, and interactive way based on the input training data. Generally, these systems facilitate dealing with different types of knowledge, such as memory-based, statistical, and symbolic. ANN and genetic algorithm (GA) combinations can be used in the following ways:

- Neural networks generated by genetic algorithms, where network weights or the structure naturally evolve.
- Neural networks tuned by genetic algorithms, where genetic algorithm operations and functions encompass neural network characteristics like learning.
- Collaborative and hybrid neural networks and genetic programming, where genetic trees and local neural networks act as agents, performing tasks in collaboration with one another.

Kitano (1990) discusses the studies on neural network training using genetic algorithms. Figure 9.11 illustrates the cost improvement by using ANN and GA hybridization.

FIGURE 9.11
Genetic and
connectionist
hybridization

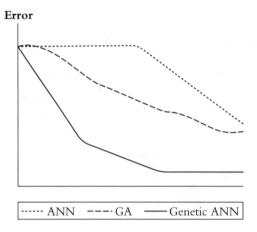

Neuro-evolution (NE) is the application of a genetic algorithm to evolve one or more combinations of the following parameters of the neural network: connection weights, network topologies, and learning rules. The two most important aspects of NE are the choice of suitable genetic representation, which will encode weights and topologies, and the types of genetic operators used to evolve these representations.

There are three challenges with NE methods:

1. *Premature convergence*: Premature convergence is a common problem that occurs when the population of chromosomes reaches a generation where offspring can no longer improve on their parents, resulting in a suboptimal solution. It is related to population diversity, where the decrease in population diversity is considered the primary reason for premature convergence. Therefore, a homogeneous population—that is, one with little diversity—is the main reason for premature convergence.

2. *Competing conventions*: The competing conventions problem, also known as the permutation problem, is caused by many-to-one mapping from the representation genotype to the actual ANN phenotype. Any permutation of the hidden nodes will produce a functionally equivalent ANN with different chromosome representation. When these chromosomes are crossed over, it will likely result in damaged offspring. To illustrate the problem, consider the following example:

Parent 1: A B | C D
Parent 2: C D | A B
Offspring: A B A B or C D C D

The letters A, B, C, and D represent hidden neurons with specific functions. When we cross over the parents, the resulting offspring will be missing some of the functionality present in the parents. There are some proposed solutions to the competing convention problem. However, these solutions generally involve simplifying assumptions about the topology and layers of the networks, and are computationally expensive; hence, they cannot be applied to the topology-evolving neural network.

3. *Code bloat*: Code bloat is a problem in NE methods that results from a genome increasing in size without a corresponding increase in fitness. Most of the encoding strategies incorporate the network size in the evaluation function to favor a smaller network.

■ 9.6.1   Neural Network Weight Training

As stated earlier, artificial neural network parameters can be naturally evaluated for fast and efficient training of the network and to enhance learning. Sajja (2007) introduced a neural network that utilizes "naturally selected" parameters as inputs and weights of the neural network instead of random selection. Figure 9.12 shows the broad paradigm used in the application (Sajja, 2007).

An evolutionary algorithm can be used to train the weights of the neural network on a fixed network topology. A genetic algorithm is used by Seiffert (2001) to train a neural network to solve the XOR problem. A population of 50 neural networks with a fixed topology of two inputs, one output, and a two-node hidden layer is trained up to 500 iterations, or a mean network error of 0.01 is achieved over all four training patterns. Two-point uniform

■ FIGURE 9.12
Structure of the neuro-genetic system

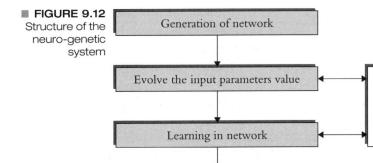

■ **FIGURE 9.13**
Evolving weights
for neural network

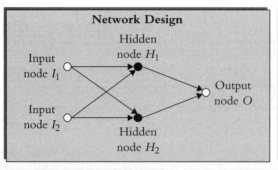

Network Design

Training Data

I_1	I_1	O
0	0	0
0	1	1
1	0	1
1	1	0

Encoding of Weights

I_1H_1	I_1H_2	I_2H_1	I_2H_2	H_1O	H_2O

crossover with a probability of 0.8 and Gaussian mutation with mean of 0 and a standard deviation of 1.0, with a probability of 0.1, are the operators employed with an elitism of 1. The results are compared to back propagation on the same network topology. Both approaches found solutions easily, with the genetic algorithm being faster.

Figure 9.13 shows the mapping of the weights of the neural network from the problem space (top side) into a chromosome by means of a neural network. Including the bias, six weights are coded into the linear chromosome. The order of weights within the chromosome is chosen arbitrarily, but must be left unchanged while the network is trained.

■ 9.6.2   Evolving Neural Nets

Neural network structures can evolve through the process of natural selection. The EPNet algorithm (Yao & Yong, 1997) is such a hybrid algorithm used to evolve feed-forward artificial neural networks. It combines the architectural evolution of a neural network with its weight learning. Two mutation operators used to modify ANN weights in EPNet are modified back propagation (MBP) and simulated annealing algorithm. Here, the genetic algorithm is used to evolve neural network node density, connectivity, and weights.

The EPNet algorithm is comprised of the following steps (Yao & Yong, 1997):

Step 1: Generate an initial population of M networks at random. The number of hidden nodes and the initial connection density for each network are uniformly generated at random within certain ranges. The random initial weights are uniformly distributed within a small range.

Step 2: Partially train each network in the population on the training set for a certain number of epochs (may be determined by users, for example, k_0) using a variant of back propagation (modified back propagation), with adaptive learning rates. The error value E of each network on the validation set is checked after partial training. The error E is expected to be significantly reduced to avoid trapping the network into the local minimum. The network is marked with "success" if error reduction is according to expectations.

Step 3: Rank the networks in the population according to their error values, from best to worst.

Step 4: If the best network found is acceptable, or if the maximum number of generations has been reached, stop the evolutionary process and go to Step 11; otherwise, continue.

Step 5: Use rank-based selection to choose one parent network from the population. If it is marked with "success," go to Step 6; otherwise, go to Step 7.

Step 6: Partially train the parent network for K_1 epochs using the MBP to obtain an offspring (child) network, and mark it in the same way as in Step 2, where K_1 is a user-specified parameter. Replace the parent network with the offspring in the current population, and go to Step 3.

Step 7: Train the parent network with a simulated annealing (SA) algorithm to obtain an offspring network. If the SA algorithm reduces the error E by the following equation of the parent network significantly, mark the offspring with "success," replace its parent with it in the current population, and then go to Step 3. Otherwise, discard this offspring and continue to the next step.

$$E = 100 \frac{O_{max} - O_{min}}{Tn} \sum_{t=1}^{T} \sum_{t=1}^{n} \left(Y_i(t) - Z_i(t) \right)^2$$

where O_{max} and O_{min} are the maximum and minimum of output values, n is the number of output nodes, and $Y_i(t)$ and $Z_i(t)$ are the actual and expected outputs of node i for pattern t.

Step 8:   First, decide the number of hidden nodes N_{hidden} to be deleted by generating a uniformly distributed random number between 1 and a user-specified maximum number. N_{hidden} is normally quite small in the experiments—not more than three in most cases. Then delete N_{hidden} hidden nodes from the parent network uniformly at random. Partially train the pruned network by the MBP to obtain an offspring network. If the offspring is better than the worst network in the current population, replace the worst with the offspring and go to Step 3. Otherwise, discard the offspring and continue to the next step.

Step 9:   Calculate the approximate importance of each connection in the parent network. Decide the number of connections to be deleted in the same way as described in Step 8. Delete the connections from the parent network according to the calculated importance. Partially train the pruned network by the MBP to obtain an offspring network. If the offspring network is better than the worst network in the current population, replace the worst with the offspring and go to Step 3. Otherwise, discard this offspring and continue to Step 10.

Step 10:   Decide the number of connections and nodes to be added. Calculate the approximate importance of each virtual connection with zero weight. Randomly add the connections to the parent network to obtain Offspring 1 according to their importance. The addition of each node is implemented by splitting a randomly selected hidden node in the parent network. The network after node additions is Offspring 2. Partially train Offspring 1 and Offspring 2 by the MBP. Replace the worst network in the current population by the better of the two offspring and go to Step 3.

Step 11:   After the evolutionary process, train the best network further on the combined training and validation set using MBP until it "converges" (there is no further significant improvement in the accuracy after a certain number of epochs/cycles). A direct encoding scheme is used in EPNet to represent ANN architectures and connection weights, including biases. The sigmoid transfer function can be utilized here. The selection mechanism is rank-based, with high-fitness individuals having a higher probability of selection.

The EPNet was terminated after the maximum number of generations was reached or if the average error of the population had not decreased by more than a threshold value after G_0 consecutive generations. The back-propagation algorithm is modified to include a heuristic of the developer's choice to adjust the learning rate of each ANN. The learning rate is adjusted by checking the error E after every k epochs. If the error decreases, the learning rate is increased; otherwise, the learning rate is decreased. The simulated annealing algorithm is applied when the MBP algorithm fails to decrease the error in the ANN. If simulated annealing also fails to decrease the error, architectural mutations will be attempted.

■ 9.7   GENETIC-FUZZY-NEURAL NETWORKS

The genetic-fuzzy-neural network hybridization offers the ultimate advantages of natural evolution, fuzziness, and an artificial neural network; however, such hybridization is complicated and application-specific.

Typically, genetic-fuzzy-neural networks are the fuzzy neural networks working on the back-propagation method with implicit learning and explicit representation of knowledge with the help of fuzzy rules and/or a user interface achieved via fuzziness. Such systems are augmented with the evolutionary learning method, which can be used to evolve weights or structures/topologies of the network.

Genetic-fuzzy-neural networks incorporate fuzzy numbers as weights, perform fuzzy operations in the neurons of the network, and/or use fuzzy neurons to represent membership functions. In addition, the learning process uses GAs to obtain the weights of the neural network, adapt the transfer functions of the nodes, and/or adapt the topology of the network.

See and Openshaw (1999) have applied soft computing approaches for river-level forecasting. A methodology is outlined in which the forecasting data set is split into subsets before training with a series of neural networks. These networks are then recombined via a rule-based fuzzy-logic model that has been optimized using a genetic algorithm. The overall results indicate that this methodology may provide a well-performing, low-cost solution, which may be readily integrated into existing operational flood forecasting and warning systems.

Figure 9.14 illustrates the working methodology of the neuro-fuzzy-genetic system employed for water-level forecasting.

In this methodology, a special type of neural network is employed, known as a self-organizing map (SOM). It is another type of artificial neural network developed by Kohonen (1984), which differs from the MLP in both the configuration of the neurons and in the training algorithm. The neurons in a SOM are usually arranged in a two-dimensional grid, where each neuron has an associated vector of weights that corresponds to the input variables. The weights are first initialized randomly. Training of the network consists of selecting a data case, determining the neuron that is the closest in Euclidean distance (or another measure of similarity), and updating the winning neuron and those within a certain neighborhood around the winner. This process is repeated over several iterations until a stopping condition

■ **FIGURE 9.14**
Soft computing methodology for water level forecasting

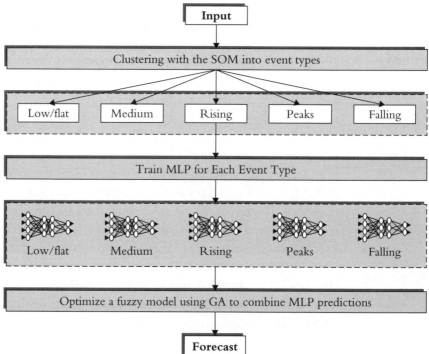

is reached. When training is completed, the weight vectors associated with each neuron define the partitioning of the multidimensional data.

■ 9.8 CHAOS THEORY

Chaos originates from the Greek and more often refers to unpredictability. The roots of chaos theory date back to around 1900, in the works of Henri Poincaré on the problem of the motion of three objects in mutual gravitational attraction, the so-called three-body problem. Poincaré established that there can be orbits which are nonperiodic, and still not forever increasing or approaching a fixed point. Later studies, also on the topic of nonlinear differential equations, were carried out by G. D. Birkhoff, A. N. Kolmogorov, M. L. Cartwright, J. E. Littlewood, and Stephen Smale (Strogatz, 1994).

A nonlinear dynamic system can show one or more types of behavior such as everlastingly at rest, everlastingly expanding, periodic motion, quasi-periodic motion, and chaotic motion. The type of behavior a system may demonstrate depends on the initial state of the system and the values of its parameters. The complex type of behavior to characterize and predict is chaotic motion for which the theory is named.

Chaos is a phenomenon that has deterministic underlying rules behind an irregular appearance. So far, no one has given a standard accepted definition of chaos. However, the usual features are:

- It has deterministic rather than probabilistic fundamental rules, which every upcoming state of the system must follow.
- It has sensitive dependence on initial conditions.
- The fundamental rules are nonlinear.
- Minor changes in the initial state of chaotic systems can lead to thoroughly different behavior in the final state.
- The behavior of the system shows sustained irregularity. Thus, long-term prediction is nearly impossible in most of the cases.
- The transition to chaos is preceded by infinite levels of bifurcation.

■ 9.8.1 Basic Constructs

There are six basic constructs in connection with chaos theory—namely, strange attractors, fractals, self-similarity, bifurcation, self-organization, and unpredictability.

In general, there are two types of equilibrium solutions in a dynamic system, namely, stable and unstable. An equilibrium solution is stable if any solution in close proximity of the equilibrium solution gets nearer and nearer to the equilibrium solution as time advances. This stable equilibrium solution is also known as an *attractor* in graphical context. Though there are very simple attractors, such as points and circle-like curves called limit cycles, chaotic motion gives rise to what are called *strange attractors*. *Strange* or *chaotic attractors* are focal points for patterns generated by dynamic systems. Their basins of attraction are the areas containing those patterns within their boundaries. Chaotic attractors and their basins are similar to homeostatic points in general systems theory. We can illustrate the concept of attractors by an example. Consider an open barrel drain when the water is being run fast enough to fill the barrel. Suppose a ping-pong ball is dropped in the barrel. It will immediately continue to move in a quasi-predictable manner. It is predictable in the sense that it will not be able to escape the barrel and so its general location is well established (at least until the barrel is filled to overflowing); quasi in the sense that how near to or how far from the drain hole (strange attractor) it will be at any time cannot be readily foreseen, especially for times in the distant future. Strange or chaotic attractors and basins of attraction capture the realism—consistencies and vagaries—of human behavior patterns. The Lorenz attractor (Lorenz, 1963) is perhaps one of the most well-known chaotic system diagrams, possibly because not only was it one of the first, but it is one of the most complex and as such gives rise to a very remarkable pattern which looks like the wings of a butterfly.

Fractal boundaries are the irregular lines of demarcation between separate units. Actually, fractals are geometric objects of static images, whereas chaos is a dynamic system in which the motion of a point is our interest. Fractal boundaries and their measure—dimensions—convey in a systematic manner that veracity is often not as clear as we picture it. Unlike the dimensions with which we usually deal, fractal boundaries can have fractional dimensions. Consider an example of a seashore. From a far distance, the edges may look like continuous, curved lines constituted of long, fairly smooth segments. Walking the seashore, however, gives quite a distinct impression. At each level, what becomes apparent is that all the long, smooth segments are actually made up of many shorter convoluted pieces. Measuring the overall length of the seashore will vary with the "fineness" and applicability of the measuring instrument.

A fractal is an object that displays self-similarity. Fractals are related to chaos because they are complex systems that have definite properties. Fractals suggest two very important concepts. First, what you see depends largely on your perspective. Second, accuracy of measurement often depends on the definition of the process. Fractal boundaries and dimensions capture the fuzzy, gray areas of behavior patterns.

Self-similarity (and self-affinity) denotes the tendency for processes and other phenomena to evidence recurring patterns. The constructs of self-similarity and self-affinity capture the sense that patterns seem to be part of nature. Patterns tend to repeat themselves, not exactly, not perfectly, but still enough to be recognizable. Similarities, not only of boundaries but of patterns in general, have proved fascinating, valuable, and enlightening. Consider a case of parenting, both on a reproductive and a behavioral level. We tend to resemble our parents genetically, physically, and behaviorally. Behavior patterns have a tendency to repeat themselves, though not exactly.

Bifurcation means to divide into two branches. It refers to an unexpected, qualitatively different appearance in the solution of a nonlinear dynamic system as a parameter is varied. When a process or pattern bifurcates, complexity is added to a system, which means adding strange attractors. A bifurcation cascade is when bifurcations happen at such a rate that no discernable patterns are in evidence. After a time, many natural processes tend to bifurcate as the type of process changes. Then, after another period of stability, another bifurcation takes place. As long as the bifurcations stay within limits or happen at long enough intervals so that the system's resources can accommodate the new conditions slowly, stability can be maintained. However, if either of these conditions is violated, bifurcation cascade occurs. The system goes out of control—that is, it becomes chaotic.

While such a state may seem catastrophic, it need not be. At that disastrous point, the system must reorganize into a different, though perhaps similar, pattern—essentially creating a new strange attractor. Thus, these "confused" states can serve as opportunities for creative, functional change. Consider an instance of organizational growth. If the tasks demanded of an organization exceed its capacity to adjust, overload causes the system to become chaotic.

Self-organization is the inherent tendency for dynamic systems in a chaotic state to form a new coherent pattern. An important characteristic of chaotic systems is their inherent power to reorganize based only on the interactions of their components. Self-organization establishes new patterns of behavior, particularly after chaos has been reached, accommodating the new demands on the system. The example of an organization that has undergone bifurcation cascade demonstrates this attribute.

Chaotic systems are unpredictable. *Unpredictability* is the inability to state with certainty the next state of a system given the knowledge of its present state. One aspect of unpredictability, defined from a chaos theory perspective, is similar in a sense to that conveyed by Heisenberg's uncertainty principle—that is, everything about a system cannot be known with absolute certainty.

■ 9.8.2 Hybridization

When we can model a chaotic system, it can be used to analyze the time series of the system. This is useful in making the design of the system better. For example, machine operations can be gently analyzed to detect near-future failure in order to avoid an expensive repair process. There are many potential application domains, such as ecology, cardiology, financial markets, economy, and weather.

It is also possible to employ neural networks, fuzzy logic, and genetic algorithms together with chaotic systems. This is helpful to balance each other's strengths.

Complex tasks, such as speech production and video and audio pattern recognition, are difficult to achieve by manufactured systems. Chaotic systems, however, are capable of performing such tasks. Neural networks are modeled on the human brain, which displays chaotic behavior. Thus, integrating chaos with a neural network can be effective in performing complicated tasks.

The chaotic modeling of genetic algorithms can be considered a promising exercise of chaos as a means to analyze genetic algorithms. Conversely, genetic algorithms can be a helpful in expressing a complex chaotic system where a standard mathematical model is difficult. Similarly, fuzzy logic may be employed to describe a complex chaotic dynamic system.

Here are some potential application areas of chaotic systems:

- Economic forecasting, financial analysis, and market predictions
- Switching of packets in computer networks
- Cardiology—namely, prediction and control of heart activity
- Information compression and storage

■ 9.9 ROUGH SET THEORY

Rough set theory is a relatively recent development in the field of artificial intelligence. The notion of rough sets was introduced by Zdislaw Pawlak in his seminal paper (Pawlak, 1982). This theory is useful for discovering relationships in data and to reason about incomplete data. It is a formal theory derived from basic research on logical properties of information systems. Rough sets are built on ordinary sets. Obviously, rough sets and fuzzy sets are complementary generalizations of classical sets. The approximation spaces of rough set theory are sets with multiple memberships, while fuzzy sets are concerned with partial memberships. The speedy progress of the rough set approach provides a vital basis for soft computing.

In order to understand and use raw data, we derive essential knowledge about it. This knowledge can be represented in various forms, such as rules, algorithms, and equations. However, it is not always essential to derive conclusions from whole data. This means that only *rough* data or *coarse* data may be enough. Sometimes, such approximate rough data may be better than detailed data. The rough set theory presents a novel approach for reasoning from imprecise and ambiguous data.

The ultimate application domains of rough sets have been in symbolic approaches. For instance, databases, knowledge-based systems, machine learning, and data analysis. The rough set theory has also shown application in medicine, engineering, and operations research. The theory can efficiently perform knowledge acquisition and machine learning. Rough set theory has been implemented successfully in knowledge-based systems in medicine and industry.

The important merit of rough set theory in data analysis is that it does not need any preliminary or additional information, such as probabilities in statistics or basic probability assignments in Dempster-Shafer theory, grade of membership, or the value of possibilities in fuzzy set theory.

■ 9.9.1 Pawlak's Information System

This information system represents what is called *instance space* when learning from examples. The concept of a rough set is a mathematical tool to deal with uncertain and imprecise data.

Definition 9.1

A *relationship* consists of maps, $t: A \dashrightarrow V = \cup V_a s$, where $t(a) \in V_a$, $A = \{a, b, \ldots.\}$ is a set of attributes, V_a = attribute domains. A *relational data model* consists of the following:

- a collection of relationships
- a set of constraints (e.g., keys, functional dependence)
- a set of relational operators

Two such models are equivalent if and only if the set of relationships, constraints, and operators can be expressed by the other set of relationships, constraints, and operators using relational algebra. For any two equivalent models, their set of all view instances is the same at all times.

The difference between the entity-attribute database and the relational database is that the entities of the information system do not need to be distinguished by their attributes or by their relationship to entities of another type. In the information system, entities are called objects. The main goal of the information system is the basis for knowledge acquisition: to help discover new rules from examples. In the 1970s, Pawlak and his colleagues studied logical properties of information systems, which are instances of relational databases.

Definition 9.2

The *Pawlak information system* consists of the following:

- $U = \{x, y, \ldots.\}$ is a set of entities of S
- $A = \{a, b, \ldots.\}$ is a set of attributes
- V_a = attribute domain; V = union of all $V_a s$

For each x, there is a map:

$$x: A \dashrightarrow V; x(a) \in Va$$

Note that the two distinct x's may define the same map, which is not allowed in the relational model.

Definition 9.3

An information system is called a *decision table* if $A = CUD$ and $C \cap D = \phi$, where C is conditional attributes and D is decision attributes.

Let B be a nonempty subset of A. B induces an equivalence relation, denoted by $IND(B)$, on U:

$$x \cong y \ (\text{mod } B) \text{ if } x(b) = y(b) \text{ for } \forall \, b \in B$$

The partition induced by B is called a *classification* of U created by B. The ordered pair $A = (U,B)$ is called an *approximation space*. Conceptually, let R be a collection of equivalence relations on U; then the pair (U,R) is called the *Pawlak knowledge base*.

■ 9.9.2 Rough Sets

The rough set theory (Pawlak, 1991) is not an alternative to classical set theory, as is fuzzy set theory, but rather is embedded in it. Rough set theory can be viewed as a specific implementation of Frege's idea of vagueness. This means that imprecision in this approach is expressed by a boundary region of a set and not by a partial membership, as in fuzzy set theory.

The rough set concept can be defined by means of topological operations, *interior* and *closure*, called *approximations.*

Suppose we are given a set of objects U, called the *universe,* and an indiscernibility relationship $R \subseteq U \times U$, representing our lack of knowledge about elements of U. For the sake of simplicity, we assume that R is an equivalence relationship. Let X be a subset of U. We want to characterize the set X with respect to R. To this end, we will need the basic concepts of rough set theory, given as follows:

- The *lower approximation* of a set X with respect to R is the set of all objects, which can be for *certain* classified as X with respect to R (are *certainly* X with respect to R).
- The *upper approximation* of a set X with respect to R is the set of all objects that can be *possibly* classified as X with respect to R (are *possibly* X in view of R).
- The *boundary region* of a set X with respect to R is the set of all objects that can be classified neither as X nor as not-X with respect to R.

Let us now define rough sets.

Definition 9.4

1. Set X is *crisp* (exact with respect to R) if the boundary region of X is empty.
2. Set X is *rough* (inexact with respect to R) if the boundary region of X is nonempty.

Thus, a set is *rough* (imprecise) if it has a nonempty boundary region; otherwise, the set is *crisp* (precise).

This is the idea of vagueness proposed by Frege. However, the approximations and the boundary region can be defined more precisely. In order to do this, we need some additional notation. The equivalence class of R determined by element x will be denoted by $R(x)$. The indiscernibility relationship, in certain a sense, describes our lack of knowledge about the universe. Equivalence classes of the indiscernibility relationship, called *granules* generated by R, represent the elementary portion of knowledge we are able to perceive due to R. Thus, in light of the indiscernibility relationship, in general, we are able to observe individual objects, but we are forced to reason only about the accessible granules of knowledge.

Formal definitions of approximations and the boundary region are as follows:

Definition 9.5

1. *R-lower approximation* of X

$$R_*(x) = \bigcup_{x \in U} \left\{ R(x) : R(x) \subseteq X \right\}$$

2. *R-upper approximation* of X

$$R^*(x) = \bigcup_{x \in U} \left\{ R(x) : R(x) \cap X \neq \varnothing \right\}$$

3. *R-boundary region* of X

$$RN_R(X) = R^*(X) - R_*(X)$$

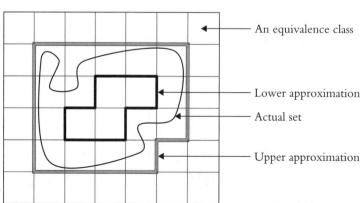

■ **FIGURE 9.15**
The rough set

An equivalence class

Lower approximation

Actual set

Upper approximation

The definition of a rough set is illustrated in Figure 9.15 (Akerkar & Lingras, 2008).

■ 9.9.3   Rough Logic

Rough set theory is based on a known equivalence relation. But the equivalence relations are mostly unknown in applications. Therefore, the concept of rough logic based on the notions of lower and upper approximations without explicit equivalence relation was introduced. Rough logic (Lin, 1996) is an S_5 modal logic because the language structure is the same. The model theory of rough logic has a similar possible-world model structure as S_5, but is different in its semantics.

A *relational structure* on E is a four-tuple:

$$E = (E, N, R, F)$$

where

- E is a set of entities $\{e, e1, ...\}$, the domain of objects
- N is a set of distinguished entities, the domain of constants
- R is a set of relationships
- F is a set of partial functions

We have used the same notation for the set of entities and the relational structure. The relational structure will be referred to as the ideal universe or ideal world. We assume that there is an equivalence relationship of R on E, and hence, two rough operators: the upper approximation (denoted by H) and the lower approximation (denoted by L).

Let $P = \{Hi, i = 1, 2, ...\}$ be the partition. Let W_h, $h > 0$ be a representative set that consists of one representative from each H_i:

$$W_h = \{e \mid \text{a unique } e \in Hi, i = 1, 2, ...\}$$

Each W_h inherits a relational structure from E:

$$W_h = (W_h, N_h, R_h, F_h)$$

1. $N_h = N \cap W_h = N$
2. R_h is a set of relationships restricted to W_h
3. F_h is a set of partial functions restricted to W_h (if any function values are outside of W_h, they are undefined). W_h is called a possible world.

The pair $W_0 = (E, P)$ is an approximation space of E. Its relational structure is induced from E.

$$W_0 = (W_0, N, R, G)$$

W_0 is called an approximation world.

For any given two observable worlds, W_h, W_k, we can define a binary relationships as follows: For each element x in W_h, x belongs to at least one of the R-elementary sets, say, H_i, In this H_i, there is a unique y in W_k. The set of such pairs (x, y) forms a binary (equivalence) relationship that relates the two possible worlds.

■ 9.9.4   Rough Models

A rough model (Lin, 1996) is a six-tuple

$$RM = (E, N, R, F, RO, W)$$

where:

1. E is a set of entities with a partition
2. N is a set of distinguished entities
3. R is a set of relationships
4. F is a set of partial functions
5. RO is a set of rough operators induced from the partition—that is, $RO = \{H\}$; (H = upper approximation)
6. W is a set of possible worlds $W_h = (W_h, N_h, R_h, F_h)$

■ 9.9.5   Rough-Set-Based Systems

We now present a concise survey of current rough-set-based systems. The development of an efficient knowledge-based system (KBS) involves the development of an efficient knowledge base that must be complete, coherent, and nonredundant. Knowledge acquisition is one of the major bottlenecks in the stage of knowledge base development. Usually, for each application domain, there are several sources of knowledge (human experts; the specialized literature, which includes textbooks, books, reviews, collections of data during the run of similar systems, etc.). In order to make knowledge extraction as correct as possible, different techniques could be applied. Among these techniques, data mining techniques and more general knowledge-discovery techniques became the most used in recent years. The following rough-set-based tools play a prominent role in such a context:

- *ROSETTA* (http://www.lcb.uu.se/tools/rosetta/) is a freely distributed toolkit for analyzing tabular data within the framework of rough set theory. It consists of a computational kernel and a graphical user interface (GUI) front end. Downloadable versions for both the Windows and Linux operating systems are available. The software supports the complete data mining process, from data preprocessing (including handling incomplete data), data discretization, and generating reduct sets that contain essential attributes for the given data set, to classification, rule generation, and cross-validation evaluation. Some discretization and reduct-generation packages are from the RSES library.
- *RSES* stands for Rough Set Exploration System (http://alfa.mimuw.edu. pl/~rses/). There are downloadable versions for both the Windows and Linux operating systems. It is still maintained and being developed. The system supports data preprocessing, handling incomplete data, data decomposition, reduct generation, classification, and cross-validations.
- *ROSE* stands for Rough Sets Data Explorer (http://www.springerlink. com/content/fkh4g1yr9mxg42ag/). This software is designed to process data with large boundary regions. It supports data preprocessing, data discretization, handling missing values, core and reduct generation, classifications, and rule generation, as well as evaluations. This software provides not only the classical rough set model, but also the variable precision model.
- *Rough Enough* is a software system developed by Anders Torvill Bjorvand. The present version was developed under the 4GL DBMS Paradox for Windows. The newest version is available for download at http://www. trolldata.no/renough/
- *Rough Analysis* is List Processing (LISP) software by Enrique Alvarez (http:// www.lsi.upc.es/~ealvarez/rough.html). This is a simple LISP code for analyzing data within the framework of rough set theory. It calculates relative reducts and partial dependency between two classifications. With this code, you are not allowed to search reducts of one classification with more than eight features because it applies an exhaustive search method. However, you can use some heuristics.

- LERS stands for Learning from Examples based on Rough Sets (http://citeseerx.ist.psu.edu/showciting;jsessionid=F38C13EFEB056A9FA3C6E 8148BC329CA?cid=2038213). It is not publicly available. The system was designed especially to process missing values of attributes and inconsistency in the data set. Certain rules and possible rules are extracted based on the lower and upper approximations.

Numerous types of problems can be addressed with rough set theory. During the last few years, this formalism has been approached as a tool used in connection with many different areas of research. The relationships between rough set theory and the Dempster-Shafer theory and between rough sets and fuzzy sets have been investigated. The basic difference between the Dempster-Shafer theory and rough set theory is that the former uses belief functions, whereas the latter makes use of relationships among attributes such as the lower and upper approximation sets.

Rough set theory has also provided the necessary formalism and ideas for the development of some propositional machine learning systems. It has also been used for, among other things, knowledge representation, data mining, dealing with imperfect data, reducing knowledge representation, and analyzing attribute dependencies. Such types of operations lead to the approximation domains, such as knowledge-based systems and application areas of various engineering branches. The notions of rough relationships and rough functions are based on rough set theory and can be applied as a theoretical basis for rough controllers.

■ 9.10   APPLICATIONS OF SOFT COMPUTING

As we have discussed in this chapter, soft computing is the branch of computer science that allows uncertainty, imprecision, and partial truth to process. Soft computing systems can be applied to problems that are difficult to solve with the existing models. In many situations, one solution modeling strategy may not completely solve the problem, specifically when the nature of the problem is interdisciplinary and requires help from multiple solution paradigms. Among the various soft computing fields, neural networks, fuzzy systems, and genetic algorithms are most popular in today's scientific research. In particular, these models support powerful properties and distinct advantages such as: neural networks facilitate a system to learn, fuzzy logic integrates expert knowledge into a system with ease, and genetic algorithms permit a system to be self-optimizing. Therefore, one can build powerful hybrid systems by combining them to solve complex problems. The *rough sets theory* has recently emerged as another major scientific tool for managing uncertainty that arises from granularity in the domain of discourse. Hybridizations for rule generation, which utilize the characteristics of rough sets, include the *rough-neuro, rough-neuro-fuzzy, rough-neuro-genetic,* and also *rough-neuro-fuzzy-genetic* approaches. The key tasks of rough sets here is to manage uncertainty and extract domain knowledge.

Here are some applications where soft computing can be applied:

- Image processing and data compression
- Automotive systems and manufacturing
- Soft computing to power systems and process control
- Speech and vision recognition (classification) systems
- Optimizing software projects, risk profile analysis
- Multicriteria optimization
- Time series forecasting in finance, weather, and so on
- Customer targeting, job sequencing, scheduling
- Foreign exchange trading, trading surveillance, investor classification, and so on
- Decision-support systems and knowledge-based diagnosis
- Fuzzy cluster analysis, fuzzy associative memory, and fuzzy filtered neural networks
- Evolving neural networks, recurrent networks
- Knowledge refinement, data mining, and ontology mapping
- Process control, such as nonlinear and multivariable control of chemical plants, power stations, and missiles
- Rule generation and fuzzy system development through evolution
- Neural network that learns and generates the FS through training sets
- Machine-learning applications
- Financial forecasting, such as credit worthiness, etc. Data mining, data segmentation, and segmentation of customer data
- Tree grammars and tree automata
- Social sciences, behavioral sciences, biology, and medicine

In some areas of applications, neural networks and fuzzy-logic models outperform conventional statistical methods; for example, they show promising application in robotics and financial services. Due to various shortcomings of individual constituents of soft computing and the advantages of combining them with other technologies, soft or hybrid solutions are becoming popular.

■ 9.11 WARM-UP QUESTIONS, EXERCISES, AND PROJECTS

Warm-up Questions

1. How did soft computing come to be called this?
2. What are the reasons for creating hybrid or soft computing systems?
3. What are the implications of soft computing?
4. What is the difference between fuzziness and probability?
5. Consider Rossum's playhouse, which is a simulator designed by Gary Lucas. (It is available at http://sourceforge.net/projects/rossum/) You can use it as a general simulation tool for designing a simple autonomous robot navigation and control logic.
6. Search the Internet to find various classes of neural networks.
7. What is a hybrid neural network?
8. Can we combine the advantages of expert systems and neural networks to create a more powerful and effective knowledge-based system? Can you envisage the fundamental structure of such a system?

Exercises

1. What is a hybrid knowledge-based system?
2. What is the difference between soft computing and hard computing?
3. State the important properties of soft computing.
4. What are the guiding principles of soft and hard computing?
5. What are the advantages of integrating knowledge-based reasoning with case-based reasoning?
6. Explain the concepts of the concurrent neuro-fuzzy model, the cooperative neuro-fuzzy model, and the hybrid neuro-fuzzy model.
7. Explain the difference between *possibility* and *probability* in fuzzy logic.
8. What are the main sources of uncertainty in knowledge-based systems?

9. Explain the term chaos, and discuss the advantages of chaos in artificial intelligence.

10. Discuss the advantages of rough set theory in data analysis.

Projects

1. Explore the Internet for the following examples of hybrid systems, and prepare a report on what different knowledge-based systems they incorporate into their hybrid structure, as well as the knowledge domain in which they are used:

   a. SCREEN

   b. General Fuzzy Min Max

   c. CPD Connectionist Deterministic Parsing

2. Prepare a short term paper on the RUBICON hybrid system. You can use any search engine and collect literature on it.

References

Abraham, A. Neuro-fuzzy systems: State-of-the-art modeling techniques. In the proceedings of the *6th International Work-Conference on Artificial and Natural Neural Networks: Connectionist Models of Neurons, Learning Processes and Artificial Intelligence—Part I*, pp. 269–276; 2001.

Akerkar, R. & Lingras, P. *Building an Intelligent Web: Theory & Practice*, Sudbury, MA: Jones and Bartlett Publishers, 2008.

Halgamuge, S. K. & Glesner, M. Neural networks in designing fuzzy systems for real-word applications, *Fuzzy Sets and Systems*, vol.65, pp.1–12; 1994.

Jang, R. Neuro-fuzzy modeling: Architectures, analyses and applications, PhD Thesis, University of California, Berkeley; 1992.

Kitano, H. Empirical studies on the speed of convergence of neural network training using genetic algorithms. In the proceedings of the *8th National Conference on Artificial Intelligence*, Boston, pp. 789–795; 1990.

Kohonen, T. *Self-organization and Associative Memory*, Berlin: Springer; 1984.

Lin, T. Y., Chris Tseng H., & Teo, D., Fuzzy control and rough sets. In the proceedings of the *International Conference on Circuits and System Sciences,* Shanghai, China; June 20–25, 1996.

Lorenz, E. N., Deterministic non-periodic flow, *Journal of the Atmospheric Sciences*, vol. 20, pp. 130–141, 1963.

McGarry, K., Wermter, S., & MacIntyre, J. Hybrid neural systems: from simple coupling to fully integrated neural networks. *Neural Computing Surveys,* vol.2, pp. 62–93; 1999.

Nauck, D. & Kruse, R. NEFCLASS, A neuro-fuzzy approach for the classification of data, In the proceedings of the *1995 ACM Symposium on Applied Computing*, Nashville, TN; pp. 461–465; 1995.

Nauck, D. Beyond neuro-fuzzy: Perspective and directions, In the proceedings of the *3rd European Congress on Intelligent Techniques and Soft Computing (EU-FIT'95)*, Aachen, Germany: pp.1159–1164; 1995.

Negnevitsky, M. *Hybrid intelligent systems: Neural expert systems and neuro-fuzzy systems*, 2002, Retrieved from www.se.fsksm.utm.my/~saberi/files/ai/lecture_notes/Hybrid_system-Neuro_Fuzzy.ppt

Pawlak, Z., Rough sets. Basic notions. *International Journal of Computer and Information Science*, vol.11, pp. 341–356; 1982.

Pawlak, Z., *Rough sets: Theoretical Aspects of Reasoning About Data*, Dordrecht, The Netherlands: Kluwer Academic Publisher; 1991.

Rutkowski, L. & Cpałka, K. Flexible neuro-fuzzy systems, *IEEE Transactions on Neural Networks*, vol.14, no.1, pp. 554–574; 2003.

Sajja, P.S. A fuzzy agent to input vague parameters into multi-layer connectionist expert system: An application for stock markets, *ADIT Journal of Engineering*, vol.3, no.1, pp. 30–32; 2006a.

Sajja, P.S. Fuzzy artificial neural network decision support system for course selection, *Journal of Engineering and Technology*, vol.19, pp. 99–102; 2006b.

Sajja, P.S. An evolutionary computing approach for multi-layer connectionist system, *Journal of Computer Science*, vol.2, no.4, pp.325-331; 2007.

Sajja, P.S. An evolutionary fuzzy rule based system for knowledge based diagnosis, *Journal of Hybrid Computing Research*, vol.2, no.1; 2009.

See, L. & Openshaw, S. Applying soft computing approaches to river-level forecasting, *Hydrological Sciences Journal*, vol. 44, no.5, pp. 763–778; 1999.

Seiffert, U. Multiple layer perceptron training using genetic algorithms. *European Symposium on Artificial Neural Networks ESANN, 2001*, pp. 159-164; 2001.

Strogatz, S. H., *Nonlinear Dynamics and Chaos*, Reading, MA: Addison-Wesley Publishers; 1994.

Tschichold-Gurman, N. Generation and improvement of fuzzy classifiers with incremental learning using fuzzy rulenet, In the proceedings of the *1995 ACM Symposium on Applied Computing*, Nashville, TN: pp. 466–470; 1995.

Wermter, S. & Ron, S. Overview of hybrid neural systems. In *Hybrid Neural Systems, 1:13*, New York: Springer, Heidelberg; 2000.

Xu, H.Y. & Vukovich, G. A fuzzy genetic algorithm with effective search and optimization, In the proceedings of the *1993 International Joint Conference on Neural Networks*, pp. 2967–2970; 1993.

Yao, X. & Yong, L. A new evolutionary system for evolving artificial neural networks, *IEEE Transactions on Neural Networks*, vol.8, no.3; 1997.

Zadeh, L.A. Fuzzy logic, neural networks and soft computing, One-page course announcement of CS 294-4, Spring 1993, The University of California at Berkeley; 1992.

Zadeh, L.A. Fuzzy Sets, *Information and Control*, vol.8, pp. 338–353; 1965.

CHAPTER 10

Knowledge-Based Multiagent System Accessing Distributed Database Grid: An E-Learning Solution

■ 10.1 INTRODUCTION AND BACKGROUND

Information technology (IT) is being used widely to improve the quality and effectiveness of every aspect of our lives, including education. Traditional learning models, such as classroom teaching and distance learning, have their limitations. Above this, it is becoming increasingly harder to maintain the standards of education due to limitations on infrastructure, finances, and other resources, including a skilled work force.

Learning that is empowered through IT ensures that it is of a high quality by providing necessary information, stepwise assistance, and timely advice for decision making in cost-effective ways. Technology is being used for the effective utilization of educational resources to enhance reusability and interoperability. Today's workforce has to process more information in a shorter amount of time. New products and services are emerging with exponential speed. As production cycles and life spans of most of the products continue to become shorter, any product including information systems and problem-solving knowledge for a given domain quickly becomes obsolete (Bachman, 2000). In the competing and continuously changing world, it is the learner who inherits the future. Technologies are also rapidly changing, and the current structure of the Internet is facing drastic changes. This leads to the need for more flexible methods of learning and training on a global scale.

■ 10.1.1 E-learning Defined

E-learning is a step toward a learning economy (Bachman, 2000), emphasizing online delivery of information and hence, an accelerated learning process in a cost-effective way through IT (Gotschall, 2000; Sajja, 2008a; Shreiber & Berge, 1998). According to Drucker (2000), e-learning is just-in-time education integrated with high-velocity value chains. It is the delivery of individualized, comprehensive, dynamic learning content in real time, aiding the development of communities of knowledge, linking learners and practitioners with experts. E-learning also is the acquisition and distribution of multimedia knowledge through electronic means—specifically, through networks of computers via a variety of channels and technologies.

■ 10.1.2 Major Components of E-learning

The major components of an e-learning system are subject experts, media developers, instructors, editors, designers, and technical experts (Kanendran et al., 2004) contributing in three different aspects—content, service, and technology—as shown in Figure 10.1.

There is a need to bring learning to people instead of bringing people to learn. Technology has revolutionized business—now it is education's turn. To improve the overall quality of an e-learning solution, the three basic aspects of the methodology—service, content, and technology—need to be strengthened. Improving the quality of each aspect individually increases the quality of the integrated-solution framework, thereby satisfying users at various levels.

■ **FIGURE 10.1**
Components of an
e-learning solution

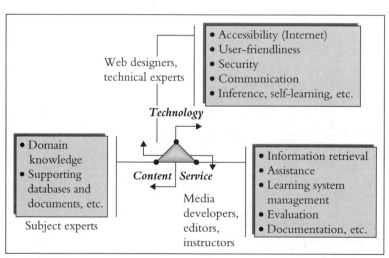

■ 10.1.3 Objectives of E-learning

The prime objectives of any technique that provides e-learning are as follows (Unwin, 2003):

- Ensure that access to high-quality information is integrated into course provisions
- Equip e-learners with the skills to exploit that information
- Provide appropriate assistance to e-learners in information searching and utilization
- Address issues related to communications and cost

■ 10.1.4 Advantages of E-learning

A complete e-learning system offers the following advantages:

- Consistent information presented in a customized way according to need (broad and easy access to information)
- Content is timely, accurate, and reliable
- Ability to upgrade instantly and quickly
- Documentation of knowledge for future use
- Anywhere and anytime learning by anybody
- E-learning is Web-enabled to take advantages of global platforms
- Scalability
- Cost-effective solutions by saving infrastructural cost and time
- Collaborative online communities
- Conforms to standards, if any

■ 10.2 EXISTING E-LEARNING SOLUTIONS: WORK DONE SO FAR

Various e-learning systems and models have been developed to capitalize on the advantages of e-learning. Zahm (2000) described multimedia computer-based training (CBT) via CD-ROM or as a Web download. Urdan and Weggen (2000) shared that e-learning covers a wide set of applications and processes, including computer-based learning, Web-based learning, virtual classrooms, and digital collaborations via the Internet, intranets, and extranets. Shreiber and Berge (1998) and Gotschall (2000) proposed that online learning is a technology-based solution to make information currently available for direct access. In his work, Hall (2000) proposed distance learning for a planned interactive course, using the e-learning concept to teach technical skills effectively.

All of these solutions offer many advantages of e-learning; however, the quality of the e-learning solution can be further enhanced by making effective utilization of Information and Communication Technology (ICT). Most of the traditional computer-aided software developed so far are typical full-fledged systems based on specific databases, providing only static presentation of information. The system developed for adult literacy, "Parichay" (Sajja, 2006), calculates a learner's level of capability using domain heuristics and presents material according to the learner's need and capability. However, this solution is a single personal computer-based system and has limited scope. Due to this limitation, learners cannot take advantage of building communities and groups for discussion.

According to Kuan-Ching et al. (2006) and Foster et al. (2001), existing solutions have focused mainly on the content delivery for a specific domain and are based on client–server, peer-to-peer, and Web service architecture. Such systems lack personal attention, and learners are not motivated to educate themselves. The software should be user-friendly, easy to operate (preferably in users' native language), able to present information dynamically in a multimedia format, and capable of explaining its decision-making process. In short, the strategy needs to satisfy different user groups in different ways by identifying the user's interests and capabilities.

■ 10.3 REQUIREMENTS FOR AN IDEAL E-LEARNING SOLUTION

Most of the e-learning solutions provide an online repository of the material, but not individual advice and step-by-step assistance to help learners. Those who want to learn about technical subjects, such as the implementation of array data structures in computer science, how titration experiments can be done in chemistry in simulative environments, and how practical problems can be solved based on a mathematical problem, find difficulties in learning using the static material provided to them.

Users learn in different ways: visual, referential, sequential, active/reactive, and so on. A good teacher identifies a suitable style for learners and presents the subject in a more effective fashion. The typical e-learning solutions cannot convert content represented in one ontology into another one. Thus, it becomes necessary to store the same content in a redundant fashion to achieve such effectiveness.

Teachers need to understand students' needs and inspire them to learn and solve problems in an interesting way. Utilizing users' own terminology in their own style plays an important role in developing the required attitude for learning. Existing e-learning solutions provide limited help by letting the users carry out predefined commands for further actions instead of providing a friendly interface to learners and necessary justification for the decisions that are made.

Moreover, standard e-learning solutions are not integrated with functions like student monitoring, mail and chatting, reporting, evaluation of quizzes and assignments, and so on. One might think that an institute-level Enterprise Resource Planning (ERP) system would encompass all such supporting agents, which are independent for ease of development and control, and that it would work in conjunction with other domain systems. For an academic institute, a typical e-learning system generally encompasses agents like tutorials, mail and chat, drills and quizzes, and learning material and student data management. Such enterprise-wide e-learning systems can be generic and can be used for any academic institution.

In addition, many parameters that can affect IT-enabled e-learning must be identified according to the perspectives of different users, such as e-learners, administrators, teachers, support staff, students, visitors, guests, and parents. These different users have different perspectives and requirements. An ideal e-learning solution would consider these major objectives and quality constraints, and handle them accordingly.

■ 10.3.1 Quality Parameters for an Ideal E-learning Solution

With the objectives to develop an ideal e-learning solution in mind, a survey was carried out to determine necessary quality parameters along with the required IT support (Sajja, 2008a). This survey was carried out at the Post-Graduate Department of Computer Science, Sardar Patel University, India. Students, faculty members, and nearby experts were engaged in short-listing a few critical parameters through discussions and walkthroughs. Table 10.1 lists the parameters identified through the experiment, with technology support and orientation required. This table also shows the technological support that users were currently receiving and highlights the advanced needs and improvements required.

■ Table 10.1 Quality Parameters and Technological Support for E-learning

Parameter that Affects Quality (listed alphabetically)	Technology (ICT) Support	Orientation Required
Availability of material and question bank	Provided through database tables, document files, and rich-text files	Knowledge-based approach is required to select questions for examinations, quizzes, and practice according to learner's level
Availability of teacher/technology and collaboration	Static knowledge is available through Internet and distributed systems	To make dynamic knowledge from multiple expers available
Consistency, regularity, and trustworthiness	Back-ups, manuals, and expert knowledge	Requires efficient structures to represent expert knowledge and appropriate knowledge-based processes to store, retrieve, use, and infer knowledge
Correct and fast evaluation of examination/assignments	Computer programs, scripts, and macros; however, limited to objective-type answers	Theoretical and technical experiment-oriented questions need to be addressed
Efficient information retrieval	Efficient search techniques and filtering	Requires intelligent approach to enhance effectiveness and suitability of the retrieved content
Ease of documentation, cloning, and extensibility	With necessary hardware support and protocols	Intelligent protocols for web-based systems and security algorithms are required for restricted cloning and extensibility
Flexibility, reusability, and frequency of revision	Through program	Reusability can be increased by independent lower-level components (agents) for each specific task
Knowledge management and systems learning	Typically supported by files and databases	Knowledge base can be utilized for partial self-learning, user-friendliness, and justification of the decisions made by the system
Machine independence, portability, and scope of system	Independent programming languages and packages Scope of such system can be further increased by making content and system centrally available on Internet with multilingual interface	Intelligent information retrieval, native language interface, and other protocols for portability and machine independence are required

(continues)

■ Table 10.1 Quality Parameters and Technological Support for E-learning (continued)

Parameter that Affects Quality (listed alphabetically)	Technology (ICT) Support	Orientation Required
Multimedia support and effective presentation	Multimedia and computer graphics	Knowledge-based approach required to determine media and sequence of presentation according to user's level and learning style
Performance (cost, time savings, etc.)	High processor ability of computing resources	Cost can be further reduced by introducing reusable lower-level entities called learning objects (LOs)
Safety and security	Hardware locks and software validation in procedures Access rights to different user groups	Optionally intelligent encryption algorithms can be applied to sensitive information
Specificity (level of content relevance and completeness)	Verification and validation by multiple experts	Optional automatic self-learning support from knowledge-based approach
Support of standards	Software engineering models and tools	Knowledge engineering models required
Users' ease of learning and user-friendliness	Through user profile and interface	Knowledge-based approach further improves friendliness by providing explanation and reasoning, along with step-by-step assistance in user's native language

■ 10.4 TOWARD A KNOWLEDGE-BASED MULTIAGENT APPROACH

Some of the parameters listed in Table 10.1 can be satisfied with traditional development strategies, such as databases and Internet tools. However, parameters like user-friendliness, effective presentation of material in different media according to learners' levels, explanation and reasoning to satisfy users' queries, efficient information retrieval, and self-learning can be better supported through a knowledge-based approach to developing an ideal e-learning solution according to users' perspectives.

Since e-learning encompasses multiple independent tasks, there is a need for various independent lower-level components called agents. Some agents contain a knowledge-based approach, and some are utilizing typical development strategies like databases and files. Since most organizations already have some data in electronic form, the proposed solution should take advantage of this to increase reusability, adoptivity, and flexibility of the system. Moreover, the knowledge base and database should be available on the Internet to satisfy the "anytime" and "anywhere" conditions for content presentation (system operation).

Inspired by the requirements obtained as a result of the previously mentioned survey, the case of a multiagent e-learning system using a knowledge-based approach to access a distributed database grid is presented here. The case discusses the detailed structure of the solution, methodology, and an experiment with the knowledge-based multiagent system.

■ 10.4.1 Objectives of a Knowledge-Based Multiagent E-Learning Solution

When designing a suitable knowledge-based e-learning strategy, the following objectives were kept in mind:

- Help users (e-learners, administrators, teachers, support staff, students, visitors, guests, and parents) to learn by accessing existing databases through the grid
- Provide high-quality information and effective course material, with explanation and reasoning customized to each learner's level
- Provide drill, quiz, and question bank facilities to e-learners and quick evaluation of the same
- Provide assistance in information searching

The following section introduces the technologies necessary for the proposed solution.

■ 10.4.2 Introduction to Multiagent Systems

The term "agent" refers to a component of software and/or hardware that is capable of acting exactly as required to accomplish tasks on behalf of the user. KBS tools used as agents are autonomous, cooperative, and able to learn. A multiagent system can be considered a loosely coupled network of problem-solving agents that work together to find answers to problems that are beyond the individual capabilities or knowledge of each entity alone (Durfee et al.,

■ **FIGURE 10.2**
Multiagent system

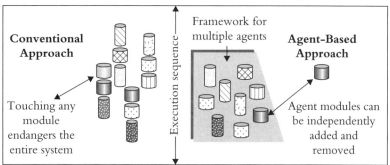

1989; Sajja, 2005). Such a framework presents a useful software engineering paradigm, where problem-solving components are described as individual agents pursuing high-level goals. Because agents are independent and proactive entities, the system built from such multiple components becomes modular and structured when compared to conventional systems, as denoted in Figure 10.2 (Sajja, 2007).

All agents, because they are part of a system under consideration, need to communicate with each other using special tools like Knowledge Query and Manipulation Language (KQML). Some of them require a special ontology to represent knowledge for intelligent behavior.

■ 10.4.3   Advantages of a Knowledge-Based Multiagent Approach for E-learning

Intelligent agents are artificial intelligence (AI) tools that can manage the information overload, serve as academic experts, and create programming environments for the learners. According to Hill (2003) and Dan (2003), vortals and intelligent agents are the two most promising technologies in which e-learning could be practically accomplished. Vortals (*vertical or niche portals*) are specialized, dedicated portals that adapt specific learning collaborative strategies aimed at gaining performance and providing needed information.

Anane et al. (2003) described agent technology as a critical factor in knowledge acquisition in semantically rich environments, as exemplified by the Semantic Web. Giotopoulos et al. (2007) has described a genetic algorithm-based e-learning approach through various assessment agents and resource retrieval agents. This effort partially fulfills the need for different agents, but cannot access the existing databases available on a distributed environment.

Ammar and Neji (2007) introduced an emotional multiagent system for peer-to-peer e-learning that identifies the facial expression of learners through emotional agents for a more personalized learning experience. This approach has its specific requirements and may be a cost-prohibitive solution.

Since an e-learning solution encompasses multiple independent tasks, resulting in a large, complex system, it is highly advisable to identify multiple independent lower-level solutions that perform specific tasks related to the e-learning process and integrate them into a framework-enabling operation. Such a multiagent knowledge-based approach offers the benefits of an intelligent system as well as the basic functionality of an ideal e-learning solution. Having such independent components brings increased reusability, structure, and an ability to isolate and repair the agents, and hence, provides ease of development and control. The most important requirement of an e-learning solution is high availability of material on demand according to users' needs and capabilities. Thus, the multiagent paradigm accessing distributed databases through a grid on the World Wide Web can serve as an ideal platform for implementing an e-learning solution.

The proposed approach here, enabling us to take advantage of properties like common meanings and machine-processable metadata, enabled by a set of suitable agents to establish a powerful approach, satisfies the e-learning requirements. Since the proposed methodology is intended to access existing databases in a distributed grid on the Internet or an intranet, it offers the benefit of easy accessibility to the databases; hence, a great deal of effort can be saved by not having to re-enter the information.

■ 10.5   SYSTEM ARCHITECTURE AND METHODOLOGY

To achieve the best of these three worlds—knowledge-based, multiagent, and available on the Internet—and to meet the objectives of an ideal e-learning solution discussed earlier, a collaborative structure is designed that accesses the databases (also called information repositories) on the Web. A prototype model has been developed by the Department of Computer Science, Sardar Patel University, India. The department is running Master of Computer Applications (MCA, 100 students), Post-Graduate Diploma in

■ **FIGURE 10.3**
System
architecture

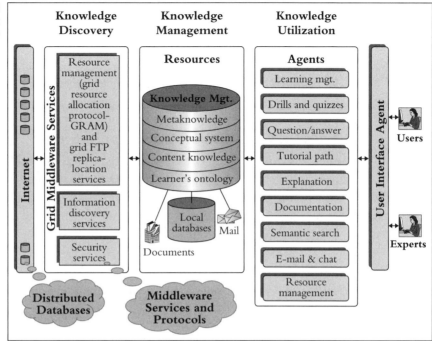

■ **FIGURE 10.3** System architecture

Computer Applications (PGDCA, 115 students), MSc Bioinformatics (30 students), M.Phil, and PhD programs in computer science. Prior to implementing this system, the department was using a networked computer server to share static documents containing course material. However, this content could not be integrated with tasks like mail, learning content management, customized material management, semantic search, and so on.

Figure 10.3 describes how different agents with a particular functionality form a multiagent system, accessing available distributed databases through grid middleware services.

■ 10.5.1 System Agents

The proposed system encompasses different agents for activities like learning management; tutorials; quizzes, drills, and practice assignments; performance evaluations; information retrieval and semantic search; explanation and user's query management; electronic notice board for mail; documentation; and resource management. All of these agents are working in collaboration with two main agents. One of them is an interface agent, which provides a user-friendly interface by managing a user's profile. Another is a knowledge management agent. The prime objective of this agent is to retain the meta-knowledge (also known as knowledge about the content/knowledge) and the ontology—the fashion in which the knowledge is stored. It also controls other agents of the system and local databases/documents, if any.

■ 10.5.2   Interaction Between Agents

Agents in a multiagent system should recurrently interact to share information and perform tasks to achieve their goals. All the agents of this system can communicate with other agents with ease, if they are following a common language. Many tools are available for this; the declarative communication language KQML (Genesereth & Fikes, 1992) is one of the more popular tools. It was conceived both as a message format and a message-handling protocol to support runtime knowledge sharing among agents (Finin et al., 1997). An example of a KQML block is shown in Figure 10.4 (Sajja, 2008b).

■ 10.5.3   Middleware Services

Since the system is intended to use the readymade databases available on the Web to minimize redevelopment effort, grid middleware services are required. Examples of available toolkits include UNICORE, Globus, Legion, and Gridbus (Asadzadeh et al., 2006). Among them, UNICORE, Globus,

■ FIGURE 10.4
An example KQML block

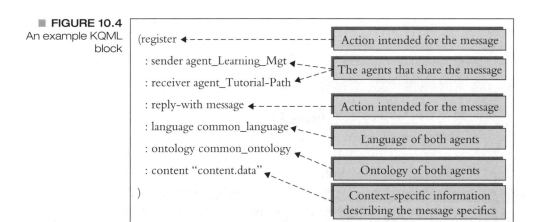

and Gridbus are open-source and freely available. The protocols used at this stage are Grid Resource Allocation Protocol (GRAM) and Grid FTP Replica-Location Services.

■ 10.6   KNOWLEDGE REPRESENTATION AND SYSTEM OUTPUT

Agents of a multiagent system can communicate with ease if a similar ontology is followed by all the agents. An ontology is a way of formally describing the vocabulary and set of symbols. In fact, an ontology constrains the set of possible mappings between symbols and their meanings (Stojanovic, 2004; Noy & Klein, 2004). Figure 10.5 shows an example of knowledge representation for a programming language tutorial. The knowledge of an integer array is represented in the form of a semantic network showing objects and their relationships. Arrays are the basic unit of any programming language, encompassing the same size and type of elements under a common name. Figure 10.5 explains that array A is an integer variable, represented as "A[i]," where "i" represents the index of referred variables within the group. This is a semantic representation of the topic "arrays of programming language" in a knowledge-based structure.

Such semantic representations have their well-defined representation criteria and reasoning schemes, so further management and explanation becomes easy. Similarly, all of the tutorial topics can be represented in suitable knowledge representation schemes to access the system in a knowledge-based way. Figure 10.6 presents a sample screen design from the programming language tutorial. Figure 10.7 shows how the system calculates the learner level by considering the number of questions answered correctly within a given time

■ **FIGURE 10.5**
Representation of the topic "array of integers"

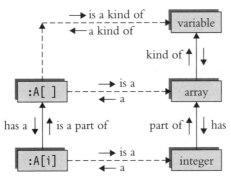

FIGURE 10.6
Screen design of programming language tutorial

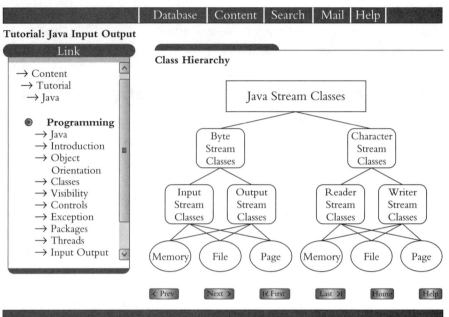

FIGURE 10.7
Speed correctness ratio and learner's level identified by the system for the given student batch

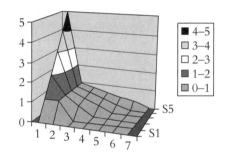

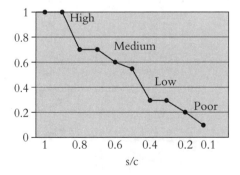

FIGURE 10.8
Screen design
of student's
performance in
the programming
language

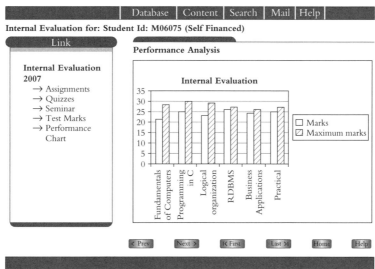

(speed–correctness ratio). This helps in determining the sequence of presentation items and their repetition using some practice screens, if necessary. Figure 10.8 describes students' performance in comparison with the maximum marks obtained in the subject.

■ 10.7   RESULTS OF THE EXPERIMENT

The prototype model of the system is developed and tested by the post-graduate computer science students and teachers. Figure 10.9 presents the results of the survey after implementation.

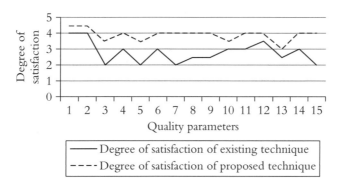 **FIGURE 10.9**
Comparison
between existing
techniques and
modified e-learning
prototype

■ 10.7.1 Advantages Achieved

The prototype model has satisfied the selected population of users at the site, and based on this, remaining modules are being prepared. The system design is flexible in the sense that an agent can be isolated and repaired or replaced easily through the knowledge management agent with which different agents are working. The following are the advantages of the proposed model:

- Learning through a database grid on the Web is a highly accessible and relatively inexpensive solution, as it saves time, reduces cost, provides ease of documentation, efficiently maintains records, and provides a quick assessment of user answers in friendly way.
- It identifies a learner's level and provides specific step-by-step assistance.
- The system provides knowledge-based access of distributed databases on the Web, which provides further advantages, such as:
  - Reusing the available information in the database format and benefiting from both centralized and decentralized resources at once
  - Effective information retrieval
  - Explanation/reasoning for the decision made
  - Built-in knowledge management facilities such as self-learning and inferencing

The multiagent environment helps in strengthening the structure and reusability of the system so that the modules can be used as independent components with little enhancements.

■ 10.8 CONCLUSION

This system can be used for students, trainers, and the development of virtual classrooms as a parallel teaching and learning aid with traditional classroom teaching and distance learning.

As stated earlier, the quality of an e-learning system directly depends on its content, service, and technology. The domain knowledge and its effective representation through suitable technology increase the system's usability and reliability. The self-learning facility of the knowledge-based management agent partially updates the domain knowledge. However, such self-learning supports only partial learning and is limited. Sometimes, experts and administrators need to update the system. Because the system supports any existing databases containing material and user information, it provides a flexible platform for any course learning for a given institution. This is the maximum level of flexibility, adoptivity, and generalization that this system may offer.

However, to increase the scope of the system, it may be enhanced with an interactive editor agent to edit the domain knowledge and provide an interface to add to and update the existing database repository on a distributed environment. This leads to a generalized (and commercial) e-learning product with empty domain knowledge and databases, which turns the system into an ERP solution with different roles and modules, such as admission, tutoring, assistance, evaluation, and performance monitoring, by centralizing and decentralizing resources through a distributed environment. Converting the system into such a generic product increases the cost when compared to development efforts and benefits. Developers may consider this trade-off when designing a solution.

The scope and benefits of the proposed system can be increased by different language-specific or audience-specific agents, such as a multilingual or Braille interface (with suitable hardware and software). Many system agents can be isolated and used in a patchwork fashion with similar types of systems, with only minor changes.

This case considers a maximum of learner perspectives to improve quality. Still, there is a need to consider the perspectives of administrators and domain experts. There is a need for self-learning from cases and available knowledge through a friendly editor. Since the proposed system follows a knowledge-based approach, it must document domain knowledge in suitable knowledge representation schemes. Using symbolic artificial intelligence techniques, one may discover flexible ontologies that can efficiently store, retrieve, and use domain knowledge. One issue that may appear at this stage is the redundant knowledge stored in different ontologies. If one can define an ontology mapping function to utilize knowledge stored in another ontology, such duplication can be avoided and material can be presented in multiple context/format according to users' needs.

An independent e-learning solution is not affordable or practical for all subjects, especially when the content for a given course must be represented in different ways, based on each student's style, or the same content is used for different courses. In such cases, a reusable lower-level learning object repository (LOR) is prepared and shared for increasing the cost-effectiveness of the e-learning solution. With a LOR, it is possible to gather a pool of information objects and make them available for reuse in a variety of learning delivery contexts. The development of such LORs and their interoperability is another aspect that needs serious consideration when designing a cost-effective e-learning solution.

References

Ammar, M. & Neji, M. Emotional multiagent system for peer-to-peer e-learning, Proceedings of *ICTA'07*, April 12–14, Hammamet, Tunisia, pp. 201–206, 2007.

Anane, R., Chao, K., Hendley, R., & Younas, M. An agent-mediated approach to e-learning, Proceedings of *Internet and Multimedia Systems and Applications*, pp. 183–188, 2003.

Asadzadeh, P., Buyya, R., Kei, C., Nayar, D., & Venugopal, S. Global grids and software toolkits: A study of four grid middleware technologies, 2006. Retrieved from http://www.utpl.edu.ec/upsiblog/?cat=18

Bachman, K. Corporate e-learning: Exploring a new frontier, 2000. Retrieved from http://www.spectrainteractive.com/pdfs/CorporateELearingHamrecht.pdf

Dan, G., Florin, L., & Mihai, H. E-learning distributed framework using intelligent agents, *New Trends in Computer Science and Engineering*, Anniversary Volume, Technical University Gh. Asachi, Polirom Press, Iasi, pp. 159–163, 2003.

Drucker, P. Need to know: Integrating e-learning with high-velocity value chains, A Delphi Group White Paper, 2000. Retrieved from http://www.delphigroup.com/research/whitepaper_request_download.htm

Durfee, E. H., Lesser, V. R., & Corkill, D. D. Trends in cooperative distributed problem solving, *IEEE Transactions on Knowledge and Data Engineering*, vol.1, no.1, pp. 63–83, 1989.

Finin, T., Labrou, Y., & Mayfield, J. KQML as an agent communication language, In J. M. Bradshaw, ed., *Software agents*, Menlo Park, CA: AAAI Press, pp. 291–316, 1997.

Foster, I., Kesselman, C., & Tuecke, S. The anatomy of the grid enabling scalable virtual organizations, *International Journal of Supercomputer Applications*, vol.15, no.3, 2001.

Genesereth, M. & Fikes, R. Knowledge interchange format, *Version 3.0 Reference Manual, Technical Report Logic 92-1*, Computer Science Department, Stanford University, 1992.

Giotopoulos, K., Alexakos, C., Beligiannis, G., & Likothanassis, S. Integrating computational intelligence techniques and assessment agents in e-learning environments, *International Journal of Computational Intelligence,* vol. 3, no.4, pp. 328–337, 2007.

Gotschall, M. E-learning strategies for executive education and corporate training, *Fortune*, vol. 141, no.10, pp. S5–S59, 2000.

Hall, B. How to embark on your e-learning adventure: Making sense of the environment, *e-Learning*, January–March, 2000. Retrieved from http://www.cnssystech.com/infozone/Technology_eLearningAdventure.asp

Hill, L. Implementing a practical e-learning system, 2003. Retrieved from http://agora.lakeheadu.ca/pre2004/december2002/elearning.html

Kanendran, T. A., Johnny, S., & Durga, B.V. Technical report: Issues and strategies of e-learning, *Sunway College Journal*, vol.1, pp. 99–107, 2004.

Kuan-Ching, L., Chuan-Ko, T., Yin-Te, T., & Hsiao-His, W. Towards design of e-learning platform in grid environments, Proceedings of the *2006 International Conference on Grid Computing & Applications*, Las Vegas, Nevada, 2006.

Noy, N. & Klein, M. Ontology evolution: Not the same as schema evolution, *Knowledge and Information Systems*, vol.6, no.4, pp. 428–440, 2004.

Sajja, P. S. Multi-layer knowledge-based system: A multiagent approach, *Proceedings of the Second Indian International Conference on Artificial Intelligence*, Pune, India, pp. 2899–2909, 2005.

Sajja, P. S. Parichay: An agent for adult literacy, *Prajna*, vol.14, pp. 17–24, 2006.

Sajja, P. S. Multiagent system for dairy cooperatives, *Cooperative Perspective*, vol.42, no.3, pp. 24–30, 2007.

Sajja, P. S. Enhancing quality in e-learning by knowledge-based IT support, *International Journal of Education and Development Using Information and Communication Technology*, vol.4, no.1, 2008a.

Sajja, P. S. Multiagent system for knowledge-based access to distributed databases, *Interdisciplinary Journal of Information, Knowledge, and Management*, vol.3, pp. 1–9, 2008b.

Shreiber, D. A. & Berge, Z. L. Distance training: How innovative organizations are using technology to maximize learning and business objectives, San Francisco: Jossey-Bass, 1998.

Stojanovic, L. Methods and tools for ontology evolution, PhD Thesis, Universitat Karlsruhe, 2004.

Unwin, D. Information support for e-learning: principles and practice, UK eUniversities Worldwide Summer, 2003.

Urdan, T. A. & Weggen, C. C. Corporate e-learning: Exploring a new frontier, WR Hambrecht + Co., 2000. Retrieved from http://www.wrhambrecht. com/research/coverage/elearning/ir/ir_explore.html

Zahm, S. 2000. No question about it—e-learning is here to stay: A quick history of the e-learning evolution, *e-Learning*, vol.1, no.1, pp. 44–47.

CHAPTER 11

Knowledge-Intensive Learning: Diet Menu Planner

■ 11.1 INTRODUCTION

This chapter describes a case-based reasoning (CBR) approach to knowledge-intensive learning. The motivating force behind case-based reasoning in knowledge-based systems comes from the machine learning community, where case-based reasoning is regarded as a subfield of machine learning. The basic idea of CBR is to solve a current problem by reusing solutions that have been applied to similar problems in the past. Therefore, the current problem has to be compared with problems described in past cases. Solutions contained in cases that represent similar problems are then considered candidates for solving the current problem, too.

Case-based reasoning (Aamodt, 1990, 1994) simulates a type of human problem-solving behavior. It is useful whenever it is difficult to formulate domain rules and when cases are available. It is also useful when rules can be formulated but require more input information than is typically available because of incomplete problem specifications or because the knowledge needed is simply not available at the time. Other indications for CBR are when general knowledge is not sufficient because of too many exceptions, or when new solutions can be derived from old solutions more easily than from scratch. Many successful commercial applications, such as CLAVIER (Hennessy & Hinkle, 1992) and FormTool (Cheetham & Graf, 1997), have proven the utility of this paradigm.

We will illustrate a framework for knowledge-intensive learning (Akerkar, 2004) using diet menu planning as an example. We call the designed system *DietMaster*. We have already introduced the concept of case-based reasoning in Section 4.7.4. The framework discussed here represents a perspective on knowledge, reasoning, and learning that aims to satisfy fundamental system requirements. The knowledge-based systems should function within a continually evolving environment, and thus, their knowledge needs to be updated and refined constantly. Methods for automated *learning from experience* are especially essential. The ability to learn from each problem-solving experience is called *sustained learning*.

The case base in our system is a representative set of cases. This set covers the goals and subgoals that arise in reasoning, and both successful and failed attempts at achieving those goals. A case is a piece of knowledge representing an experience in a particular context. Typically, a case consists of (Kolodner, 1993):

- **The problem statement**, including contextual information (e.g., invariant and preconditions)
- The **solution** to the problem
- The **outcome** of applying the solution (e.g., post-conditions)
- Any underlying **facts and supporting reasoning** that the system knows how to make use of

The problem statement is a description of the situation or problem. It lists the goals of the system, constraints on the situation, and features of the problem. The solution to the problem may consist of other exponents that aid in adaptation and critiquing, such as:

- Diagnosis, plan, and explanation of the solution
- The steps used to solve the problem
- The justifications for decisions that were made in solving the problem
- Acceptable solutions that were not chosen
- Unacceptable solutions that were ruled out
- Expectations of what the solution will achieve

The outcome is the resulting state of the world when the solution was carried out. If expectations are violated, or if the solution failed, the outcome might include an explanation of how this method will be repaired. The outcome has several parts:

- The outcome itself
- Whether the outcome fulfilled or violated expectations
- Explanation of the expectation violation and/or failure
- Repair strategy

- What could have been done to avoid the problem
- Pointer to the next attempt at a solution

Cases can be represented in variety of forms, such as frames, semantic networks, predicate notation rules, or mixed formats. Cases should be organized in memory for effective retrieval and reuse. There are different case organization methods. Two influential case memory models are the dynamic memory model and the category exemplar model.

■ 11.2 CASE RETRIEVAL

This step gives the best-matching previous case. Its subtasks are referred to as identify features—match, search, and select—and are executed in that order. The identification task comes up with a set of relevant problem descriptors, the matching task returns a set of cases that are sufficiently similar to the new case (using a similarity threshold of some sort), and the selection task works on this set of cases and chooses the best match.

■ 11.2.1 The Identify Features

At a basic level, this task involves noticing input descriptors; however, a more elaborate approach is needed to understand the problem within its context. Unknown descriptors may be disregarded, or the user may be asked to provide an explanation. Noisy problem descriptors are filtered out to infer other relevant problem features and to check whether the feature values make sense within the context. This generates expectations of other features. Descriptors other than those given as input may be inferred by using a general knowledge model or by retrieving a similar problem description from the case base and using its features as expected features.

■ 11.2.2 Matching

This task involves finding a good matching previous case. It is divided into subtasks—namely the initial matching process, which retrieves a set of plausible candidates, and the more elaborate process of selecting the best one among this subset.

Using the problem descriptors as indexes to the case library in either a direct or indirect way does find a set of matching cases. There are three ways of retrieving a case or a set of cases: following direct index pointers from problem features, searching an index structure, or searching in a model of general domain knowledge. Cases may be retrieved solely from the input features or from features inferred from the input. Cases that match all input features are, of course, good candidates for matching, but depending upon the strategy, cases that match a given fraction of the problem features (input or inferred) may also be retrieved.

Some tests for relevance of a retrieved case are often executed, particularly if cases are retrieved based on a subset of features. The matching process will be easy if the case representation is properly designed. This can be a problem with indexing vocabulary, however. A way to assess the degree of similarity is needed, and several "similarity metrics" have been proposed based on surface similarities between the problem and case features.

The next task involves finding the best match from a set of similar cases. The best matching case is usually determined by evaluating the degree of the initial match more closely. If a match turns out not to be strong enough, an attempt to find a better match by following difference links to closely related cases is made. The selection process typically generates consequences and expectations from each retrieved case, and attempts to evaluate consequences and justify expectations. This can be done by using the system's own model of general domain knowledge or by asking the user for confirmation and additional information. The cases are eventually ranked according to some metric or ranking criteria. Knowledge-intensive selection methods typically generate explanations that support this ranking process, and the case that has the strongest explanation for being similar to the new problem is chosen.

■ 11.3 CASE REUSE

Using the past case obtained through the "retrieve" step, a solution to the current problem is proposed that considers two aspects: the differences among the past and the current case, and what part of a retrieved case can be transferred to a new case.

The past case may be reused either by applying its solution to the new case or by considering differences in both cases, adapting the relevant part of the past case, and applying it to the new case.

■ 11.4   CASE REVISION

When the solution generated by the reuse phase is not correct, one needs to revise the retrieved case. This consists of two tasks: evaluating the case solution and learning from it if successful, and repairing the case solution using domain-specific knowledge.

Evaluating the solution is accomplished by taking feedback from the "real world" and applying it to the solution. The result may take some time to appear, depending on the type of application. The case may still be learned from, and be available in the case base in the intermediate period, but it has to be marked as a nonevaluated case.

When repairing the case solution, feedback from the evaluation phase is applied to modify the solution in such a way that failure does not occur. The repair module of a CBR system possesses general causal knowledge and domain knowledge about how to disable or compensate causes of errors in the domain. The revised plan can then be retained directly if it is correct; otherwise, it can be evaluated and repaired again. The evaluation and repair tasks are recursive, occurring until a correct solution is achieved.

■ 11.5   CASE RETENTION

The outcome of the evaluation and possible repair tasks helps one to learn from the success or failure of the proposed solution. This involves selecting the desired part of the case to retain, in what form to retain it, how to index the case for later retrieval, and how to integrate the new case into the memory structure.

Extract

If the case was solved by using a previous case, a new case may be built or the old case may be generalized to subsume the present case as well. If the problem was solved by other methods, including asking the user, an entirely new case will have to be constructed. Now the question: Which part of the case is to be retained? Problem descriptors, problem solutions, and explanation or justification of the solution to the problem-solving method are the structures that may be extracted for learning. Information about the repair may also be extracted and retained, either as separate failure cases or within the total problem case, which will help to improve understanding or correct the present case, if failure has occurred.

Index

Here, the type and structure of indexes is determined. This is actually a knowledge acquisition problem, and should be analyzed as part of the domain knowledge analysis and modeling step. A trivial solution to the problem is to use all input features as indexes. This is a syntax-based method. In a memory-based method, relevant features are determined by matching all the cases in the case base and filtering out features that belong to cases that have few features in common with the problem case.

Integrate

Here, the knowledge base is updated with the new case when the index is modified. The importance of a particular case or solution to the index is adjusted based on the success or failure of the case to solve the input problem. The features relevant for retrieving successful cases strengthen the case, while it is weakened for features that lead to unsuccessful cases being retrieved. Thus, the index structure helps tune and adapt the case memory for its use.

In the knowledge-intensive approach to CBR, learning may also take place through interaction with the user or other machine-learning methods (e.g., the rule-based approach).

■ 11.6 ORGANIZATION OF CASES IN MEMORY

A case-based reasoner is heavily dependent on the structure (and content, of course) of its case memory. Since a problem is solved by recalling a previous experience suitable for solving the new problem, the case search and matching processes need to be both effective and reasonably time-efficient. Furthermore, since the experience from a problem just solved has to be retained in some way, these requirements also apply to the method of integrating a new case into the memory. How the cases should be organized and indexed—for example, how cases should be described and represented, how they should be interrelated, and how they should relate to entities like input features, solutions, and problem-solving states—have been (and continue to be) a major research topic.

■ 11.7 DIETMASTER

The DietMaster (Jamsandekar, 2000) follows a *knowledge-intensive* approach to problem solving and learning. It is an approach that is based on an intensive use of domain knowledge and relevant parts of the surrounding world in its problem-solving and learning methods.

The knowledge representation system is an open, extensible system. A knowledge base may be viewed as representing a tightly coupled network of concepts—that is, physical entities, relations, processes, and so on—where each concept is defined by its relationships with other concepts. The DietMaster knowledge base contains *general domain knowledge* in the form of concept classes and relationships and *specific domain knowledge* in the form of concept instances and previously solved cases. The general knowledge consists of deeper, fundamental knowledge in terms of the functional model, as well as shallower associations in the form of heuristic rules. Within the DietMaster architecture, a simple heuristic association is represented merely as a particular relationship, called *implies*. More complex heuristic rules are represented as particular frames, called *rule frames*. Thus, concept definitions, rules, and cases are all represented as frames. A frame is a four-level structure that contains slots, which in turn, contain facets, which contain a value or a list containing values.

The basic reasoning approach in DietMaster is case-based reasoning from previously solved problem cases, supported by model-based reasoning within the knowledge network. In addition, heuristic rules may be used for associational reasoning when the case base is still small and covers few actual problems, or if case-based problem solving fails. DietMaster is designed for classification type problems, and incorporates a generic model of planning tasks, which is used to guide the actual problem-solving process.

Since a knowledge base in DietMaster is supposed to be rather extensive—representing different types and aspects of knowledge—some way to direct the reasoning according to the current purpose and context is needed. This is achieved by a method called *goal-focused spreading activation*, in which only the part of the knowledge base that is semantically and pragmatically related to the current goal is activated.

The case-based learning method in DietMaster is supported and guided by the network model of specific (case) and general knowledge. All four modules share an underlying model of descriptive knowledge called the fundamental knowledge (FK). Upon this fundamental knowledge, each of the four submodels may express operational knowledge, such as heuristic associations (cases and rules) and procedures (e.g., strategies, action sequences).

In addition to the object-level concept descriptions, the object-level knowledge model includes the previously solved cases and the object-level rules. At the control level, the combined reasoning model has knowledge about what type of reasoning method—and associated knowledge structure—to activate at a given point in time. The kinds of reasoning used by the combined reasoning model are case-based-reasoning, model-based-reasoning, concept-network, rule, case, and so on. The planning model represents the problem-solving process through a set of actions and their conditioned execution—for example, when to apply a particular piece of domain knowledge, when to look for more evidence, when to hypothesize, and so on. The sustained learning model (SLM) contains the algorithms (procedures) for knowledge-supported case-based learning and a collection of rules to guide the matching and feature generalization processes. This model describes the internal organization and structuring of representational terms, such as the types of frames, slots, and facets that the system contains.

Knowledge-intensive reasoning and learning at the object level requires as complete a domain model as possible, while reasoning at the control level needs to know about the level, depth, role, and form of the object knowledge structure in order to apply appropriate inference and learning methods to different knowledge types. Since the DietMaster will contain several types of reasoning and learning methods, as well as different types of knowledge, each reasoning type needs to be associated with its appropriate knowledge type.

■ 11.7.1   General Menu-Planning Process for Diabetic Patients

The process of menu planning is derived using data collected from experts (dietitians, physicians, medical practitioners, and home science departments of various colleges running undergraduate and postgraduate courses) and literature of the Indian Medical Council. The menu-planning process is divided into five major steps:

- Determine the total calories required for an individual according to his or her physical state and activities he or she is doing.
- Determine the nutrient requirements with regard to carbohydrates, proteins, and fat to suit the person's health state and overcome the energy requirement.
- Determine the proportions of eleven food groups to fulfill total carbohydrate, protein, and fat requirements as well as restrictions that should be followed to improve the health state.
- Divide these proportions into multiple intakes among a 12-hour period.
- Plan a sample menu by assigning proper food items to each intake, which will match the food group requirement.

■ 11.7.2 The DietMaster Architecture

DietMaster integrates both problem-solving and learning architectures. The flow of control and information between the knowledge base and the processes of problem solving and learning is shown in Figure 11.1. The figure illustrates that problem solving in DietMaster is performed by a combination of model-based reasoning (MBR), case-based reasoning (CBR), and rule-based reasoning (RBR). The learning combines case-based learning (CBL) and rule-based learning (RBL) methods.

FIGURE 11.1
The DietMaster
architecture

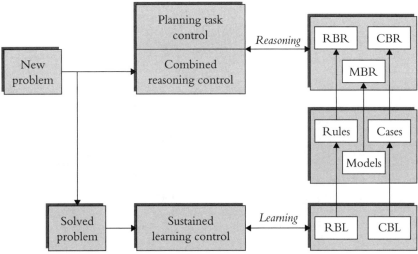

At a high level of abstraction, DietMaster is an integrated architecture containing three building blocks: an object-level knowledge base, a problem solver, and a learner. The object knowledge base contains a conceptual knowledge model, a collection of past cases, and a set of heuristic rules. DietMaster contains multiple methods for reasoning and learning, where each method communicates with a part of the knowledge base.

The planning task controller and the combined reasoning controller use knowledge in the planning and reasoning modules, respectively (see Figure 11.2). For example, the planning module initializes the problem-solving process through the start-up task "understand problem," which activates a set of relevant features. This is followed by the task "retrieve candidate solutions," which triggers the reasoning model, whose initial task is to decide whether the case base or heuristic rules should be used in the initial attempt to solve the problem. When presented with a new problem, the reasoning controller receives a problem frame containing the input features and the current goal.

■ **FIGURE 11.2**
Functional
architecture of
DietMaster

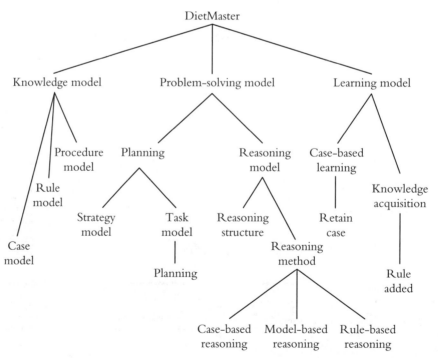

In a system for planning a diet menu, for example, the initial goal could be "Find total calories required." If a feature is known to the system, it will have a frame that describes its current properties. If a feature is not available, the system uses rules to generate it and creates the corresponding slots. The system checks whether this description violates any constraints or current facts. The input features (observed features, also called *findings*) trigger a chain of activations along a particular subset of relationships in the knowledge model. This process establishes a context for further inferencing, which is guided by the current goal and subgoals and the current state of the planning model. The planning model continually updates the subgoals as the problem-solving process proceeds.

The process of selecting the initial reasoning paradigm starts when a set of relevant features of a problem has been identified. This feature set typically contains input features as well as inferred features—that is, features that the system derives from the input features by using its knowledge. If the set of relevant features gives a reminder of a previous case that is above a particular strength—called the *reminding threshold*—case-based problem solving is tried; otherwise, activation of the rule set is attempted. Relevant features may be input features or features inferred from the object domain model. For example, if an application system has a well-developed collection of rules but has not seen many problems yet, the user may want to optimize performance by setting the threshold level to a high value—close to 1.0. The rule base will then be used in the initial attempt to solve the problem, unless there is a strong reminder to a case. As more cases are added, the ratio of case-based to rule-based successes is likely to increase, and the system will gradually lower the threshold value. The exact flow for this process will depend on the actual application system.

The sustained learning control module is the operational part of the learning model. The learning controller guides the learning process by providing a strategy for when to perform particular learning tasks and how to combine them. DietMaster learns from every problem-solving experience. If a successful solution was copied from a previous case, the reminder to that case from each relevant feature is strengthened. In this situation, no new case is stored, but an attempt is made to merge the two cases by generalizing their feature values. If a solution was derived by revising a previous solution, a new case is stored. A new case is also created after a problem has been solved, whether from rules or the deeper knowledge model. Thus, the main target for the learning process in DietMaster is the case base. But Diet-Master may also learn general knowledge through interactions with the user during problem solving.

Heuristic rules are integrated within the conceptual model and are available for the same tasks as the conceptual domain model in general. A rule may be used to support learning, for example. Even if the explanatory strength of a shallow relationship like a rule in general is low, it may add to other explanations for the same hypothesis and, thus, contribute to a justification of a hypothesis.

■ 11.8 KNOWLEDGE MODEL

DietMaster's combined approach to problem solving and learning requires a representation system that is able to express conceptual models, heuristic rules, and previously experienced cases. The representation must be able to adequately express deep as well as shallow knowledge at the object level as well as at the control level.

■ 11.9 REPRESENTATION OF DIFFERENT KNOWLEDGE TYPES

Figure 11.3 illustrates the different types of knowledge at the object and control levels. Domain knowledge at the object level consists of a conceptual domain model in which specific experiences (past cases) and general heuristics (premise-conclusion rules) are integrated. Explicit knowledge about how to use domain knowledge for problem solving and learning is described partly as control level concepts, partly as control rules. The general definitions of concepts and relationships at this level are part of the unified conceptual fundamental knowledge. This enables an explicit definition of each type of concept that will be reasoned about. A function, for example, may be explicitly defined by describing its input arguments, output, side effects, contextual constraints, dependencies on other functions, and so on. In this way, the system is able to understand the effect and operation of a function and use this understanding in its reasoning at a higher level (control level).

There are two types of heuristic rules within the DietMaster architecture: the premise-conclusion rule—called the *conclusive rule*—and the

FIGURE 11.3
Dimensions of
knowledge

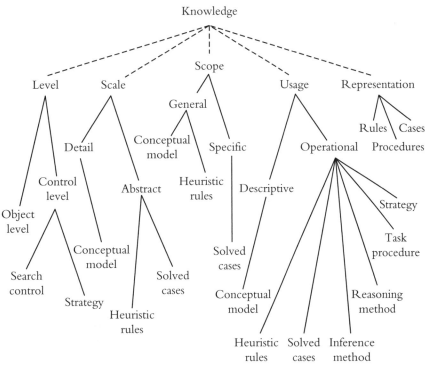

premise-action rule—called the *conditioned procedure*. While a conclusive
rule expresses a *premise → conclusion* statement, a conditioned procedure
represents a *premise → action sequence* structure. The conclusion part of a conclusive rule contains an assignment of a value to some variable (a frame-
slot pair), which is a different type of knowledge than a specification of a
sequence of steps to follow in order to reach a (sub)goal.

Thus, although they both are regarded as heuristic rules, conclusive rules
and conditioned procedures are different types of knowledge, used for different purposes. Both types of heuristic rules are used at the control level,
while, as noted previously, the type of rule at the object level is the conclusive rule.

Knowledge representation in DietMaster constitutes a tightly coupled,
semantic network of frames. As previously emphasized, every entity and every relationship that has meaning within the knowledge model is explicitly defined in a separate frame. Relationships tie concepts to each other,

whereby the semantic network is formed. The meaning of each concept is defined through the concept's relationships with other concepts.

■ 11.9.1 Case Structure

The structure of a case is considered in three different modes—namely, input case, case in process, and output case. When a new client accesses Diet-Master and asks for a diet recommendation, this person has to feed his or her personal information to the system. The system collects some features that describe the case—this is the *input case*. When the diet-planning process starts, it generates some intermediate results describing the client in more detail. Those are called *derived descriptors* of the case, and along with input descriptors, forms the *case in process*. After completion of the planning process, the case will be stored in the case base for future reuse. Here, only required information for reuse gets stored in the case base and becomes the *case to store*.

■ **Table 11.1 The Structure of a Case**

Input Case	Case in Process	Learned Case
Input findings	Input findings	Relevant findings
Goal	Derived findings	Case(s) reused for generating a plan
	Solution constraints	Explanation of successful plan
	Planning states	Successful diet plan
	Possible planning	Differential cases
	Explanation of planning	Book-keeping information
	Possible diet plan	
	Explanation of plan	
	Similar cases	

■ 11.9.2   General Knowledge

General knowledge of DietMaster is stored in terms of rules and models. These rules are mostly fixed. Some rules apply to input descriptors of the

client (new case) and generate either a permanent or an intermediate result. Intermediate results form case descriptors for solving further problems.
These are referred to in the model as derived descriptors, which will be
further used to generate output. Some of these rules are conclusive rules,
whereas some are conditioned procedures.

■ 11.9.3 Rules

Rules are associations of knowledge units. They are described as follows:

1. The standard weight for a given height, age, and gender has been stored
   in terms of associated rules. There are two sets of rules, one of which
   maintains the standard weight for children. These are maintained in the
   form:

   1.1 (Age, Height, Gender) $\longrightarrow$ Standard Weight

Another set maintains the standard weight for adults, with a reference to
gender, which is then converted to the current age with the help of formu-
las. These are maintained in the form:

   1.2 (Height, Gender, Body Frame) $\longrightarrow$ Standard Weight

2. Depending on the age of person, decide his or her age group. This is a
   conclusive rule.

   (Age) $\rightarrow$ Age Group
       If Age < 12 months
   Age Group $\rightarrow$ Infant
       If Age >= 1 and Age <= 6 years
           Age Group $\rightarrow$ Preschooler Child
       If Age > 6 and Age <= 12 years
           Age Group $\rightarrow$ School-age Child
       If Age > 12 and Age <= 18 years
           Age Group $\rightarrow$ Adolescent
       If Age > 18 and Age <= 59 years
           Age Group $\rightarrow$ Adult
       If Age > 59 and Age <= 120 years
           Age Group $\rightarrow$ Old Age

3. This rule checks the physical state of a person and decides whether he or she is underweight, overweight, or obese (recognized with obesity status).

   (Standard Weight, Actual Weight, Body Frame, Waist-to-Hip Ratio) →
   Obesity Status

4. Each exercise consumes some energy. This statement is being maintained as rule in terms of calories consumed per minute. These are stored as:

   (Exercise for a Minute) → Calories Consumed

5. The main output (Step 1) of the diet-planning process is to decide total calories required.

   (Standard Weight, Obesity Status, Activity, Exercises, Female Status) → Total Calories Required

6. Restrictions on nutrients are stored as minimum and maximum levels of carbohydrates, proteins, and fats for certain diseases. These are stored in terms of rules maintained in one-to-many relationships, as one disease can restrict multiple nutrients. Those are stored and defined as:

   (Symptoms, Other Health Complaints) → Minimum, Maximum Levels of Carbohydrates, Proteins, and Fats

7. The output of Step 2 of the diet-planning process is to decide nutrient requirements. This stepwise conditioned procedure is explained in the next section as a ratio of carbohydrates, proteins, and fats.

   (Obesity Status, Female Status, Other Health Complaints, Standard Weight) → Protein Required

   (Protein, Total Calories Required) → Carbohydrates

   (Protein, Carbohydrates, Total Calories Required) → Fats

8. Restrictions on food groups are also defined as minimum and maximum levels of food groups, which suit the health state of the client and help to improve it. These are conclusive rules and are in the following format:

   (Obesity Symptoms, Other Health Complaints) → Restrictions on Food Group[1]

---

1. Food groups are cereals, pulses, milk, eggs, meat, green vegetables, other vegetables, roots and tubers, fruits, sugar, and oil.

9. The nutrient contents of food groups are defined in terms of conclusive rules:

(Food Group Proportion) $\longrightarrow$ Energy, Carbohydrates, Proteins, Fats

10. Step 3 of the diet-planning process is to plan the proper proportions of 11 food groups to gain required nutrients and total calories. These rules are stored in the form:

(Age Group, Gender, Activity, Female Status) $\longrightarrow$ 11 Food Group Proportions

A conditioned procedure is being defined to adjust the food group proportions to fulfill nutrient requirements and to follow restrictions on food groups.

11. The insulin treatment the client undergoes defines his or her intake proportion. Some insulin types propose three intakes, whereas some suggest five intakes. These rules are stored in a table, in the form:

(Insulin Type) $\longrightarrow$ Intake Proportion

12. Step 4 of the menu-planning process is to distribute food group portions into different intakes. The intake proportion suggested is mainly for carbohydrates, since the preference is to distribute carbohydrate-rich food groups according to the intake proportion given and other food groups according to the regular eating habits of the client. This is also a conditioned procedure, and its construction can be defined as:

(Intake Proportion, Health Complaints, 11 Food Group Proportions) $\longrightarrow$ Intakes [Cereals, Pulses, Milk, Sugar, Fruit, with Reference to Insulin Type]

[Eggs, Meat, Green Vegetables, Other Vegetables, Oil, with Reference to Regular Meal Pattern]

13. People are asked not to eat some food items but are permitted to eat some food items in greater quantities and to eat some food items in moderate quantities to treat certain diseases. Those are defined as contraindicators and indicators of the disease. The extent of diabetes, hypertension, cholesterol level, and obesity are also considered health complaints.

(Other Health Complaints) $\longrightarrow$ Restrictions on Food Items

14. The final step of menu planning is to generate an intake-wise menu plan as follows:

(11 Food Group Proportions in Intakes, Restrictions on Food Items) → Assign Food Items for Each Intake

15. According to the occupation or type of work the user is doing, five work groups are formed: Sedentary, Moderate, Hard, Bed Patient, Loss of Weight. Association of occupation and work group is stored in terms of rules in the knowledge base.

Occupation → Work Group

16. Any person requires some energy to do his or her day to-day activities and basal metabolic activities.

Work Group → Caloric Factor

If Activity = "Bed patient" then Caloric Factor = 25

If Activity = "Loss of Weight" then Caloric Factor = 27

If Activity = "Sedentary" then Caloric Factor = 30

If Activity = "Moderate" then Caloric Factor = 35

If Activity = "Hard Work" then Caloric Factor = 40

■ 11.9.4 Procedures

General knowledge is also stored in terms of procedures that partially solve a problem whenever past cases are not available. These procedures are also used in the adaptation process. The five major operations in diet menu planning, along with supportive processes, are generalized and kept available. These can also act as fundamental knowledge and at times with conditioned rules. An example algorithm for the five major procedures is provided here.

This procedure performs the initial step of menu planning to calculate total calories.

Input: Age, Height, Weight, Gender, Female Status, Activity, and Waist-to-Hip Ratio
Output: Total Calories Required Per Day for the Client

Calculate Total Calories: (Age, Height, Weight, Gender, Female Status, Activity, Waist-to-Hip Ratio)

1. Start.

2. Calculate BMI.
   BMI = (Weight in kg)/(Height^2 in meters)

3. If Age <18 then
   Apply Rule 1.1 to find standard weight
   Otherwise
   Apply Rule 1.2 to find standard weight

4. Decide weight status
   a. Actual Weight is less than 20% of Standard Weight and Age < 18
      then
      Weight Status <- Underwt
   b. If Age > 18 and Actual Weight exceeds Standard Weight by 20%
      and BMI > 29 then

If Gender = Male and Waist-to-Hip Ratio > 1 then
Weight Status <-Overwt
               Otherwise
               If Gender = Female and Waist-to-Hip ratio > 0.9 and
               Female Status = Normal then
Weight Status <-Overwt
               end if
               end if
   c. According to Weight Status decide calorie change
If Weight Status = Underwt then
Caloriesded = -500
Otherwise
Caloriesded = Ø
               If Weight Status = Overwt then
Caloriesded = 500

5. Apply Rule 16 to check activity and decide caloric factor

6. Calculate Total Calories
   Total Calories = (Standard Weight in Kg) * Caloric Factor

7. If person does exercise, apply Rule 4 and calculate sum of
   calories consumed for all exercises. This is considered as
   'Extra' calories

8. Total calories required = Total calories - Caloriesded + Extra
   calories from Steps 4, 6, and 7

9. Decide additional calories required for female client [NIN- a]
   If Female Status = 1st Trimester Pregnancy then E= 10 cal.
   If Female Status = 2nd Trimester Pregnancy then E= 90 cal.
   If Female Status = 3rd Trimester Pregnancy then E= 200 cal.

   If Female Status = 0 - 6 Mon Lactation then E = 550 cal.
   If Female Status = 7 - 12 Mon Lactation then E = 400 cal.

   Total Calories = Total Calories + E

10. Stop

■ 11.10 PROBLEM SOLVING IN DIETMASTER

Problem solving in DietMaster is controlled and guided by the planning model. This generic model specifies a goal and task structure for the planning process. The planning model considers planning a major task that is further decomposed into subtasks. These steps should be executed in sequence, as they are dependent on each other. The underlying methods within each of these steps are then described and related to the control structure defined by the planning model.

In this respect, DietMaster has to go through five major steps when planning a diet. It applies a combined approach to solving each individual task based on the retrieve–reuse/generate–revise cycle. This is a combination of case-based and rule-based approaches. The CBR cycle generally consists of four steps, called the REs: retrieve, reuse, revise, and retain. Out of those four, three REs—retrieve, reuse, and revise—are adopted here. Generate is the phase where calculations are done using general knowledge to solve the problem and generate a result. DietMaster selects appropriate features and sets an index parameter and then retrieves the matching case. It proceeds with the next step after solving the previous step; at the same time, it passes matching cases of the previous step to be used as a search space for the next step. This way, it reduces the search space and increments the search criteria until it reaches the last step. If DietMaster could not find a matching case to solve a subproblem, it solves the subproblem with the generate phase satisfying that subgoal. When a step is solved with the generate phase, DietMaster uses the complete case base as a search area for solving further steps.

While solving the problem, DietMaster maintains the explanation regarding phases undergone through the problem-solving process. The output generated is displayed and an expert user is asked to revise it to properly suit the current client. After solving the problem, the output is evaluated for relevant information, which is retained, if necessary.

■ 11.11 INTEGRATED REASONING IN DIETMASTER

Now we will describe how the planning model works. As mentioned earlier, DietMaster works in four phases: retrieve, reuse/calculate, revise, and retain. All of these phases use general knowledge stored in the form of rules whenever required. The system accepts the input in the form of physical state, physiological state, and current menu. The system searches for a previous matching case in the retrieve phase. It checks for the availability of previous matching cases (with the same features) used for the diet plan and tested to be successful. If such a case is available, DietMaster enters the reuse phase and applies the diet plan of the previous case as output to the current problem. Otherwise, the system searches for a previous case nearly matching the current case. If such a case is found, it is partially used where applicable, and the remaining part is calculated according to the general knowledge. This is the revise phase. If no case matches the current case even partially, the system switches to the generate phase and solves the subtask using procedures and rules. An expert user is allowed to revise the suggested plan, and the final plan is given as an output of the system. The diet plan generated through the revise phase is followed for a test period and stored as an under-observation plan. Integrated reasoning in the planner is shown in Figure 11.4.

Following the test period, the system enters the retain phase and evaluates the physiological state of the client. If the current physiological state is better than the previous state of the client, he or she is asked to continue the same plan and the diet plan is stored as a successful solution for future reuse. But if the diet plan does not suit the client—that is, his or her physiological state is aggravated, the plan stored as under observation is removed from the case base so that it is not accessed in the future for reuse. The case-based reasoning in DietMaster is shown in Figure 11.5.

■ FIGURE 11.4
Integrated reason-
ing in DietMaster

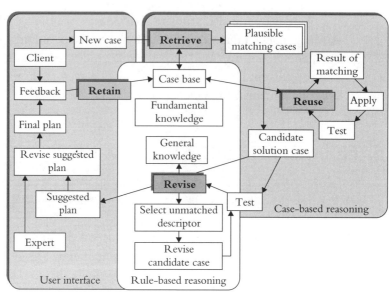

■ FIGURE 11.5
Case-based
reasoning in
DietMaster

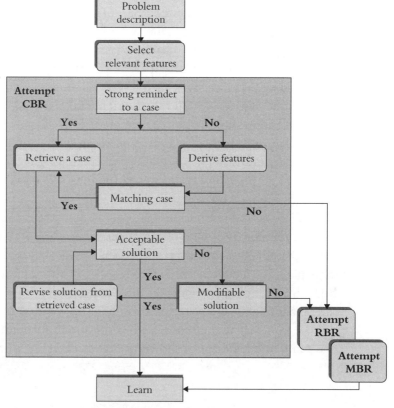

■ 11.12   PROBLEM SOLVING AND REASONING ALGORITHM

Problem solving and reasoning in DietMaster are shown in Figure 11.4 and reviewed in Section 11.11. The reuse phase of the CBR cycle works at each step of planning. In the adaptation phase, we propose a strategy of using experiences in multiple levels. The old cases get reused in the same way as in the diet planning process. DietMaster decides up to which step the current matching case (old case) can be reused. This is done by comparing corresponding features. There are two types of matching processes implemented in DietMaster: direct matching and relative matching. The direct matching method is used to find candidate-matching cases. The relative matching method selects the most desirable case. In this method, the selection of the most successful case is made from the candidate case set. If old plans are not available to solve a step, DietMaster uses general knowledge as discussed in the Sections 11.8 and 11.9. In this way, DietMaster uses multiple reasoning methods to solve the problem.

■ 11.13   THE LEARNING PROCESS

The primary machine-learning method in DietMaster involves obtaining problem-specific knowledge by retaining experience in the form of cases. However, the DietMaster system is also able to take part in the refinement of its general knowledge model. This ability is due to its knowledge-intensive methods for generating and evaluating explanations, which also has the side effect of checking coherence and integrity in the knowledge base, as well as suggesting possible ways to resolve conflicts. Unresolvable contradictions discovered during problem solving or case learning is reported to the user, who decides the proper actions to take. This refinement process is a manual process, however, while the research reported here focuses on methods for sustained learning in which the computer plays a much more active part.

■ 11.13.1 The Learning Algorithm

The DietMaster system learns by retaining cases, whether representing a single problem-solving experience or merged into slightly generalized cases. The criteria for when to store a new case, when to modify an existing case, and when to update indexes only are as follows: a new case is created if no similar past case was found, a past solution needed modification, or the new case has a set of relevant findings significantly different from those of the matching case. In this context, "significantly different" means that the two sets have different values and the corresponding findings cannot be generalized. If both cases have the same findings and their values are close enough to be generalized, the two cases are merged. If their values are close enough to be regarded equal, the only update made is adding "book-keeping" information to the case and adjusting the relevance factors. If a past case leads to a successful solution to the new problem, this leads to a strengthening of the relevance factor for each finding. If a past case leads to an unsuccessful solution, this leads to a weakening of the relevance factors.

As the system gains experience, the frequency of problem cases that lead to the storing of a new case will gradually decrease, implying a flattening of the knowledge base growth curve over time.

■ 11.14 FEEDBACK ON DIET PLAN

The final step of CBR is *retain*. The first phase of retain is learning, and the relevant phase in DietMaster is feedback on the diet plan. After retaining a problem-solving attempt as an experience, it is applied for the test period and then checked whether it worked properly for the client.

In order to retrieve the appropriate case, cases are being indexed in multiple ways. Those are broadly categorized into three types:

- Relevant input features: This is the subset of the input descriptors that have been explained to be relevant for solving the problem. If a numeric descriptor was transformed into a symbolic value, this becomes the value of the index feature.
- Derived findings: These findings may disqualify a case, since they point to cases that probably are better matches if such a finding is involved. Differential findings are inserted in a case reminder when this case does not lead to a successful solution. Hence, they are indexes between similar cases, albeit different enough to associate different solutions.
- Plan: Successful as well as failed solutions provide indexes to the cases. The primary use of indexes is to retrieve suitable cases efficiently. Indexes that are failed solutions are used to avoid retrieving similar failures while solving new problems.

Each case is a separate entity, and the collection of cases constitutes what is referred to as the case memory. The cases are integrated into the model of

■ **FIGURE 11.6**
Structure of the
learning process in
DietMaster

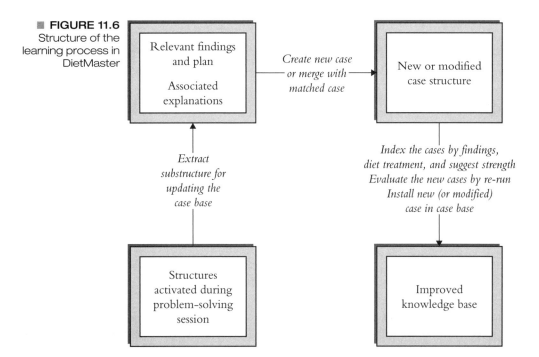

■ **FIGURE 11.6**
Structure of the
learning process in
DietMaster

general domain knowledge, with all descriptors defined within the semantic network structure, which constitutes the general knowledge. Cases are organized according to classification, resulting in a hierarchical structure of the case base.

As indicated in Figure 11.6, the extraction process will necessarily extract different items from a problem-solving process involving case-based reasoning than it would if rule-based or model-based reasoning was used. The subsequent process description assumes that the problem has been solved by use of previous cases. The user may assist in the construction of a new case.

The case generalization method in DietMaster improves the matching process and reduces the growth of the case base. Cases are only generalized if they match exactly on feature values. If a case is used to solve the new problem completely, the new case will not get stored as a new experience; rather, the additional attempt of the old case to solve the new problem is retained.

DietMaster uses multiple cases to reuse and generate solutions for current cases. Features from multiple objects are inherited, thus the term hybrid inheritance. The relationship used for generalization is the subclass of relationship. The specific values may be retained in a particular facet of the finding slot.

■ 11.15 CONCLUSION

We have discussed a case study for developing a knowledge-based diet-planning system using case-based reasoning. CBR is an essential technology for building intelligent systems for medical diagnoses that can aid significantly in improving physicians' decision making. These systems help physicians and doctors to check, analyze, and repair their solutions.

References

Aamodt, A. A Computational Model of Knowledge-Intensive Learning and Problem Solving; Current Trends in Knowledge Acquisition. In: Bob Wielinga, et al. (eds.), Amsterdam: IOS Press, pp. 1–20, 1990.

Aamodt, A. & Plaza, E. *Case-Based Reasoning: Foundational Issues, Methodological Variations and System Approaches*; AI Communications, IOS Press, Vol. 7: pp. 39–59, 1994.

Akerkar, R. Knowledge-Intensive Learning, Tutorial Talk: International Symposium on Knowledge Systems, Germany, 2004.

Cheetham, W. & Graf, J. Case-based reasoning in color matching. In Leake, D. & Plaza, E. (eds.) Proceedings of the *Second International Conference on Case-Based Reasoning, ICCBR-97*, Berlin: Springer, pp. 1–12, 1997.

Hennessy, D. & Hinkle D. Applying Case-Based Reasoning to Autoclave Loading, *IEEE Intelligent Systems*, vol. 7, no. 5, pp. 21, 24–26, Oct. 1992.

Jamsandekar, P. & Akerkar, R. Dietary Planner, A Case-Based Reasoning System. In the proceedings of *Recent Trends in IT, A National Conference*, Amaravati, India, 2000.

Kolodner, J. *Case-based Reasoning*. San Mateo, CA: Morgan Kauffmann Publisher; 1993.

CHAPTER 12

Natural Language Interface: Question Answering System

■ 12.1 INTRODUCTION

Natural language processing (NLP) is a theoretically motivated variety of computational techniques for analyzing and representing naturally occurring texts at one or more levels of linguistic analysis for the purpose of achieving human–like language processing for a range of tasks or applications. The basic objective of NLP, as stated, is to accomplish human–like language processing. There are some other practical objectives of NLP, many related to the specific application for which it is being utilized. For instance, an NLP-based information retrieval system has the purpose of providing more precise and complete information in response to a user's real information need. The question answering (QA) system, a type of NLP-based information retrieval, is a study of the methodology that returns exact answers to natural language questions rather than a list of potentially relevant documents, which users have to scan through in order to dig out the necessary information (Joshi & Akerkar, 2008a, 2008b). The challenge with QA systems is how to return answers to users' natural language questions. The whole process is quite complicated, as it requires a number of different techniques working closely together in order to achieve the goal, including query rewrites and formulations, question classification, information retrieval, passage retrieval, answer extraction, answer ranking, and justification.

The research on *natural language interface to databases* (NLI2DB) has recently received attention from the research communities. The purpose of natural language interfaces is to allow users to compose questions in natural language and to receive responses in the form of tables or short answers. Due to the implicit ambiguity of natural language, current natural language interfaces are often implemented in a specific domain and can only understand a subset of a natural language.

In this case study, we will discuss interesting facets of question answering systems. In general, QA systems are natural language interfaces to knowledge-based systems that are adapted to particular domains. However, currently, QA systems use text documents as their basic knowledge source and bring together different NLP techniques to search for the answers. The idea of a QA system is simple: given a set of documents and a question, find the answer to the question in the set of documents. This task would usually be performed by an individual, who indexes the set of documents with an information retrieval system. However, this is a time-consuming method. When a question needs to be answered, a query will be created to retrieve documents relevant to the question, and each document retrieved will be read manually until the proper answer is found. With this process, there is a chance of missing a correct answer. In order to overcome such problems, a QA system is the best option.

Such systems employ information retrieval to obtain documents relevant to the question, and then use information extraction techniques to determine the answer from those documents. As it becomes more difficult to find answers on the World Wide Web using standard search engines, question answering technology will become increasingly important.

Example

Looking at different examples of questions and their answers, we can sense the complexity of research into question answering systems. For instance:

Question: When was Mozart born?

This question requires a single fact as an answer and, moreover, the answer may be found verbatim in text—that is, Mozart was born in 1756.

Question: How did Socrates die?

This question may require reasoning. In this example, die has to be linked with drinking poisoned wine.

Question: How do I assemble a computer?

The complete answer to this question might require combined information from many different sources. The complexity can range from simple lists to script-based answers.

Question: Is the moon flat?

This question requires a simple yes/no answer.

The concept of natural language is studied at different levels. Liddy (2003) proposed the following seven levels for linguistic analysis. Bhattacharyya (2003) elaborated on how these levels of linguistic analysis are useful in the interlingual approach for machine translation.

Phonological

Phonetics is the interpretation of speech sounds within and across words. It is the study of language in terms of the relationships between phonemes—the smallest distinct sound units in a given language (Matthews, 1997). Phonetic knowledge is used, for example, for building speech-recognition systems. Though most natural language processing systems do not need to operate at this level, speech-recognition systems depend heavily on this analysis.

Morphology

Morphology is the study of the meaningful parts of words. It deals with the componential nature of words, which are composed of morphemes. Morphemes are the smallest elements of meaning in a language. Morphological knowledge is used, for example, for automatic stemming, truncation, or masking of words.

Lexicology

Lexicology is the study of words. The lexical level of analysis is defined as "of or relating to words or the vocabulary of language as distinguished from its grammar and construction." This level refers to parts-of-speech tagging or the use of lexicons (dictionaries, thesauri, etc.). Lexicons are utilized in information retrieval (IR) systems to ensure that a common vocabulary is used in selecting appropriate indexing or searching terms and phrases.

Syntactic

The syntactic level of linguistic analysis is concerned with how words arrange themselves in construction. Syntax is the study of the rules, or "patterned relationships," that govern the way words in a sentence are arranged. Syntactic rules are used in parsing algorithms. Meaning can be derived from a word's position and role in a sentence. The structure of a sentence conveys meaning and relationships between words, even if we do not know what the dictionary meanings are. All this is conveyed by the syntax of the sentence. Natural language processing systems, in their fullest implementation, make good use of this kind of structural information.

Semantics

Semantics involves the meaning of a word. This is more complex level of linguistic analysis. The study of the meaning of isolated words may be termed lexical semantics. The study of meaning is also related to syntax at the level of the sentence and to discourse at the level of the text. The level of processing can include the semantic disambiguation of words with multiple senses; in an analogous way to how syntactic disambiguation of words that can serve as multiple parts-of-speech is accomplished at the syntactic level. Semantic disambiguation permits just a single sense of polysemous (the existence of multiple meanings for a single word or phrase) words to be used in the semantic representation of the sentence. For instance, along with other meanings, "nature" as a noun can mean either a character of a person, or the physical world including all natural phenomena and living things, or a sort of thing. If information from the remaining part of the sentence were required for the disambiguation, the semantic (not the lexical level) would do the disambiguation.

Discourse Analysis

Although syntax and semantics work with sentence-length units, the discourse level of NLP works with units of text longer than a sentence. This level relies on the concept of predictability. It uses document structure to further analyze the text as a whole. By understanding the structure of a document, NLP systems can make certain assumptions. Examples from information science are the resolving of anaphora and ellipsis and the examination of the effect on proximity searching.

Pragmatics

Pragmatics is often understood as the study of how the context (or "world knowledge") influences meaning. This level is, in some ways, far more complex and effort-intensive than all the other levels. This level depends on a body of knowledge about the world that comes from outside the document. Though it is easy for people to choose the right sense of a word, it is extremely difficult to program a computer with all the world knowledge necessary to do the same.

These levels of linguistic processing reflect an increasing amount of unit analysis as well as increasing complexity and difficulty as we move from the phonological level to pragmatics. The larger the unit of analysis becomes (i.e., from morpheme to word, to sentence, to paragraph, and to full document), the less precise the language phenomena. This decrease in precision results in fewer discernible rules and more reliance on less predictable regularities as one moves from the lowest to the highest levels. In addition, higher levels presume reliance on the lower levels of language understanding, and the theories used to explain the data move into the areas of cognitive psychology and artificial intelligence. As a result, the lower levels of language processing have been more thoroughly investigated and incorporated into NLP–related systems (Liddy, 1998).

■ 12.1.1 Open-Domain Question Answering

The taxonomy of existing open-domain QA systems is based on the following criteria:

- Linguistic and knowledge resources
- Natural language processing involved
- Document processing
- Reasoning methods
- Assumptions about answers being explicitly stated in documents
- Necessity to generate answers

The five classes of systems identified in this taxonomy are strongly associated with the types of questions and the available test collections.

Class 1 Systems are capable of processing factual questions and typically extract answers using keyword matching.

Class 2 Systems use semantic alternations, world knowledge axioms, and simple reasoning to relate snippets of text containing answers with the questions.

Class 3   Systems generate answers to list, script, or template-like questions from parts found in several documents.

Class 4   Interactive systems answer questions in the context of previous interactions, which involve complex reference resolution.

Class 5   Systems answer speculative questions, which involve knowledge extraction from relevant documents and case-based, temporal, spatial, and evidential reasoning.

■ 12.1.2 Closed-Domain Question Answering

Closed-domain question answering has recently regained the interest of researchers. The definition of the closed domain ranges from working in a specific domain to using closed document collections restricted in size and subject. The term restricted domain is often used interchangeably with the term closed domain.

Besides relying upon domain ontologies, the emerging closed-domain systems share such features as:

• Concept recognition and matching in questions and documents
• Utilization of the domain-specific document structure and features such as tense, voice, and style
• Logical representation of documents
• Mapping questions to restricted sets of semantic frames
• Modeling questions as syntactico-semantic patterns

■ 12.2   NATURAL LANGUAGE INTERFACE TO STRUCTURED DATA

Using natural language to communicate between a database system and its human users has become increasingly important since database systems have become widespread. In order to facilitate full use of the database systems, its accessibility to nonexpert users is desirable. In the late 1960s, BASE-BALL (Green, 1961) and LUNAR (Woods, 1972) emerged as the first usable NLI2DBs. The BASEBALL system was designed to answer questions about baseball games that were played in the American League during any one season. LUNAR contained chemical analyses of moon rocks, and had a significant influence on subsequent computational approaches to natural language. LUNAR is an interface system to a database that deals with information about lunar rock samples using augmented transition network and procedural semantics.

PLANES, LADDER, and REL systems were developed by the late 1970s. Some of these systems used semantic grammars. This is an approach in which nonterminal symbols of the grammar reflect categories of world entities (e.g., student_name, designation_of_employee) instead of purely syntactic categories like noun phrase, verb phrase, etc.

Subsequently, several NLI2DBs appeared with different approaches toward handling natural language. By the mid-1980s, NLI2DB had become a popular research area, and numerous research prototypes were implemented.

Historically, computing scientists have divided the problem of natural language access to a database into two subproblems: the linguistic component and the database component. The database component performs traditional database management functions, whereas the linguistic component is responsible for translating natural language input into a formal query and generating a natural language response based on the results from the database search. A lexicon is a table that is used to map the words of the natural input onto the formal objects (relation names, attribute names, etc.) of the database. Both parser and semantic interpreter make use of the lexicon. A natural language generator takes the formal response as its input and inspects the parse tree in order to generate adequate natural language response.

Natural language database systems make use of syntactic knowledge and knowledge about the actual database in order to properly relate natural language input to the structure and contents of that database. Of course, the system expects the user to ask questions pertaining to the domain of the database, which in turn represents some aspect of the real world. Syntactic knowledge usually resides in the linguistic component of the system—in particular, in the syntax analyzer—whereas knowledge about the actual database resides to some extent in the semantic data model used. Knowledge about the user and goals of his or her speech act are required if a user-friendly dialogue is to be carried through. Questions entered in natural language are translated into a statement in a formal query language. Once the statement is unambiguously formed, the query is processed by the database management system in order to produce the required data. These data are then passed back to the natural language component, where generation functions produce a surface language version of the response.

NLI2DBs were seen as a promising way to make databases accessible to users with no programming expertise, and there was an extensive optimism about their commercial prospects. Linguistic Technology's ENGLISH

WIZARD was among the systems claimed to have been commercially successful.

The use of NLI2DBs, however, is much less widespread than it was once predicted, mainly because of the development of alternative graphic- and form-based database interfaces. However, these alternative interfaces are less natural to interact with and queries that involve quantification or that require multiple database tables to be consulted are difficult to formulate with graphic- or form-based interfaces, whereas they can be expressed easily in natural language.

In order to illustrate the general idea of how an NLI2DB works, we present one of the more successful NLI2DBs developed. We discuss a template-based system for translating English sentences into SQL queries for a relational database system. The input sentences are syntactically parsed using the link parser and semantically parsed using domain-specific templates. The system is composed of a preprocessor and a runtime module. The preprocessor builds a conceptual knowledge base from the database schema using WordNet. This knowledge base is then used at runtime to semantically parse the input and create the corresponding SQL query. The system is meant to be domain-independent and has been tested with the CINDI database that contains information on a virtual library. The general architecture of the system is shown in Figure 12.1.

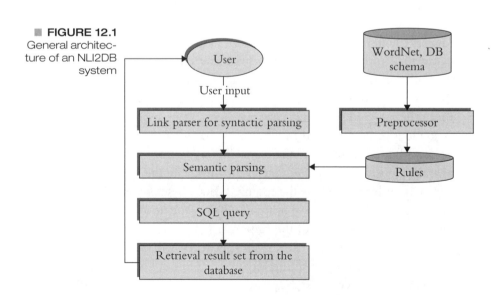

■ **FIGURE 12.1** General architecture of an NLI2DB system

In order to tolerate lexical variations in the input questions, the preprocessor builds a semantic knowledge base composed of interpretation rules and semantic sets for all possible relationship and attribute names in the database. This helps to build the same semantic representation, and hence, the same SQL query for various questions.

In the preceding NLI2DB example, we saw that the link parser, which collects information at a syntactic level, also can be used at a semantic level. The focus of NLI2DBs today has shifted to handle problems at a higher level of linguistic analysis. Therefore, the development of NLI2DB systems that handle language-related phenomena is an active area of research.

■ 12.3   NATURAL LANGUAGE INTERFACE TO UNSTRUCTURED DATA

The process of establishing an interaction between human being and machine was made successful in 1966 with the ELIZA system, which was developed by Joseph Weizenbaum (Weizenbaum, 1966). ELIZA worked by simple parsing and substitution of keywords into phrases stored in a knowledge base. Though ELIZA did not employ any language-related phenomena, it still remains a milestone simply because it was the first time a programmer had attempted such a human–machine interaction with the goal of creating the illusion of human–human interaction.

Dialogue systems were historically the domain of artificial intelligence (AI) researchers. These systems are a sort of natural language interface to unstructured data. These systems do not restrict themselves to interacting with data in database tables only; data from various sources can be used and accumulated.

Moving forward through the history of the natural language interface to unstructured data research brings us to SHRDLU and GUS. Both of these systems are dialogue systems interacting on information about a restricted domain. The difference between these systems and systems such as LUNAR lies in their dialogue capabilities. GUS was designed to simulate a travel advisor and had access to a database containing limited information about airline flight times. SHRDLU is probably the better known of these two systems. It controlled a robot arm in a virtual microworld consisting of a tabletop strewn with colored blocks of varying shapes and sizes and a box into which the blocks could be placed. While example conversations with SHRDLU are generally impressive, the system is still severely limited to only discussing the microworld it inhabits.

In 1971, a program called PARRY was also developed by Kenneth Colby. This program attempted to embody a theory of paranoia (psychiatric disorder) in a system. Instead of a single keyword, the program used groups of keywords, and used synonyms if the keywords were not found. Researchers claimed that PARRY passed the Turing test. But the system received criticism from the scientific world. Currently, there is a vast amount of NLP-based research carried out for the development of natural language interfaces.

One modern natural language system is Jupiter, probably best described by its product page (http://groups.csail.mit.edu/sls/research/jupiter.shtml) at MIT: "Jupiter is a conversational system that provides up-to-date weather information over the phone. Jupiter knows about 500+ cities worldwide (of which 350 are within the United States) and gets its data from four different Web-based sources." Clearly, Jupiter is more complex than systems such as SHRDLU, as the system is dealing with input via the telephone and hence has to cope with the added problem of robust speech recognition to provide a reasonable input to the dialogue system. Note, however, that just as SHRDLU was limited to questions about the block world it inhabited, Jupiter is limited to questions about weather reports for the cities of which it is aware.

Boris Katz at MIT's Artificial Intelligence Laboratory developed the SynTactic Analysis using Reversible Transformations (START) natural language system. It is a software system designed to answer questions that are posed to it in a natural language. START uses several language-dependent functions, such as parsing, and natural language annotation, to present the appropriate information segments to the user.

Since information is largely available in unstructured manner, retrieving relevant documents containing the required information was the primary goal of the natural language interfaces. This task is known as information retrieval. Pinpointing the exact information required—information extraction—is the next step, and the development of a question answering system is an advanced step toward human–machine interaction.

Information extraction is the task of locating specific pieces of data from a natural language document, and has been the focus of the Defense Advanced Research Project Agency (DARPA) Message Understanding Conference (MUC) program. The extracted information can then be stored in a database, which could then be queried using either standard database query languages or a natural language database interface.

However, a limitation with information extraction systems is that they are difficult and time-consuming to build, and they generally contain highly domain-specific components, making porting to new domains also time-consuming. Thus, more efficient means for developing information extraction systems are desirable.

A question answering system establishes nonformal communication with the user and tries to answer to the natural language queries asked by the user. These question answering systems are a sort of natural language interface to unstructured data.

The Text REtrieval Conference (TREC), co-sponsored by the National Institute of Standards and Technology (NIST) and the U.S. Department of Defense, was started in 1992 and has been organized regularly ever since. Question answering is one of the important aspects of text retrieval, and several groups present their current work in this conference. The KUQA system presented at TREC-9 (2000) developed by Soo-Min Kim and his colleagues categorized questions based on an expected answer and then used NLP techniques as well as WordNet to find candidate answers that suit the corresponding category. However, the system did not handle any linguistic phenomena.

At TREC-13 (2004), Michael Kaisser and Tilman Becker presented their QuALiM system that used complex syntactic structure. Based on certain syntactic descriptions, question patterns were identified. Syntactic descriptions of prospective answers were also maintained based on documents retrieved using answers generated by the Google search engine.

The concept of combining NLP techniques with large-scale information retrieval and information extraction is not new, yet it is not successful to the desired extent. Fagan (1987) experimented with indexing noun phrases and prepositional phrases. Many researchers experimented with indexing syntactically derived word pairs; the types of constructions examined in the context of indexing include linguistically motivated pairs such as head/modifier and adjective/noun. Some have tried full linguistic trees and case frames as units of indexing. However, none of these experiments resulted in a dramatic improvement in precision or recall, and often resulted in degraded performance.

In all of these studies, the word-level index was directly augmented with linguistically derived representations. Often, this caused performance issues because the creation of an index is limited by the speed of the parser and because sophisticated linguistic representations were not amenable to large-scale indexing. The current generation of question answering systems that employ NLP alleviate performance problems by delaying linguistic analysis until the corpus has been narrowed down to a small set of candidate documents or passages. The MURAX system is an early example of such an approach. After retrieving a set of candidate documents, the system parses both the questions and the passages, and attempts matching at the relationship level.

However, a drawback of this two-step paradigm is low recall: If the keyword-based document retrieval system does not return *any* relevant documents due to such problems as synonymy, anaphora, or argument alternations, any amount of additional processing is useless. The current workaround to this problem is to implement feedback loops that relax the query set if the results are too restrictive. Not only does this introduce complex dependencies in a system's architecture, it also necessitates the addition of new modules to assess the quality of the result sets.

However, Katz and Lin (2002, 2003, 2004) of MIT showed that NLP technology, in general, is not powerless. On the contrary, performance drop or improvement depends on the manner in which NLP techniques have been applied. Katz and Lin identified two broad linguistic phenomena that are difficult to handle with the simple keyword matching–driven paradigm. Recently, Joshi and Akerkar (2006, 2008a, 2008b) tackled the problem caused by linguistic phenomena of semantic symmetry and ambiguous modification.

Large numbers of experiments are being carried out worldwide to develop effective natural language interfaces. Though several different approaches are exploited to achieve success, every system has certain shortcomings.

We will now present various approaches available to deal with language.

■ 12.4 DIFFERENT APPROACHES TO LANGUAGE

Natural language is a topic of interest from a computational viewpoint due to the implicit ambiguity that language possesses. Several researchers have applied different techniques to deal with language. The next few subsections describe the diverse strategies that are being used to process language for various purposes.

■ 12.4.1 Symbolic (Rule-Based) Approach

Natural language processing appears to be a strongly symbolic activity. Words are symbols that stand for objects and concepts in the real world, and they are put together into sentences that obey well-specified grammar rules. Hence, for several decades, research on natural language processing has been dominated by the symbolic approach.

Knowledge about language is explicitly encoded in rules or other forms of representation. Language is analyzed at various levels to obtain information. On this obtained information, certain rules are applied to achieve linguistic functionality. Because human language capabilities include rule-based reasoning, it is well supported by symbolic processing. In symbolic processing, rules are formed for every level of linguistic analysis. It tries to capture the meaning of the language based on these rules.

■ 12.4.2 Empirical (Corpus-Based) Approach

Empirical approaches are based on statistical analysis as well as on other data-driven analyses, of raw data which is in the form of text corpora. A corpus is a collection of machine-readable text. The approach has been around since NLP began in the early 1950s. Only in the last 10 years or so has empirical NLP emerged as a significant alternative to rationalist rule-based natural language processing.

Corpora are primarily used as a source of information about language, and a number of techniques have emerged to enable the analysis of corpus data. Syntactic analysis can be achieved on the basis of statistical probabilities estimated from a training corpus. Lexical ambiguities can be resolved by considering the likelihood of one or more interpretations on the basis of context.

Recent research in computational linguistics indicates that empirical or corpus-based methods are currently the most promising approach to developing robust, efficient NLP systems. These methods automate the acquisition of much of the complex knowledge required for NLP by training on suitably annotated natural language corpora (e.g., tree-banks of parsed sentences).

Most of the empirical NLP methods employ statistical techniques, such as n-gram models, hidden Markov models (HMMs), and probabilistic context-free grammars (PCFGs). Given the successes of empirical NLP methods, researchers have begun to apply learning methods to the construction of information extraction systems (McCarthy, 1995; Soderland, 1995). Several different symbolic and statistical methods have been employed, but most of them are used to generate one part of a larger information extraction system. Majumder (2002) experimented with n-gram-based language modeling and claimed to develop a language-independent approach to IR and natural language processing.

■ 12.4.3 Connectionist Approach (Using a Neural Network)

Since human language capabilities are based on a neural network in the brain, artificial neural networks (also called connectionist networks) provide an essential starting point for modeling language processing. In recent years, the field of connectionist processing has seen a remarkable development. The subsymbolic neural network approach holds a lot of promise for modeling the cognitive foundations of language processing. Instead of symbols, the approach is based on distributed representations that correspond to statistical regularities in language.

There has also been significant research applying neural network methods to language processing. However, there has been relatively little recent language research using subsymbolic learning, although some recent systems have successfully employed decision trees, transformation rules, and other symbolic methods. The SHRUTI system is a neurally inspired system for event modeling and temporal processing at a connectionist level.

■ 12.5 SEMANTIC-LEVEL PROBLEMS

Any natural language application based on the concept of keyword matching has to face some common problems at the semantic level. We have decided to put an emphasis on problems caused by linguistic phenomena of semantic symmetry and ambiguous modification. This section describes problems due to these phenomena, and we elaborate on the use of shallow parsing-based algorithms to deal with them.

Semantic symmetry and ambiguous modification are linguistic phenomena that occur quite often. Semantic symmetry is a linguistic phenomenon in which word order matters. Two sentences with the same keywords may have different meaning. For example, the sentence "The bird ate the snake" and "The snake ate the bird" are similar at word level but they have different meanings. Similarly, even though the questions "What do rats eat?" and "What eats rats?" are the same at the word level, they have completely different meanings and should be answered in a different way.

At the word level (lexical level), two sentences look the same, but at the semantic level, these two sentences vary. An interface for a natural language or a question answering system has to consider this fact, and answers generated by the system must drop the sentence with the wrong meaning and present only the sentence with the correct meaning.

Ambiguous modification is a process that needs to be handled carefully. Instead of modifying the actual expected noun from the sentence, the adjective in the question modifies another unexpected noun, which results in the infiltration of wrong sentences into the answer. Because of this, the interface performance becomes degraded.

Both of these linguistic phenomena cause problems that directly affect the overall performance of the system, and they occur at a semantic level. Most of the systems tackling any problem at a semantic level (such as machine translation, writing theme of the document, etc.) need information collected at a syntactic level (syntactic analysis). Even the only system currently tackling problems caused by semantic symmetry and ambiguous modification (Katz & Lin, 2003) collects information at a syntactic level and builds ternary relationships based on the output obtained from a Minipar parser.

Katz and Lin (2003, 2004) have implemented Sapere, a prototype natural language, question answering system that retrieves answers by matching ternary expressions derived from the question with those derived from the corpus text. They compared the results obtained from the Sapere system with a simple Boolean retrieval engine that uses standard inverted keyword index-to-index documents at the sentence level.

Sapere is primarily a relationship-indexing engine; it stores and indexes ternary expressions extracted from the corpus text and performs matching at the relationship level between questions and sentences stored in its index. Ternary expressions are generated from text by postprocessing the results of

Minipar, a fast and robust functional-dependency parser. The Sapere system detects the following types of relationships: subject-verb-object (including passive constructions), adjective-noun modification, noun-noun modification, possessive, predicate nominatives, predicate adjectives, appositives, and prepositional phrases.

Ternary expressions are similarly derived from the question, with the *wh*-entity left as an unbound variable. Sapere attempts to match relationships in the question with those found in the corpus text, thereby binding the unbound variable in the question with the actual answer. If such a match occurs, the candidate sentence is returned.

The system developed by Katz and Lin generates an appropriate answer, but at the cost of time and a delay in returning an answer to the user's question: time required for the Minipar parser is followed by time required for developing ternary relationships.

■ 12.6 SHALLOW PARSING

This section helps understand the effect of semantic symmetry and ambiguous modification phenomena, and describes shallow parsing-based algorithms to overcome problems caused by these phenomena.

■ 12.6.1 Semantic Symmetry

Semantic symmetry occurs when an entity is used as the subject as well as an object in different sentences. In a question answering system, selectional restriction (keyword matching) in different sentences is based on such entities, thus, the wrong answer is generated. The following example (Joshi & Akerkar, 2005) illustrates the phenomenon of semantic symmetry and demonstrates the problems this causes.

Question: Who <u>killed</u> <u>militants</u> ?

Candidate Answer 1: National army soldiers <u>killed</u> six <u>militants</u>.

Candidate Answer 2: <u>Militants</u> <u>killed</u> 13 bus passengers.

In the previous sentences, "militants" is an entity (POS[1]—Noun) that acts as a subject in Sentence 2 and as an object in Sentence 1. The selectional

---

1. Part-of-speech

restriction for the subject of "kill" is the word "militants" in one sentence, and the selectional restriction for the object is also the word "militants" in another sentence. Thus, a semantically symmetric relationship involves sentences where one can swap the subject and object and still end up with a sentence that makes sense.

Hence, candidate answers fetched on the basis of keyword matching need to be monitored carefully, as these sentences may have different meanings. In the previous example, the system returns two sentences based on mere keyword matching. The question in this example is referring to the sentences, which contain a semantic symmetry relationship.

Two sentences—"National army soldiers killed six militants" and "Militants killed 13 bus passengers"—are similar at the word level, but they have very different meanings and should be presented as an answer by considering the meaning of these sentences. In these cases, lexical content is insufficient to determine the meaning of the sentence.

■ 12.6.2 Sentence Patterns and Semantic Symmetry

All sentences are categorized as either active or passive. Sentences in active voice follow an SVO structure—that is, Subject followed by Verb followed by Object—whereas sentences in passive voice have an OVS structure: Object followed by Verb followed by Subject. The sentence in active voice can also be presented in passive voice by changing position of Subject and Object and changing the Verb to a past participle form.

Questions may be of type XVO, where X is the subject for which we want to find an answer, V is the verb, and O is the object. "Who killed militants?" is an XVO-type question. In this case, only those active sentences in which the object does not come before the verb is the order VO maintained. If this sentence was in passive voice form (OVS), the sequence of the verb and object will not match, but we can understand that this sentence is in passive voice by looking at the verb, which is in past participle form. Hence, the sequence does not match and the POS of the verb does not point to the correct answer. So, we can formulate the rule that emphasizes the sequence and tense of the verb.

This same logic can be applied to questions of type SVX—that is, X is the object entity that we want to obtain as an answer, V is the verb, and S is the subject entity. "Militants killed whom?" is an example of such a category.

Any sentence in which the word "militants" appears after the verb "killed" is an object entity, whereas we are looking for sentences in which "militants" is the subject. This example emphasizes the importance of the sequence of words in a sentence. In a passive sentence, the SVO sequence is not followed but the passiveness of the sentence can be determined by the tense of the verb, which helps in deciding whether the sentence is correct. This fact underlines the importance of verb tense (past tense or past participle). If the question is in passive voice, this logic also works. XOV* type questions fall in this category. "By whom were militants killed?" is an example of this type of question. X is the subject that we expect from the question answering system, O is the object, and V* is the past participle verb tense used in the question.

■ 12.6.3 An Algorithm

Based on the study of patterns of questions and the sentences, Joshi and Akerkar (2006, 2008a, 2008b) have formulated rules that select exact sentences as answers from a number of candidate answer sentences. The following algorithm gives the procedure for solving semantic symmetry.

Two important factors considered are:

- The sequence of keywords in the question and in the candidate answer sentence
- The POS of keywords (especially the verb keyword)

The algorithm scans each candidate answer sentence and applies the following rule to check whether that sentence is the correct answer or not.

Rule 1

```
If (sequence of keywords in question and candidate answer matches)
then
   If (POS of verb keyword are same) then candidate answer is correct;
Otherwise
   candidate answer is wrong.
```

Rule 2

```
If (sequence of keywords in question and candidate answer do not
match)
   then
```

```
    If (POS verb keyword are not same) then candidate answer is
correct;
  Otherwise
  candidate answer is wrong.
```

■ 12.7 AMBIGUOUS MODIFICATION

In this section, we will consider the concept of ambiguous modification and devise rules to handle ambiguous modification as shown in Joshi and Akerkar (2008). Adjectives are often ambiguous modifiers. If a paragraph contains a pool of adjectives and nouns, any particular adjective could potentially modify many nouns. Under such circumstances, a natural language interface system cannot achieve high precision without exactly identifying the association between adjectives and nouns. Ambiguous modification occurs when an entity behaves in an unrestrictive manner and can be associated with more than one noun in a particular sentence.

Definition

Katz and Lin (2003) stated that a word w, involving a relation R, is an ambiguous modifier if and only if there exist at least two words, w_1 and w_2, such that $S(R(w,w_1)) = S(R(w,w_2)) = 1$, where S is a function defined on any logical expression e. The value of function S depends upon the semantic validity of the function. If S is semantically valid, its value is one; otherwise, it is zero.

In short, if an adjective word w can fit well with two different words in different sentences and still make sense, we can say that w is an ambiguous modifier.

Example

This example illustrates the ambiguous modification.

Question: Which is the longest river in India?

Candidate Answer 1: The Ganges River is the longest river in India.

Candidate Answer 2: The Mahatma Gandhi Setu, the longest bridge in India, constructed over the river Ganges connecting Patna at the south end to Hajipur at the north in Bihar.

Candidate Answer 3: The longest river forms the bridge between two provinces, Uttar Pradesh and Bihar, in India.

Candidate Answer 4: Ganges, which flows east through the Gangetic Plain of northern India into Bangladesh, is the longest river in India.

Candidate Answer 5: In India, Ganges, which rises in the western Himalayas in the Uttarakhand province and drains into the Sunderbans delta in the Bay of Bengal, is the longest river.

Candidate Answer 6: In India, the longest bridge, the Mahatma Gandhi setu, spans over 5575 km on the south bank of river Ganges.

This example lists different answers generated by the system in response to the question asked. In these answers, "longest" is the adjective that modifies the noun "river" correctly in Candidate Answer 1, Candidate Answer 4, and Candidate Answer 5. But in case of Candidate Answer 2, Candidate Answer 3, and Candidate Answer 6, the adjective modifies the noun "bridge." Sentences in which the adjective "longest" modifies the noun "river" and sentences in which the same adjective modifies another noun "bridge" are semantically valid. Though these sentences are semantically valid, not all of these sentences are correct when presented as a possible answer to the question that is asking for longest river.

This example illustrates the phenomenon of ambiguous modification and demonstrates the problems it can cause. Ambiguous modification as it relates to adjectives occurs when an entity behaves in unrestrictive manner and can be associated with more than one noun in a particular sentence. The adjective "longest," involved in an adjective-noun modification relationship, is not constrained in its possible choices of head nouns,[2] and hence, is free to float among nouns.

In the previous example, "longest" is the adjective that acts as a modifier in the adjective-noun modification relationship, whereas "in India" is used to specify scope. Candidate Answers 2 and 3 are correct at a lexical level, but wrong at a meaning level. In Candidate Answer 2, "longest" modifies the incorrect head noun. In Candidate Answer 3, "in India" does not modify the correct head noun.

Now we can devise a method to handle ambiguous modification. We can formulate rules, while studying the structure of sentences, which are

---

2. A *head noun* is the word that is modified by an adjective clause. For example, in the sentence "I like the book that you wrote," "book" is the head noun because the adjective clause modifies it. Normally, the head noun is the noun that comes right before the adjective, but not always.

based on shallow parsing. Candidate answers that are fetched based on keyword matching can be tested for correctness using these rules. Every sentence that is amenable due to Ambiguous Modification contains one adjective and more than one noun. One of these nouns is used for defining the scope whereas the other is pointing to the identifier we are looking for. These nouns can easily be distinguished and the sequence of these two nouns and the adjective is the important factor that is used in the formulation of rules. The algorithm scans each candidate answer sentence and applies the following rules to check whether that sentence is the correct answer sentence or not. We have identified the adjective as Adj, the scope defining noun as S_N, and the identifier noun as I_N.

Algorithm (Rules)

If the sentence contains keywords in following order –

```
Adj α Sɴ    Where α indicate string of zero or more keywords,
     Then
        R₁-a →  If   α  is  Iɴ          →  Correct Answer
     Or
        R₁-b →  If   α  is  Blank      →  Correct Answer
        Else
        R₂   →  If   α  is  Otherwise →  Wrong  Answer
```

If the sentence contains keywords in following order –

```
Sɴ  α  Adj  β   Iɴ Where α and β indicate string of zero or more
keywords,
     Then
        R₃ →    If  β  is  Blank      →  Correct Answer
                (Value of  α  does not matter)
        Else
        R4  →   If  β  is  Otherwise  →  Wrong  Answer
```

Table 12.1 shows how rules R_1 to R_4 help to find the correct answer among the number of candidate answers shown.

■ **Table 12.1 Rules to Handle Ambiguous Modification**

Question : Which is the longest river in India?
Adj : **longest** S_N = **India** I_N = **river**

Candidate answer	Sequence	Rule	Is it an exact answer?
Candidate Answer 1: The Ganges River is the longest river in India.	Adj α S_N α = I_N	R_1-a	YES
Candidate Answer 2: The Mahatma Gandhi Setu, the *longest* bridge *in India*, constructed over the *river* Ganges connecting Patna at the south end to Hajipur at the north in Bihar.	Adj α S_N α = Otherwise	R_2	NO
Candidate Answer 3: The longest river forms the bridge between two provinces, Uttar Pradesh and Bihar, in India.	Adj α S_N α = Otherwise	R_2	NO
Candidate Answer 4: Ganges, which flows east through the Gangetic Plain of northern India into Bangladesh, is the longest river in India.	Adj α S_N α = I_N	R_1-a	YES
Candidate Answer 5: In India, Ganges, which rises in the western Himalayas in the Uttarakhand province and drains into the Sunderbans delta in the Bay of Bengal, is the longest river.	S_N α Adj β I_N β = Blank	R_3	YES
Candidate Answer 6: *In India, the longest* bridge, the Mahatma Gandhi setu, spans over 5575 km on the south bank of *river* Ganges.	S_N α Adj β I_N β = Otherwise	R_4	NO

■ 12.8 CONCLUSION

Due to the involvement of language-related complex phenomena, development of complete and comprehensive natural language applications has become a challenging task. The widely used rule-based approach for developing linguistic applications needs to analyze vast information gathered at a syntactic level to overcome the problems occurred at a semantic level. We have reviewed the general literature related to a natural language interface to question answering systems and discussed the issues in the shallow parsing technique in this case study. The algorithms discussed here are implemented, and verified and certainly improve the performance of the natural language interface. These algorithms not only improved the precision of the system but also performed this task in less time. Improved precision leads to improvement in the ranking of correct answer.

The way search engines function is about to change dramatically. Upcoming third-generation search engines are concentrating on linguistic aspects rather than on mere keyword matching. Given this, we feel that the shallow parsing-based approach is more effective because of two reasons: problems caused by linguistic phenomena at semantic levels are tackled without carrying in-depth parsing, and while dealing with the problems, the system does not compromise on response time.

References

Bhattacharyya, P. Natural language processing, Universal Networking Language Workshop, IIT, Mumbai, 2003.

Fagan, J. Experiments in automatic phrase indexing for document retrieval: a comparison of syntactic and non-syntactic methods, PhD Thesis, Cornell University, 1987.

Green, B. F., Wolf, A. K., Chomsky, C., & Laughery K. BASEBALL: an automatic question answerer, Proceedings of the Western Joint Computer Conference, Volume 19, pp. 219–224. Reprinted in (Grosz et al., 1986), pp. 545–549, 1961.

Joshi, M. & Akerkar, R. Algorithm to effectively handle semantic symmetry in question answering systems, CSIT-2005, Yerevan, 5-8080-631-7, pp. 246–250, 2005.

Joshi, M. & Akerkar, R. Shallow parsing–based algorithms to improve precision of question answering systems, National Workshop on Artificial Intelligence, SIGAI, C-DAC, Mumbai, 2006.

Joshi, M. & Akerkar, R. Solving semantic-level problems using shallow parsing algorithms, International Journal of Computer & Communication Technologies, Volume 1, Issue 1, 2008.

Joshi, M. & Akerkar, R. Algorithms to Improve performance of natural language interface, International Journal of Computer Science and Applications, Volume (5), Issue 2, pp. 52–69, 2008a.

Joshi, M. & Akerkar, R. Natural language interface using shallow parsing, International Journal of Computer Science and Applications, Volume (5), Issue 3, pp. 70–90, 2008b.

Kaisser, M. & Becker, T. Question answering by selecting large carpora with linguistic methods, Proceedings of the Thirteenth TExt REtrieval Conference, TREC-2004.

Katz, B., Lin, J. START and beyond, In proceedings of the 6th World Multiconference on Systemics, Cybernetics, and Informatics, 2002.

Katz, B. & Lin, J. Selectively using relations to improve precision in question answering, In proceedings of the EACL-2003 Workshop on Natural Language Processing for Question Answering, 2003.

Katz, B. & Lin, J. Sapere: From keywords to key relations, MIT Computer Science and Artificial Intelligence Laboratory, 2004.

Soo-min, K., Dae-ho, B., Sang-Beom, K., & Hae-Chang, R. Question answering considering semantic categories and co-occurence density, In the proceedings of the Ninth TExt REtrieval Conference TREC-2000.

Liddy, E. Enhanced text retrieval using natural language processing, ASIS Bulletin, 1998.

Liddy, E. Natural language processing, Encyclopedia of Library and Information Science, New York: Marcel Dekker; 2003.

Oxford Concise Dictionary of Linguistics, New York: Oxford University Press; 1997.

Majumder, P., Mitra, M., & Chaudhari, B. N-gram: A language-independent approach to IR and natural language processing, Lecture notes, 2002.

McCarthy, J. & Lehnert, W. Using decision trees for coreference resolution, In the proceedings of the Fourteenth International Joint Conference on Artificial Intelligence, pp. 1050–1055, 1995.

Soderland, S., Fisher, D., Aseltine, J. Lehnert, W. "Crystal: Inducing a conceptual dictionary," In the proceedings of the Fourteenth International Joint Conference on Artificial Intelligence, pp. 1314–1319, 1995.

Weizenbaum, J. ELIZA: A computer program for the study of natural language communication between man and machine, Communications of the ACM, 9(1), pp. 36–45, 1966.

Woods, W., Kaplan, R., N-Nebber, B. The lunar sciences natural language information system, BBN Report 2378, Cambridge, MA: Bolt Beranek and Newman; 1972.

Index